Got Enough?!

A RAGS TO REVELATION
STORY

Michael Rullo

Transcendent Press
CALGARY, ALBERTA

Transcendent Press
Email: info@michaelrullo.com
Website: www.michaelrullo.com
Second Paperback Edition – January 2019
22 21 20 19 18 — 1 2 3 4 5 6 7 8 9

Library and Archives Canada Cataloguing in Publication

Rullo, Michael –, author
Got enough?!: A Rags to Revelations Story / Michael Rullo

Issued in print and electronic formats:

ISBN: 978 – 1 – 7751494 – 0 – 8 (pbk); 978 – 1 – 7751494 – 1 – 5 (Amazon POD pbk); 978 – 1 – 7751494 – 4 – 6 (pdf); 978 – 1 – 7751494 – 2 – 2 (epub); 978 – 1 – 7751494 – 3 – 9 (mobi).

Under a Federal Liberal government, Library and Archives Canada no longer provides Cataloguing in Publication (CIP) data for independently published books.

TECHNICAL CREDITS:
EDITING: Crescent McKeag, *Calgary Writing Services*, Calgary, Alberta
    and Valerie Repnau, *Eurocom LLC,* Los Angeles, California
COPYEDITING & PROOFREADING: Bobbi Beatty, *Silver Scroll Services*, Calgary, Alberta
DESIGN & PRODUCTION: Jeremy Drought, *Last Impression Publishing Service,* Calgary, Alberta
AUTHOR PORTRAIT: Angela Chard, *Crystal Image Studio*, Calgary, Alberta
Printed on Demand for Amazon.com by CreateSpace.com a DBA of *On-Demand Publishing, LLC.*

Verified *5-Star*-Amazon Reader Reviews

"What an *amazing book!* It's not very often that you can say a book is *life-changing* but this one was so packed with information, so clearly and enjoyably written, and so filled with super-helpful insight that I find myself re-reading it and quoting it in my daily life. I've also given it as gifts to friends and family who are struggling financially, depressed, or just wondering how to live a better life. I really appreciated the author telling the story of his own personal journey through the various, often very funny anecdotes, quotes, and *"Rullo Rules,"* but I appreciated even more how he is supporting everything he said with the latest scientific discoveries about happiness, goal setting, how we manage our money and shopping impulses, how to make money and how to use failure, laughter, and creativity to finally feel like you have enough. This isn't just a self-help book but a how-to manual on life. It changed me. Very cool book!"
- ***Chris Kreed***

❄❄❄

"This book is not your standard self help business book, it far surpasses those! What caught my attention immediately was the smooth flow of the writing. This is an easy book to follow yet at the same time, it is packed with solid information on every page. Mr. Rullo's personal anecdotes are refreshing and honest, his advice is deep and insightful, and his emphasis on *"Enough"* brings a new and innovative take on success. This book is a must read for everyone from beginning entrepreneur to seasoned professional and from young adult to retiree, but the advice in this book also extends beyond business to personal life decisions. You can read the book quickly because it is written so smoothly, or you can do like I did and take your time, savour it, and highlight passages that are important to you so you can go back and reread them again and again. Whatever your business or personal situation, I recommend you get this book and start reading it today!" - ***Byrad***

Verified *5-Star*-Amazon Reader Reviews

"Purchasing this book was a big plus for me. I like to buy books about being successful in life and I read Michael Rullo's *Got Enough?!* I was quite impressed. Michael Rullo simplifies success in ways that inspired me to look at my life in a different perspective. He tells his story with humility and humour about how he went through his achievements and struggles with a series of anecdotal wisdom and traditional quotes. I recommend this book to those who are seeking a fresh voice whether you are successful or not." - ***Amazon Customer***

***

"I purchased the paperback version of this book and was very impressed. Michael's *Got Enough?!* story is an abbreviated retelling of his life. Written through the perspective of his experiences and enduring the ups and downs life throws at you, Michael's story is humble, funny and informative. It will likely cause you to re-evaluate yourself, and the book provides a valuable blueprint of how to generate real success in your own life. Without spoiling anything, I quite enjoyed the revelations Michael comes to at the end of the book, making it a satisfying read as you join him on his journey. Highly recommended, as this is definitely not your typical self-help book. *Got Enough?!* has a personality and soul that few books in the genre can match." - ***Mark***

Verified *5-Star*-Amazon Reader Reviews

"Wisdom does not necessarily come from years of aging. Michael Rullo is at least 30 years younger than me. Yet, I found his 'revelations' (word in the subtitle) insightful. Rullo's book makes accessible his significant experiences, risk taking, diligence, & thoughtful decision making. Even the title's question *'Got Enough?'* raises a deep philosophic question.

Here are five of my favourite Rullo quotations:

1) ". . . more isn't going to make me any more comfortable & content. That's what *'Enough* feels like."

2) "There's a cost to living a lifestyle you can't afford, & it never ends well. The system is designed to keep you in bad debt."

3) "Achieving greatness is not hit or miss. It's about showing up & doing!"

4) "The majority of people I encounter always seem to be looking for an external solution."

5) *"Enough* doesn't necessarily mean rich. It means finding the right balance of all the things that are important in life, of which money is only one."

If you are ready to find your *'enough'* don't hesitate to get hold of *Got Enough? A Rags to Revelations Story!"* - ***Patricia Morgan***

***

"I really liked how this book is formatted & how it flows from chapter to chapter, easy read & great insight into many ideas & concepts." - ***Alex***

Verified *5-Star*-Amazon Reader Reviews

"I got this book a few months ago and whenever I feel stuck, in a slump and lazy, I pick it up again and read a chapter or two, randomly this time. Without fail so far, this book kind of slaps me in the face and I magically get the urge to be more productive or creative, and to show my friends and family more appreciation. This book raises many important questions that each person will identify with, sparking off a lot of soul-searching (for me anyway!) and helping the reader understand the most important concepts in our society now, money, the pursuit of it, how to understand it and know when you have "*enough*", when to stop and feel content and appreciate what you have. We are all constantly brainwashed subliminally or not, to constantly chase money, which leads to endless frustration because we are always bombarded with things we're supposed to crave, when a lot of us already have things that make our lives richer than we think. This book teaches you to identify what you need to be free of the tyranny of money, how to make a plan for getting there, reach your goal, and then be content once you've achieved it. The tone of the book is down to earth, direct, and never condescending (I hate that about some other self-help books), with a good measure of humour. The author Michael Rullo is extremely relatable, calling himself an ordinary or average man, he wasn't born with a silver spoon in his mouth, which to me makes all his advice and anecdotes all the more powerful because they are all about regular people and you can totally identify with them as a reader. It makes you realize that any goal is attainable if you know how. Reading these chapters again puts me in a good space, as it forces me to re-evaluate my progress constantly but also brings me back down to reality with renewed appreciation of what I do have. The writing is direct, breezy and to the point, with a lot of humour thrown in. I like the little quotes dotting the book here and there, and all the personal anecdotes which are extremely relatable and enlightening. In the end, this is my go-to source when I need an extra kick up the butt to stay on the right track, aim for financial security and appreciate all the things and relationship treasures I do already have. I don't live in Canada where the author lives but it would be cool if he did some seminars in the US or via streaming." - *V. Apple*

Verified *5-Star*-Amazon Reader Reviews

"*Got Enough*" richly deserves to be in the same canon as Tony Robbins' "*Personal Power*", Stephen R. Covey's "*The 7 Habits of Highly Effective People*", and Dale Carnegie's "*How to Win Friends and Influence People*". In using easily relatable anecdotes from his personal and professional life, Michael Rullo is able to convey and illuminate commonsense wisdom and truths of how one can best live one's life. I constantly found myself having to return to what I had just read because of what was on the page, well, it got me thinking... Thoroughly readable, immensely relatable, and a literal page turner (provided you spring to have the paper copy!). *A 10 out of 10! - **Jeff***

***

"You will not regret buying this book. It is well written and very interesting. It is not one of those boring self help books but rather a book that teaches you about life. Got this as an early Christmas present and could not put it down." *- **Naz***

Dedication

THIS book is dedicated to my heroes—my parents Mario and Maria Rullo—my sisters Emilia and Mirella, their children, McKale, Alia, Nicole, Dana, and Mackenzie, and to all my friends and extended family who are too numerous to mention. To all those affected by the impact of losing a loved one to cancer or any other illness, tragedy, or loss, I wrote this book to share my *Enough* story with the hope that it may help others understand that they don't need more in life to be satisfied, they just need *Enough*! To everyone who has entered my life along the way—for better or for worse—thank you all, because each of you has had a role in my being where I am today, why I feel like life is great, and I feel that I have *Enough*.

About the Book

We have a better standard of living, more choices, unparalleled access to goods and services, more friends at our fingertips, and more wealth than most of the past generations combined, so why is it that we never seem to have enough?

What if someone could give examples showing you how to make more money, how to keep more of the money you do earn, what science says will make you happiest, and what other ingredients you'll need to throw into the stew of life to cook up *Enough*?

Michael Rullo is an '*Enough*' consultant who shares with others how to figure out *Enough* for themselves, but that wasn't always the case. With wit and cleverness, he intimately opens up about his story of how he came to understand *Enough*, from begging for a job at age ten to how he paid off his first home by twenty-four and retired by thirty-seven, and how money didn't buy him the happiness he thought it would. Through his personal search for *Enough*, and combined with some of the latest insights from the fields of finance, philosophy, science, and psychology, he shows you that *Enough* is attainable.

With clear how-to instructions, impactful quotes that range from wise to humorous, and so much more, *Got Enough?!* is not just another one of those books on how to get rich, although you can use it to do almost anything you set your mind to, it's a diverse life guide to

- MONEY – how to make it work for you not against you;
- GOALS – how to go from pipe dream to living the dream;
- INSPIRATION – how to reconnect with what drives you to thrive;
- MOTIVATION – how to create positive momentum in your life; and
- BALANCE – how to figure out what you need more of, less of, some of, and none of...

When Michael tells people his story of how he came to discover *Enough*, they often say, "You should write a book and show everybody how to get *enough*!"

Every once in a while, a book comes along that can genuinely make your life better. This is that book.

Our care should not be to have lived long as to have lived enough.
LUCIUS A. SENECA

Table of Contents

Introduction:
Why Me? Why You? Why Not?

You don't need to know it all;
a limited knowledge, applied well,
pays dividends in the end!

MICHAEL RULLO

T HERE are a million ways to learn something, but out of all of them, I don't recommend the hard way, even though that's how I did it. I'm hoping that the reason you've picked up this book is that you want to learn from my mistakes and better still...from my successes. My name is Michael Rullo, I paid off my first home by twenty-four, and I earned *Enough* and retired by the age of thirty-seven.

It wasn't from hitting it big in the stock market, oil and gas, tech stocks, winning the lottery, or anything else that people can read about in other books, nor were my immigrant parents wealthy. There were no rich skeletons in my closet. I made money the old-fashioned way: I worked my butt off; I rolled up my sleeves and got dirty, but this isn't a rags to riches tale. The reason I didn't retire before thirty-seven is that I didn't feel that I had *Enough*. I would have had to have lived within my means, and I wasn't even sure what *Enough* was for me back then. Some of the wealthiest people in the world don't feel like they have *Enough*, while some of the poorest feel like they have everything they could ever want. *Enough* is a tough concept to master, but what I've learned along the way from rags to revelations is going to show you a different way to think about money, and more importantly, it's going to shift your relationship with *Enough*.

What I think you'll like is that this book is your story too. It's the story of how you're finally going to understand what it is you want in life, and I wager money is a big part of that. Even if it's not the whole story, money matters for most of us. It's how most of us keep a roof over our heads and food on the table, but somewhere along the line things got tangled up, and instead of fishing for food, most of us are now fishing for a more elusive catch: *Enough.*

There's been a significant cultural about-face in the last twenty years resulting in a constant bombardment of media messages about how to live a glamorous life. It runs on a continuous loop reinforcing the same message over and over again: money, money, money, and more money! None of these glamorous people who show off how much money they have ever seem to be satisfied, and that's because, I feel, they don't understand the concept of what *Enough* is.

Money is only one component of *Enough. Enough* is also about knowing how to set your goals to achieve what you want in life. It's about trying to catch that annoyingly elusive butterfly of happiness that always seems to be fluttering just out of reach. I know that I'm happiest when I have the freedom to do the things I love to do. Doing the things I love always puts me in a positive frame of mind, and I can put myself into a state that I like to call *Spirit,* where everything seems to flow, effortlessly and smoothly. I wanted to create a life for myself where I could do the things I love most, more often, but I saw that wanting it wasn't *Enough.* I needed to figure out how to create the life I envisioned by setting goals that involved making enough money to have the freedom to pursue the activities that I loved, whenever I wanted, without worrying about not having the time or money to do them. *Enough,* for me, boiled down to worrying less and accomplishing more.

I connected the dots, and you probably have too. Goals cost money. Doing the activities you love likely costs money, and day-to-day life also costs money. But here's the thing—I have taken the time to write this book because I've learned something that you're probably just now on the road to learning. I've learned the concept of how money works, and I've learned how to get to *Enough.*

This book describes how I came to view money, and by understanding that money is a concept, I learned that there's such a thing as having enough of it! Numbers are a measurement, and money is nothing more than numbers. What I learned about money allowed me to take my life in a profitable direction and get myself to a point where money was no longer a source of stress. When I took the time to understand money, I came to know three things about it:

1. You either don't have *Enough*, or
2. You have too much, and it still feels like it's not *Enough*, or
3. You truly do have *Enough*; therefore, you don't stress or care about it.

Money is nothing more than whatever you or I believe it to be, so if you understand money, you're well on your way to learning that there's such a thing as having *Enough*!

The word *enough* is a strange concept. What one person thinks is *Enough* may be entirely different from what another person thinks. Some people feel they need that first-class lifestyle and all the things that go along with it: cars, homes, clothes, jewelry, travel, etc. Others are content living on a meagre sum, have simple tastes, and can spend a tiny amount of money and still be very fulfilled. Then there are the people who never have *Enough*, no matter how much they have; *Enough* just isn't *enough*. Either way, I had to decide for myself what my *Enough* looked like, and this book is going to make you look your *Enough* right in its cold, possibly distant eye.

I will share stories from my past and recount how, even after I made more than I ever thought possible for myself, it still felt like it wasn't *Enough*. The more money I made, the more I would spend. I learned that the money system is set up to keep you and I wanting to go bigger and better, in doing so, making us go farther into debt and constantly wanting to have the latest and greatest. I realized that with this kind of thinking, there wasn't ever going to be an end point to the way I was living. I kept acquiring *stuff*, and the concept of *Enough* never even occurred to me until, one day, I experienced an epiphany: My wanting more means my being in debt forever, but my defining what is *Enough* becomes a set end point with a clearly defined number!

This book is not just another book on how to become a millionaire or billionaire, although you can use what I've learned to do almost anything you ultimately set your mind to achieving. Plenty of millionaires think that they still don't have *Enough*, and they don't know what to do about that. When it came to an understanding of *Enough*, I needed to get under its skin, see where it comes from, and why so slippery a concept is one that controls many of our decisions, feelings, fears, and failures. This book is my understanding, and personal philosophy, of *Enough*.

This is a no-holds-barred, firsthand account of how I created the life I have for myself today. I may not be a billionaire, famous, or well known for anything in particular, but I don't need to hold down a *job*, and I'm not trapped in *the system*. The way I see it is, I've created a life for myself that is pretty impressive, in spite of the fact that I'm not that special. My upbringing, my intellect, and my level of education are all entirely average. Anybody can do what I've done, and anybody can achieve a life like mine.

When people first meet me, and the topic of "So what do you do?" comes up, I always answer, "I'm retired." The follow-up questions come at me rapid-fire: "You're too young to be retired; how did you do it?" "What's your secret? Did you win the lottery?" "Who did you know to help you do it so early in your life?" "You're joking, right? You're not retired, are you?!" When I tell them even a fraction of what I've learned about money, and how to make *Enough* happen, I always hear, "You should write a book about it and tell everybody!"

Okay. This is that book.

Michael Rullo

1

Numbers Don't Lie!
They Also Don't Tell the Whole Story!

If finances just don't sound sexy or exciting to you, well then,
think of them as tantric finances. If you can hold out & delay
gratification by not spending all your money now, you'll be
in ecstasy later on, enjoying that money when you need it.

MICHAEL RULLO

I T was Christmas 1980, and I was just ten years old when the concept of *Enough* first came down the chimney. At that time, Calgary, Alberta, where my family and I lived, was in an economic recession. Money was tight. It was affecting everybody in the city and times were tough.

I was a typical ten-year-old boy with an appetite bigger than my stomach, and I wanted lots of toys for Christmas. You know the ones. The ones they show over and over on TV to create the sense that the latest video game release is a life-changing necessity. I would pester my Mom and Dad to buy me something with practically every commercial.

I didn't know what kind of stress my Dad was under. By trade, he worked as a foreman for a road-paving crew, but the nature of this work made it seasonal. The economy was so bad that year, he didn't know whether or not he would even have a job to go back to in the spring. He was a bundle of nerves, not knowing if our family's savings would even be enough to last until spring came around. He was concerned about keeping his home, putting food on the table so his family was fed, paying his bills, and surviving the next four more months with little to no income. On my family's Christmas list, a new gaming system, (even one that put Atari to shame with its graphics), came dead last.

School had just let out, and I was at home on a Saturday with my Dad watching television, when a commercial showing the Mattel Intellivision video gaming platform came on TV. I begged my Dad for the millionth time to have that toy. Dad couldn't take it any more. I had gotten on his last nerve with all the endless Christmas begging for new toys. In a loud, exasperated tone, he told me that if I wanted those toys, I needed to figure out how to buy them myself! I was ten! What did I know about making money to buy my toys? I tried to ask in a different way, I mean we were talking video games here (Intellivision had a lot to choose from!), and yet somehow, unbelievably, the answer was still a flat out *No*!

I went to my room to sulk. Until this point in my life, I had no concept of how truly significant money was or why it even mattered. Every toy I had ever owned was suddenly not enough, and I didn't know how to go about getting *Enough*. As a ten year old, this was my version of hitting rock bottom!

Later in the afternoon, I came out of my room and my Dad gave me some money to go and buy some milk. I went to a small neighbourhood grocery store close to our home that was owned by a businessman named George. There I was, waiting to pay when I overheard George screaming on the phone at somebody, something about someone not coming into work that night for whatever reason. A light bulb appeared above my head, and mustering my courage, I asked George if I could come into work that night. He burst into laughter and told me to go home. He didn't realize that in my mind, he was standing between me and Christmas! With Santa Claus and an army of video game manufacturers on my side, I stood my ground and said, "Mr. George, give me a job; I can do it!"

When a ten year old tells somebody he needs a job, people tend to look at him a little bit more seriously. George said to me, "You can't even touch the top shelf; how can you be a stock boy and stock those shelves?" I saw a milk crate, grabbed it, flipped it over, put it on the floor, and then proceeded to stand on it, showing George I could reach the top shelf. Then he said, "You can't even lift the crate of pop bottles to replace them!" Back then, they were super heavy for a ten year old as sodas were sold in thick two-litre glass bottles and came in crates of either twelve or twenty-four bottles, weighing in at 25 to 50 lbs., if not more. It doesn't sound like much, but I would have had to carry every crate up twenty-eight steps from the basement. I took the same milk crate that I had just stood on and flipped it over. Loading it with five bottles of pop, I picked it up with no problem. I said to George, "I'll make more trips, but I'll get it done!"

> From early on, I always hated being told what to do.
> I learned how to discipline myself so others wouldn't need to.
>
> **MICHAEL RULLO**

I could see that my inventiveness and dogged persistence was starting to win him over. Suddenly, with an "Ah-ha! Gotcha!" tone in his voice, he said to me, "You're ten years old, you can't work past 9:00 p.m., and I need a stock boy until 10:00 p.m.!" I went over to the counter, asked if I could use the phone, and proceeded to call my Mom. I said, "Ma, I'm at George's grocery store, and he said I could have a job if I can work until 10:00 p.m.; is it okay if I work here tonight?" I handed the phone over to George to speak to my Mom; they talked for a while, and then George hung up the phone and just stared at me for what seemed like forever. Christmas hung in the balance. Time stood still as I stared back. I never broke eye contact. The fate of my entire gaming universe weighed heavily on my shoulders. "Be here at 5:00 p.m.," he said gruffly, "You start work tonight!"

That was my first job interview and my first encounter with the motivating power of not having *Enough*. I improvised, and I didn't take no for an answer. I got that job at George's grocery store for two dollars an hour, and I soon found out that working sucks and it's hard! I thought to myself, after that first night, "I don't want to do this for the rest of my life!" I wanted to quit straight off, but I didn't.

I figured out that if I needed to make more money, I had to learn more than they were teaching me in school, so my education outside of school never stopped. That's what contributed to a large part of my success. I was always doing more than was expected of me. I had, at an early age, the one thing every entrepreneur needs to have: A yearning to learn so that later I could earn!

> ### *Rullo Rules*
>
> Always do more than is expected of you! When I was young, I figured out that if I wanted to earn more money, I had to learn more than they were teaching me in school; I was always reading & learning outside of regular school hours. I apply the same general concept to everything I do. Always doing more than is expected of me has contributed to a large part of my success.

In addition to my first brush with the concept of *Enough*, I also learned that numbers don't lie. When I had my first paycheque in hand, my Dad took me down to Sears to realize my Christmas dream. But the numbers didn't add up. I didn't make *Enough* to buy all the toys I wanted in the two days before Christmas. Two dollars an hour wasn't going to get me any of the expensive toys. I looked over the toys and games carefully, unimpressed suddenly by their quality, especially in comparison with how hard I had worked for them. I didn't even want to spend my hard-earned money on those toys anymore. I decided that helping out my family was more important, so I gave the money I earned to my Mom and Dad to do with it whatever they thought best. I didn't buy the Intellivision that I had been so sure I couldn't live without, but I'll never forget that Christmas. My family around the dinner table was more than *Enough*.

I want you to start thinking about what *Enough* means to you. Google's dictionary defines *Enough* as "as much or as many as required." *Merriam-Webster*'s definition gets more to the root of the emotional component of *Enough*, saying that it's "an amount that provides what is needed or wanted, in or to, a degree or quantity that satisfies, or that is sufficient or necessary for satisfaction." My *Enough* started out to be Mattel's Intellivision and all their video games, but my important takeaway was that if your *Enough* involves expensive toys, you may not be getting them all by Christmas. You're going to have to crunch the numbers. Numbers don't lie.

Nowadays when I deal with numbers, the one thing I can count on is there's going to be a solution to my problem because I can calculate it. As you begin to think about what *Enough* means to you, expensive toys may come to mind. Ask yourself, "Can I afford them? If not now, when?"

Input the data correctly, and you'll get your answer. Numbers are the most accurate thing out there. I love numbers because of their simplicity. It's not something philosophical or theory based; numbers are just cold hard facts! They are a measurement I can always bank on, and the only measurement the banks will count on when dealing with me: whether my figures are to their liking!

The important thing with numbers is that they serve as a gauge. They tell a big part of the story but not the whole thing. They will only tell me what I feed into the spreadsheet. I can speculate; I can input facts and figures, but all this does is let me gauge what I've done, where I'm at, and where I'd like to be. Numbers are not the only thing I use when deciding to go for a money-related goal, but it helps to start thinking about money in terms of just numbers. Doing so will help distance you a bit from all the emotional baggage attached to thoughts of having *Enough* money.

When I decide to go for a money-related goal, I always ask myself, "What is the amount of effort, creativity, imagination, and time required of me going to be?" and, "What am I willing to give up to attain my goal?" These questions are just as important as the numbers I use to see if something's viable. My time, effort, creativity, imagination, and what I'm willing to give up all come at a cost that banks and spreadsheets don't use when making their calculations. I know that even though these factors can't be calculated, they're going to come at a high cost regarding my quality of life; I consider that before deciding either way.

I know that a steady job is great, and a form of regular income can be a beautiful thing, but it was what I did outside of my job that set me up for life. Getting to your *Enough* may also require you to think outside whatever box you've been working in. Most of the people I worked with were content with just having their one job and didn't want to think about doing anything else outside of that job or taking a chance that could pay huge dividends later on. I can't count the number of times people said to me, "What you're doing outside of your job sounds risky!" when I was buying and renting out properties. Inevitably, my reply was, "It would only be a risk if I didn't know what I was doing and if I didn't calculate the numbers right. Numbers don't lie!" I laughed when people would roll their eyes at me, and I knew that what I was doing wasn't for everybody.

When I was right about something, it paid off in a big way. I wasn't always right, but when I was, it was because I didn't let the numbers stop me. I used the numbers to motivate me to do things with an increased chance of success. Sometimes I was told, "You can't afford to do this because it costs too much." My reply was, "I can't afford not to do it!" Yes, I was sometimes burned, but even when it didn't go as planned, I still let the numbers help me figure out a way to fix my failures.

When clients would look at my bids to construct their houses and crunch their numbers, I discovered that people will pay extra for the passion I bring, the integrity I display, the reputation I've built, and the track record that I pride myself on. Some of those things aren't always quantifiable. However, people do put a value and price on them!

Imagination, creativity, character, integrity, and likeability aren't things a spreadsheet can calculate. My success depended more on these valued characteristics than the money that was changing hands, and after a while, people stopped seeing me as a risk. I continually performed at a high level of character and integrity and showed that I was a good investment, not only because of my past business dealings, but because of how I honoured my word and commitments. At times, it felt like I had developed such a positive track record, they were now investing in my imagination and creativity. They wanted to do business with me because I was reputable, even when I wasn't the most qualified or the cheapest. My career prospered not only because I had success in real estate that was quantifiable, but also because I had other things people valued such as character, integrity, and honour. My clients looked at my numbers yes, but it wasn't the whole story.

To begin the journey to *Enough*, start with the numbers, but then think about what else you bring to the table. Make a spreadsheet that details your sexy finances and think about what else you could be doing to make your version of *Enough* a reality.

I learned, at the ripe old age of ten, that there's no such thing as a free ride. If I wanted something, it was up to me to go and get it, and what I wanted might not be worth what I had to do to get it. I learned that spending my money on frivolous things such as toys wasn't necessarily worth it when I had to bust my butt to make that money and when there were better things to spend it on such as family, food, and helping out as much as I could.

That job, in George's grocery, shaped the rest of my life for the better when it came to how the world and money genuinely worked. It also helped me to understand that *Enough* is a moving target, a pop one day, a video game the next. The simple truth regarding money is this: Numbers don't lie! People can lie, the media will fib, the internet is anybody's guess, but spreadsheets don't lie—they just might not tell the whole story!

> *The only thing in life that's free are samples!*
>
> **DANA CORCORAN**
> (My nephew, as a nine year old, explaining money & life to his seven-year-old brother!)

Not Had *Enough*? Well, Here's Some More:

• thinking about *Enough,* meaning, and happiness in life:

https://www.scientificamerican.com/article/a-happy-life-may-not-be-a-meaningful-life/

• emotional baggage and the fear of not having *Enough*:

https://www.yourcourageouslife.com/fear-of-not-having-enough-money/

•America's consumer debt:

https://www.thestreet.com/story/13726509/1/surge-in-credit-card-debt-raises-red-flags-for-u-s-economy.html

• Canada's household debt:

https://beta.theglobeandmail.com/report-on-business/economy/canadians-debt-burden-still-growing-hits-record-in-fourth-quarter/article29172712/?ref=http://www.theglobeandmail.com&

https://beta.theglobeandmail.com/report-on-business/economy/canadas-household-debt-to-disposable-income-ratio-climbs/article36275898/?ref=http://www.theglobeandmail.com&

Chapter 1 • Takeaways:

1. Use not having *Enough* to motivate you rather than depress you.
2. Be persistent in the face of your goals and the roadblocks that pop up in your way.
3. Numbers don't lie, but there are things spreadsheets don't take into consideration that are important precursors of your chances for success and which are not always quantifiable. Ask yourself if you're a sound investment.
4. Numbers raise questions and help you make better decisions.
5. Money goals always come at a high cost, and that cost is not always measured in just money!
6. Don't be afraid to look at your financial numbers. Numbers don't lie. They'll tell you what you need to do to get to *Enough*, but keep in mind, they don't always tell the whole story.
7. If a ten year old can do it, you can too!

2

Your *Enough* Number:
How to Find It

*The goal is to create a life so good
you don't need a vacation from it!*
MICHAEL RULLO

The Great North American Dream

WHAT *Enough* means to you will come out of a complex combination of where you came from, how you see yourself now, and who you aspire to be. Nowadays, when I'm asked who I am, the way I view myself is simple: I'm the son of Maria and Mario who immigrated to Canada from the beautiful Abruzzo region of Italy. They happened to meet each other by chance in Canada. They fell in love and were married for just shy of fifty years. I am their third child, and I was born and raised in Calgary, Alberta, Canada. My parents had only an elementary level of education (grade three for Mom and five for my Dad), but they raised me with the most important thing a child could have while growing up: lots of love. My parents were children of World War Two and had the most difficult of childhoods with some truly awful wartime experiences. They are my heroes and the biggest influences in my life. They created an amazing life together, and though neither of them had a formal education in the traditional sense, they are some of the wisest and smartest people I've ever met. It was in following their example that I first came to examine my *Enough* number.

My parents began their lives together like most young married people starting out...in debt. However, they also had to overcome learning a foreign language and a host of new customs and traditions. Plus, they were not

> *Education opens doors!...*
> *Determination & Drive breaks through walls!*
>
> **MICHAEL RULLO**

the tallest people in the world, standing at four feet ten inches (Mom) and five feet four inches (Dad), so literally, life loomed large for them in Canada. They combined their energies, ideas, and habits, and set some goals to create together the life that they had dreamt of.

Some of their many accomplishments were raising three children, sponsoring their brothers and one sister to immigrate to Canada, and developing several successful businesses outside of their day-to-day jobs (Mom was a hairdresser, and Dad, as I mentioned before, was a paver by trade). They retired early and traveled the world, spoiled their grandkids, and lived what many would describe as the North American dream!

In today's terms, the people who are looked up to most are those in the spotlight, those who reach the masses with their omnipresent images, social media, products, songs, movies, television shows, magazine covers, etc. There has never been a famous person of any note who has had more of an impact on my life than my parents. More than any celebrity, they showed me how life could look when you have *Enough,* and I wanted that same sense of satisfaction and security for myself (and to be taller... which I am!).

I began to treat *Enough* as I would any goal, asking myself, "What is *Enough*? "How much does it cost?" "How will I know if I have it?" Everything I ever desired that was measurable, and had a price tag attached to it, made me see that there's such a thing as knowing how much my *Enough* number is. If I can quantify all the material things I feel like owning, all the homes I'd like to have, the cars I'd like to drive, the trips and adventures I'd see myself enjoying, and then add them all up, it will give me a final number. That number is my *Enough* number.

Of course, I'd also have to figure out how much I needed to make to live day to day and add that into my final *Enough* number. Anything more than my *Enough* number is not going to make me any better off concerning my fulfillment as a person. More than *Enough* doesn't mean happier. There are plenty of miserable people that are super rich.

People have said to me that this is all hypothetical and that circumstances, wants, and needs change over time, but it helps to start thinking of it as a goal rather than an abstract concept. Calculating your *Enough* number will help you to restructure your thoughts about money and lifestyle and to unearth some deeply buried notions (that may not have seen the light of day since your childhood) of what *Enough* means to you.

My *Enough* number was a revelation for me, especially when I considered what I had to do to get there. What is *Enough* for you will also be affected by your understanding of debit, credit, and the systems in place that keep you wanting more.

> *Imagination has no age limits.*
> *I feed it by being generous,*
> *forgiving, & loving,*
> *& I just go for it whenever*
> *I set out on a new goal!*
>
> **MICHAEL RULLO**

I Credit George

When I was eleven years old, and working as a part-time stock boy in the local grocery, the owner, George, asked me if I knew what credit was. I was eleven, so I said, "No, but I'm listening." George then explained it to me this way, "I'll give you anything you want inside the store when you don't have any money to buy it. If you want chips, a pop, candy, anything I sell, you can have it no problem! I'll run you up a tab, and at the end of thirty days, you must pay it back to me. If you don't pay it back, I'll charge you 20 percent a month interest. Deal?" (Note: 20 percent was what the banks were charging at the time. George wasn't trying to take advantage of me; he was using the banks' rate of interest when teaching me this lesson.)

George went on to explain how interest worked. I said to him, "I don't think I need it, but thank you anyway." George responded, "Well, I'll give it to you for the next month. You can try it and see if you like it. Then you'll know for sure."

Two days later, I went with a friend to George's store after school to buy a pop. I only had the money for the pop, but then George asked if I wanted a chocolate bar and a bag of chips. I thought to myself, "I could put it on my tab and pay it back later!" My friend said, "Go for it, and get one of each for me too!" I used my store credit for the very first time, and it gave me such a rush! I thought I had everything I could ever want.

Thirty days later, I had used a whopping forty-six dollars in store credit. I tried to use my credit on the thirtieth day, and George stopped me and said, "It's been thirty days. You owe me forty-six dollars, and it's time to pay up." I had no money on me because I had grown so accustomed to using the store credit. I had stopped paying for things with cash. I only made two dollars an hour, and I only worked two to three hours a night, two to three times a week. Forty-six dollars seemed like an astronomical amount!

> *The secret to getting ahead is getting started.*
>
> **MARK TWAIN**

It took me three months to pay off my debt to George. It had only taken me one month to get so deeply into debt. I honoured my word and paid it all back, but I remember how much it sucked knowing I had to work and put my hard-earned money towards the stuff I had so frivolously bought with my store credit.

After I was done paying the debt to the store in full, George pulled me off to the side and asked me, "Do you like credit?" I replied, "No. I hate it!" George continued, "The credit system is set up to keep you in debt and spending more than you have. If you want to be rich, remember this. If you don't have the money for something and don't need it, then don't use credit to buy it. If you can't pay it back right away, don't use credit. There's good and bad credit. Buying things you don't need is bad. Buying a home is good."

At the age of eleven, I learned a valuable lesson about want versus need. I also saw how quickly my sense of what *Enough* was could change because of outside influences, such as the availability of credit and pressure from friends. As you calculate your *Enough* number, I want you to consider why you want what you want, how much of your money is going to pay for pop that you've already drunk, so to speak, as well as how much today's pop on credit will cost you by tomorrow. There's debt that will help you to reach your *Enough* number and debt that will hurt you. I credit George with teaching me the difference.

> ### *Rullo Rules*
> Shopping messes with your brain chemistry. Overspending produces a pleasure hit of a chemical called dopamine, but if you put something you want on credit, you don't have the balancing pain of having to pay for it. The solution? Pay for your wants in cash only to balance your brain & your budget.

Debt and the System

Thanks to my lingering lesson on credit from George, I learned to distinguish the difference between good debt and bad debt from an early age, but I also noticed that the system I grew up in was designed to keep me in bad debt. The system I'm referring to is a combination of cultural, media, and financial institutions that encourage overspending, consumerism, and a constant drive to get *more* to be supposedly happier.

When people think of something that they want to buy, they seldom check to see if it fits in with any plan or budget. They usually just think about how it would make them feel. If they use credit or loans to fund these *feelings*, they end up with transitory happiness and lasting stress and unhappiness from the credit bills that they can't afford. There's always another new gadget waiting to pounce.

Consumers report feeling that they have too much and not enough at the same time, in a cycle of relentless hunger where *Enough* doesn't even show up to the dinner table. The convenient click of online shopping has contributed to a consumer debt in the U.S. amounting to $8,100 for every person as of 2009. The *Globe and Mail* reports that Canada's consumer debt has copied that of our southern neighbours and stands at $1.92 trillion as of 2015!

As much as I may have complained about having to work at an early age, I learned to suck it up. Looking back, I know I was afforded life lessons regarding money that other people my age weren't, and those experiences contributed to my success. I saw how the system sets young people up to start out in debt, which they then work and work to get out of, only to find that they will repeatedly go into debt all over again. This cycle usually goes on right up until a person's death.

So how do the elements of the *system* conspire to keep *Enough* as a vague and closeted concept and debt as a perpetual unwanted dinner guest? In school, I never received a proper education regarding debt, credit, and how money works. All I was taught were snippets of stories and fragments of fables, aphoristically offering words of wisdom such as money doesn't grow on trees (not something that I found especially helpful). Like most young people, I used the Bank of Mom and Dad to temporarily lend me money to buy the things I wanted (If simply begging for them wasn't working!). Sometimes I didn't pay them back fully, and my parents just let it go. I would later learn that banks aren't as forgiving.

Then I graduated from high school and had to pay for my higher education. Some parents foot the bill for their child's education, but that only delays life's cold, hard lessons about how money works. Young people, whose parents pay for their studies, naturally think money is just always there for them. They are not learning to be responsible for paying for their education, car, etc., and are not receiving an outstanding education in finances, nor are they learning the value that people place on what they have had to work for. This will only keep them in a debt cycle long after their parents finally do cut the purse strings.

I have seen students go to great lengths and debts for a higher education, thinking that their dream jobs will magically appear like the pot of gold (not the chocolates!) at the end of the rainbow, and the accompanying leprechaun will pay off all their debts. The reality is that it will likely take years to work up to the dream job and even more years to pay off the debt that has already been accumulated. Additionally, the sense of entitlement that develops through the "starving student" years often translates to a feeling of "I didn't have *Enough* then, but now that I've graduated I'm owed," which may further encourage a new graduate to take on even more debt.

Sooner rather than later, most young adults are exposed to the fact that life isn't cheap. It takes a long time to get out of debt, and life for adults starting out nowadays is even more expensive because they are starting out already in debt. Debt pursues them at every opportunity. For example, every second ad on TV is trying to sell them a car and the supposed *freedom* and lifestyle that said brand would bring, so it's understandable that newly fledged young adults want cars that they can't afford to pay for. They take out leases or finance loans to buy the vehicles that the media tells them they should have. This adds to their debt yet again, for the next three to eight years.

They may no longer want to rent, and they may decide to buy a home, because they are making enough money to put a down payment on a place. But, it's costly to purchase a home, and there are lots of hidden costs. When the papers are signed, they have made a personal commitment to be in debt for the next twenty to thirty-five years.

Three years later they want a newer car because the one they have is old now and they're bored with it. They buy a new car, and so it goes.

A typical pattern emerges as this mounting debt causes additional stress and pressures to the point where all they want to do is escape. A feeling of not *Enough* can quickly lead to *I deserve...*which takes the internal dialogue form of *I need....* They say to themselves, "I need to get away," and then they take a vacation, and even though they may or may not be able to afford to pay for it, the money it costs them sets them back even further. The holiday costs more than the debt they incurred to pay for it. It costs them dearly by adding to their money woes and stress.

> *The world is full of willing people; some willing to work, the rest willing to let them.*
>
> **ROBERT FROST**

They'll *need* clothes for work, new phones, bigger TVs, and at some point, they also will probably get married and start a family. Weddings, clothes, kids, vacations, new cars, things for the home, parties, everything costs lots of money, and they'll slowly realize that they are not getting ahead.

The rest of the story is equally as pretty. If they have a family, they'll now have to pay for their kids to go to school, sports practices, and other extracurricular activities, and that will keep them in debt even longer. They'll be used to collecting a paycheque, but they won't have set themselves up for a passive cash flow when and if their jobs eventually come to an end. Many will go even further in debt during their retirement years.

One poor financial decision after another becomes a pattern, a pattern of debt, a pattern of stress, and a pattern of never having *Enough*. More importantly, they never put the brakes on, to pause and consider what *Enough* is. This pattern is supported by a system of banks and credit card companies (some of which have interest rates as high as 30 percent!) as well as an endless media maelstrom. Advertisers fund the media's messages. They persistently drive home the notion that unless you have this or that new product, well you simply don't have *Enough*.

Truth or Consequences

If people lived safe, boring lives within their means, marketers would go out of business! The fact is that it's not sexy to get ahead financially. It's hard to market. Life passes by quicker than people think it's going to, and they're often faced with the cold-hearted reality that financial institutions don't care about them. They certainly aren't going to bail them out like the Bank of Mom and Dad did when they were younger!

It's not popular to think of life as a game of Truth or Consequences, especially when the truth is the sooner they decide to think about and factor in good debt vs. bad debt, as George so expertly demonstrated to me, the better their consequences will be. The consequence of not coming to terms with your *Enough* number is that life will find a way to kick you to the curb. As the famous baseball player Yogi Berra once said, "If you don't know where you're going, you'll end up somewhere else."

Regardless of how the system is set up, you do have a choice. I had a choice between whether I was going to buy into the idea of always living for today, and still be in debt until the day I died, or to pay my dues and make the tough, unsexy decisions that would get me closer to my *Enough* number. I always ask myself this question before I make a financial decision, "Will making this choice get me ahead in the long run, or am I doing it just because I want something, although I don't need it?" I have given in to my desires in the past, only to find out afterward that doing so didn't fill any void inside me. I ultimately felt worse rather than better.

My parents came from nothing, but they saw that if they listened to the advertisers, the banks, or the endless glam-show of popular culture, they would stay in debt. My parents raised me to always live within my means. I was also given an education in credit at a time in my life when it most easily influenced me, and it impacted me, for the better. When I calculated my *Enough* number, I thought about my parents and what they had together. I thought about things I'd seen over the years that I wanted, but I also thought about why I wanted them and the effects of the cyclical system of debt, want, debt, want. I could calculate my *Enough* number by facing the truth, or I could accept the consequences.

> *The price of anything is the amount of life you exchange for it.*
>
> **HENRY DAVID THOREAU**

The Power of *No*!

To reach your *Enough* number, you're also going to have to learn the power of *No*. Kids are smarter than most adults give them credit for. I learned the power of *No* when I whined for something like a toy advertised on television. My parents weren't going to buy a toy for me that they knew I'd be bored with within a couple of days. *No* meant no, but they always explained to me why I wasn't getting whatever it was that I wanted. "We don't have the money for those kinds of things right now," they'd say, but it was always said with love. Eating and keeping a roof over our heads was more important. My sisters and I grew up valuing food and the company we shared it with, and that made our family feel like we were the wealthiest people in the world!

The reality is, like most people, I want things that I just don't need. My inner dialogue sometimes goes like this, "Yeah, I get that I don't need it. But I have to have it because I want it!" The truth is, nobody cares if I have the latest and greatest gadget. I only imagine that I have an audience of judges that think this or that about my belongings, my clothes, my phone, my car, etc. Reality always hits home afterwards, when the gadget or whatever I had to have loses its lustre and I've moved on to the next thing that I must have, seduced by yet another advert in an endless series.

Peer pressure to stay in fashion with the new *in* thing is overwhelming in our society. To be in fashion and stay on top of the latest trends is daunting. It's also costly! The way I got ahead in life was by deciding I didn't want to take part in this debt-laden world! I have stylish clothes, watches, homes, but whether something is or isn't in fashion has never been important to me. What was and is important to me to this day is the knowledge that I own my things, and my things don't own me!

> *I've told so many people that money won't make them happy, but for whatever reason, they seem hell-bent on finding out for themselves!*
>
> **MICHAEL RULLO**

Many people live their lives according to the saying, "The tail wags the dog." They are not in control. The feeling of never having *Enough* that they have been sold since childhood has deprived them of their desire and ability to tell themselves *No*. It's a powerful word, and I suggest you use it to your advantage. When people go into debt to buy a car, jewelry, a vacation, or anything they can't afford, these things own them, not the other way around.

I kept my cars for years longer than most people normally did. I didn't let myself give in to wanting the latest and greatest when I knew I couldn't afford it. I learned the power of *No* and I benefited from it. The gratification I had from not always giving in to my desire to buy came when I was at a point in my life where I could buy anything I desired, but I chose not to. If you exercise the power of *No*, you'll learn that you don't need to have instant satisfaction. You'll start to get in touch with what your *Enough* is, what you want, and what your real needs are.

Being sexy and living a sexy lifestyle has a shelf life; it comes at a high price that you'll have to pay later…and keep paying! However, living a quality life without worrying about debt is priceless. It's funny that when I got to a point in my life where I knew I could buy the things I used to want so badly but couldn't afford, I just didn't do it! My reality is I'm happy, and owning more isn't going to make me any more comfortable and content. That's what *Enough* feels like.

Not Had *Enough*? Well, Here's Some More:

- the difference between good and bad credit:

  https://www.smartaboutmoney.org/Courses/Money-Basics/Credit-and-Debt/Good-vs-Bad-Credit

- the difference between good and bad debt:

  http://www.investopedia.com/articles/pf/12/good-debt-bad-debt.asp

- America's consumer debt:

  https://www.thestreet.com/story/13726509/1/surge-in-credit-card-debt-raises-red-flags-for-u-s-economy.html

- Canada's household debt:

  https://beta.theglobeandmail.com/report-on-business/economy/canadians-debt-burden-still-growing-hits-record-in-fourth-quarter/article29172712/?ref=http://www.theglobeandmail.com&

  https://beta.theglobeandmail.com/report-on-business/economy/canadas-household-debt-to-disposable-income-ratio-climbs/article36275898/?ref=http://www.theglobeandmail.com&

Chapter 2 · Takeaways:

1. Think of people in your life whose lifestyles and values you admire and use them as a model for what *Enough* means to you.

2. Every day for a week, write down at least five things that you think would make you feel like you have *Enough*, and research their current values on the internet.

3. Determine as best you can, the cost of living the lifestyle you imagine, and add that to your list to come up with your *Enough* number. Remember that this is only an exercise to take the concept of *Enough* out of the realm of the undefined and make it into a real, tangible goal. Don't skip this step. Humour me. Give it a try.

4. There's a cost to living a *lifestyle* you can't afford, and it never ends well. The system is designed to keep you in *bad debt*. Practice being more aware of ads and offers of credit from financial institutions that are pressuring you to feel like you don't have *Enough* and you *deserve more*. You'll be more likely to stick to a budget and a financial plan that works for you instead of them.

5. Most people want things they don't need and the happiness from getting them doesn't stick around. Factor debt into your *Enough* number and practice the power of *No*.

3

Growing on Trees:
Where Does Money Come From?

Always remind yourself that if 'Plan A' doesn't work out
the alphabet still has 25 more letters!
MICHAEL RULLO

THE pursuit of money is pointless without a purpose, a clear end goal in mind, and a number you realize is *Enough*; however, most people want to know: How did he do it? Where does money come from if not from trees? How do I get some, let alone get *Enough*? When it came to making money, these were the secrets to my success:

1. I was always looking for money-making opportunities.
2. I had multiple sources of income.
3. I always had a plan.
4. I worked hard!

> *A goal is not always meant to be reached, it often serves as something to aim at.*
>
> **BRUCE LEE**

The short answer to where my money came from, which is a galaxy far, far away from the whole story, is that I planned to be a successful homebuilder. Then step-by-step, I went from being an unknown, who nobody wanted to take the time to get to know, to being a well-respected builder, designer, and real-estate expert who was widely sought after for his knowledge, advice, and skill. I'm skipping over all the hard work in between for now, but I did this in less than three years and set precedents others in the industry thought were unattainable or impossible!

Money Matters!

I discovered, very early on in my life, that people throw money away all the time and if I wanted to speed up my arrival to *Enough*, I needed to take a good look at where other people were throwing their money away and where I was bleeding mine. Once again, my first mentor, George, had a lesson to teach me on the subject. He taught me how I could profit from other people's disinterest in the small amounts of money that they think are insignificant. George said, "Small amounts today add up to big tomorrows!" Go George! He was right!

George would say to me, "See how people put those bottles in the trash can over there? They could bring them in over here, and I'd pay them money to recycle them. They're throwing money away; those people don't value or understand money. When I see empty bottles, I see money, not garbage!" The amount that you got for a bottle or aluminum can return at that time was a lot when you compare it to today's value; it was anywhere from five to seventy-five cents a bottle, and back then recycling was still a relatively new concept.

Before George explained to me that there was money people didn't seem to care about, and was thrown out all the time, I was one of those wasteful people who didn't know or care about recycling. I just did what everybody else was doing. I learned the value of a dollar from George, who was always looking for ways that money could be made or saved. He opened my eyes and made me realize that there's money in all sorts of places that people ignore or overlook.

> *Small amounts today add up to big tomorrows!*
>
> **GEORGE THE GROCER**

I started to pick up bottles from trash cans, and I brought them to the store for the recycling money. I was always a bit ambitious, so I went door to door and asked all my neighbours if I could get rid of their empty bottles for them. Almost everybody I asked would give me whatever they had kicking around because they didn't want to be bothered driving to the bottle depot. I did that every Saturday afternoon, and pretty soon I was making anywhere from twenty to fifty dollars a weekend just from collecting bottles! Back then, that was a lot of money.

My little red wagon became a real moneymaker for me. The more bottles I could carry, the more I made! Some people became so familiar with me that they would put their bottles by their front door for me to pick up without me even having to ask. I was making money but also offering a service that helped them get rid of something that they didn't want to have to worry about.

I'm not suggesting that you can reach your *Enough* number by bottle picking, but I am suggesting that George's lesson is one that can be applied in the adult world too. Money matters. Little amounts add up, and moneymaking opportunities can be disguised as empty bottles or services that no one else thinks are worth doing.

> *If you're always trying to trade your time for money, you'll never have Enough time or Enough money.*
>
> **MICHAEL RULLO**

Multiple Sources of Income

If you have more than one revenue source coming in, it stands to reason that you'll be making more money. This could mean that you have multiple jobs or it could mean that you've set up sources of passive income that generate money for you while you're working on something else. The secret that most wealthy people have in common is that they are bringing in multiple sources of income, and it's never just one thing that's making them rich.

If you take a look at most corporations, you'll also notice that they don't offer just one service or sell just one product. If you start to look at where you might find another source of income, you'll get ahead quicker than just doing one primary job. Creating wealth was a goal of mine, and looking for multiple sources of revenue was the first principle I learned to master because it works.

I learned this from my parents. Recall that my Dad was a paver by trade and my Mom a hairdresser. Those were their primary jobs, but that is not what set them up for a comfortable retirement. My Dad had a dump-truck-driving business, and he did odd contract jobs after work and on the weekends. My Mom bought residential rental properties and was a landlady. My parents still had other sources of income even if their day-to-day jobs were not bringing in lots of money. Thanks to my parents' pursuit of other sources of income, I got to see firsthand how fast wealth could accumulate.

When I was younger, I didn't just work at George's grocery store to earn income. From the ages of ten to fifteen, I delivered newspapers, collected bottles, cut grass, shovelled snow, did odd jobs for my neighbours, and helped my Mom out in her beauty salon for tips. I also found things people considered to be junk, and I'd clean them up and sell them in the newspaper for some extra cash. From the ages of fifteen to nineteen, I also cleaned bars after closing time, helped set up concert stages, bussed tables in some restaurants, and packed groceries. From the ages of twenty to twenty-four, I worked for a big bulk discount store, typed up people's essays for school, and bought and sold cars, among many other things for additional sources of income outside of my primary job.

Eventually, I was able to buy rental properties and make improvements to them, which allowed me to rent them out for a higher price. I did labour jobs and personal training. I also wrote people's resumés for them and invested in the stock market, but what I was investing in was myself. I was investing in my future and my *Enough* number, even as the ever-present voice of George in my head said, "Hey! Quit daydreaming and get back to work!"

Initially, I viewed all the different things that I did to make money as a learning experience. I found out what I liked, what I didn't, and what brought in the most money. When I got a bit older, I learned another valuable lesson that the wealthy already know, which is how to have an income outside of my number-one job without being directly involved with that income every single minute of my life, such as the income from being a landlord. If you're always trying to trade your time for money, you'll never have *Enough* time or *Enough* money. To get ahead in life quickly, you too must find a way to bring in multiple sources of income, without being 100 percent involved! This is where the planning part comes in.

> *A goal without a plan is wishful thinking!*
>
> **MICHAEL RULLO**

> ### *Rullo Rules*
>
> If you want to know how to get rich, there's a simple answer: Don't stop looking for work after you have a job! It's the work outside your job that sets you up for life.

Learn to Plan (Not Planning is a Bad Idea!)

When planning to make a plan, it helps to be like a giraffe in a hamster cage. You want to think outside the box, and you also want to take on a bit of a broader, long-distance perspective. It's tricky to see your way clear to where you feel like you have *Enough*, but your *Enough* number is a good start because your *Enough* number is a concrete goal. A good plan starts with a clear goal.

For example, I was on the hunt for more ways to earn money, and I decided that one way would be to build a home. Since I had neither money nor experience, I needed a plan. My plan began with "get more knowledge and expertise," and I brainstormed how to do that, spending countless hours on the internet. By thinking outside the hamster cage, so to speak, I came up with an idea for the next step. I picked up the phone and volunteered to work for free for a builder, who in exchange, agreed to mentor me on how to build houses. I put in the time to learn as much as I could from him before trying it for myself. I went from setting a goal, which was to build a home, to making a plan to realize that goal.

A goal without a plan is just wishful thinking; it sounds nice in theory, but it's hopeless. A plan can change, but it's a start. You can modify it along the way, like a GPS navigation system does when you don't follow its directions 100 percent.

The bottom line with everything I've ever set out to accomplish is that I made a defined end point. I then took the first step by making the smallest of gestures towards the goal to create the momentum to get started. No matter how small, I just needed that little push to get going! Once you've taken that first step towards a goal, it's much easier to keep momentum going if you have a plan in place. I always have a rough map directing me to my end point, and all my end points have combined to give me *Enough*.

Learning to plan is a bit of putting pen to paper, mixed with research, then garnished with a healthy sprinkling of constant review and reassessment. The fun begins with a goal, then some hard work to build a good foundation, and finally a bit of route mapping to figure out how you'll get from (A) to (B)onus! This is followed by a rest period that I like to call, *Fuhgettaboutit,* and then eventually the necessary reassessment to see where you're at concerning the map (how to reach your *Enough* number) as well as the plan (what you're doing in the short term to help you get there).

Making plans is necessary, yet it isn't something people usually do. I've heard people tell me about their goals, and I've asked them, "What's your plan?" Then there is a long pause, and I hear, "I haven't come up with one yet." I can't set a goal if I don't also set a plan or strategy in motion soon after. If I don't set a plan in motion, I know reaching that goal is not going to happen for me because I didn't plan for it! If you won't put the time in to make a plan, how likely is it that you'll put your energy into trying to achieve your goal? Think of your plan as a dipstick that shows you if your goal is clear and worth pursuing or if it's just a pipe dream that's in need of changing.

A Plan Without a Foundation is Like a Pizza with No Crust

Whatever your talents, interests, and goals are, for any project you embark on, it's super important to start with a strong foundation! Anything that I've accomplished with any degree of success was achieved because I took the time to build a solid foundation (no home-builder pun intended!). This can also be thought of as mastering the basics.

> I didn't get there by wishing for it or hoping for it, but by working for it.
>
> **ESTEE LAUDER**

Talent and work ethic are two very different things. I can have a God-given talent, but it will only improve once I've taken the time to master the basics. Mastering the basics takes focus and hard work. With or without the talent to do something, I found out that I still needed to master the basics to be at my best. Being at my best always increases my chances for success.

Mastering the basics may, or may not, involve formal schooling. No school could ever teach me the power of a lunchtime business meeting. There aren't night classes for the art of how to joke around with suppliers and customers to put them at ease. No college covers how to negotiate with employees, suppliers, tradespeople, inspectors, city hall, and the grumpy cat at the counter who stamps the papers for my permits. School never taught me how to make money while I slept, or what a weather delay would cost me financially, or how to renegotiate a contract because of unexpected extras. The University of Trial and Error taught me plenty, and I've learned the most by working for myself.

> *It had long since come to my attention that people of accomplishment rarely sat back & let things happen to them. They went out & happened to things.*
>
> **LEONARDO DA VINCI**

No matter what it was I decided to do to make a living, I knew that it was what I did outside of my job that would increase my chances of achieving financial freedom, as would every scrap of learning along the way. My view on my free time was this: only when I was sleeping, exercising, or going out with my friends was my time truly free. Any other time, I was always figuring out how to get to my *Enough* number, what my next goals should be, what my plan was, and what knowledge or further learning I needed to have a good solid foundation.

To be financially free, I had to learn how to figure things out that were way beyond my grasp, to teach myself what did and didn't work, and then to determine how to move on. I had to learn so many different things that had nothing to do with one another, such as accounting; cleaning; dealing with employees, suppliers, and customers; inventory; contracts; and the list goes on. For every plan I implemented, I mastered the basics first, and so should you.

These are some examples of the successful plans that I've put in place for myself:

- Make a million dollars: I put down on paper what I was planning to do, why I needed to do it, and how (my plan) I was going to make a million dollars. Then I read all the books and materials I could (mastering the basics). I found mentors and did the work. I took calculated risks. I spoke with multimillionaires and asked them how they did it. I modelled what they did, which increased my chances of getting the same results they had already achieved.

- Retire at thirty-seven: I could have conveniently retired sooner, but I didn't feel that I had *Enough* yet. I put down on paper that I would be out of the rat race, no matter what, by age thirty-seven. I wrote questions and answered all of them about how much I would need financially to feel that I could retire (which was the beginning of understanding my *Enough* number and what *Enough* meant to me). Then I mastered the basics by reading everything I could about how to retire early, by speaking with people who had already done so, and by talking with my bank and learning about finances and the importance of a steady cash flow. I went from putting down an arbitrary completion date to coming up with a plan and understanding how money works so that I could retire comfortably.

- Write a screenplay: I envisioned myself writing a proper movie screenplay. I went from watching movies and thinking, "I can do that!" to making a plan to learn how it was done. I bought a book on how to write screenplays. Then I bought twenty more books, attended seminars, invested in a software program, outlined my story, and wrote my screenplay. I went on to write many others!

Building a solid foundation pushed me forwards whenever I had those moments where I felt lost. I kept in mind, at all times, "I am my own biggest obstacle." You too will have to overcome your intrinsic barriers and the natural tendency towards the inertia that handicaps a lot of people's goals right from the start. A plan that begins with getting a good grounding in the basics, which applies to whatever goal you're aiming for, is also something that will give you a quiet confidence. When you do the work, and lay a solid foundation, you've already significantly increased your chances for success. Don't be a crustless pizza!

How to Get From (A) to (B)onus!

When I'm after a goal, and it involves money, I will be overly precise about every single detail—to the point of exhaustion. Therefore, when I make a solid plan for how I'm going to reach that goal, it will usually go, mostly, as I envisioned it. Despite your best efforts, it's important to recognize from the outset that your plan is never going to go 100 percent the way you envision it. The plan is only there to help you focus on your desired end point and what steps might be needed to get there.

A plan also gives you a way to measure your progress towards its completion. When I create a plan, and set it in motion, it's so that I have some direction guiding me step by step to what it is that I'm after, instead of just hoping that my dreams come to fruition by luck! Sure, pure luck sometimes happens, for some people, but I've never been that lucky, and if the rabbit's foot had been working for you better than it did for the poor rabbit, then you probably wouldn't be reading this book!

When I make a plan, I know that life's rollercoaster ups and downs will happen, and it isn't always going to go smoothly. I try to set myself up to win even when I lose, whenever possible, so I'm happy with the outcome either way. For example, when I began to learn how homes were built, I had no guarantee that my plan to become a successful builder would pan out, but either way, I was learning a new skill. Win or lose, I always know what it is I'm after because, before I start, I have a goal or an end number in mind at all times.

Your long-range, giraffe's-eye-view plan should be a through line to your *Enough* number. It should allow you to do *Enough* of the things you see yourself doing, have *Enough* of the things you need to have, and live *Enough* of the lifestyle you see yourself living. Your plan, in

> *Learn from the mistakes*
> *of others...*
> *You can't live long enough*
> *to make them all*
> *yourselves.*
>
> **ELEANOR ROOSEVELT**

other words, is the sum of the strategies, initiatives, tools, and knowledge you'll need to get you from where you are now to where you would like to be, while still giving you the ability to be flexible and adapt to changes along the route. You'll need to come up with all sorts of short-term plans along the way that will serve as the stepping stones on your journey to *Enough*, but it's important never to lose sight of your ultimate goal and how you're going to get there. Your long-range plan should drive your shorter-term projects.

Fuhgettaboutit

I tell people to choose a goal and make a plan, which involves mastering the basics and figuring out what they need to do to get from A to B. Then, I tell them that they should start working on that plan and set it in motion. But, when I tell people to forget about their plan, as part of that same pre-determined plan, the reaction I get is usually some version of "Say what?!" The pastry of life is filled with juicy contradictions, and setting a plan aside often achieves what a world of push, pull, pure impatience simply can't. When I'm super focused on accomplishing something, and it's just not happening for me the way I had thought it would, I get frustrated. Frustration leads to bad decisions, and I might even quit!

When I feel the first twinges of frustration trying to fracture my plan, I go for a run or a bike ride, and I do my best not to think about what's bothering me. I focus on any activity that has nothing to do with my goal and just forget about it all. Your *Fuhgettaboutit* might be playing golf, going to see a movie, surfing, yoga, going out for a walk, or just doing something/anything not associated with the plan.

The oddest things happen when I'm out for a long bike ride or run: the answers to my problems miraculously appear! Your brain and body chemistry change when you exercise and so does your thinking. Levels of the neurotransmitters dopamine (a feel-good chemical) and serotonin (memory and mental sharpness) rise. I've noticed that how I approach a problem before taking a break is always different than afterwards. My thinking becomes much more concise and focused after a good run or ride. The change in how you think following a bit of exercise, or any break, is not always something that's huge, but it's a change, and that creates a new, positive, much needed shift in the right direction. It may just give you a fresh perspective.

This fresh perspective is a critical part of the planning process. The problem with focusing too much attention on a goal, like making lots of money, is that it can consume you, especially if the aim is a general or unfocused one or if you don't have an end point in mind. After I set my end number, (either short term or long term), I will put a plan in place, and only then will I take my first steps towards achieving my financial goal. What I do next seems implausible to some. I just let my plan go to the back of my mind, and I try not to think about it!

I go about my life and do all the other things I need to do at the same time as working to reach my financial goal. No one can do only one thing 24/7, and this kind of obsessive focus won't make a goal happen all at once anyway. What it will do is lead to exhaustion, frustration, and to throwing in the proverbial towel. You need to take breaks, do other things, and not always think about your goal. You need to *Fuhgettaboutit.*

When people ask me what my financial goals are, I share this with them, "I try not to think about money too much. The seeds are planted for various goals, and they'll happen when they're supposed to." That answer drives people crazy, but I learned a long time ago that if I wanted to make God laugh, I'd tell him my plans! It would drive me crazy if I obsessed about them. I just need to *Fuhgettaboutit* from time to time and say enough is *Enough*!

> *Exercise is always a winning financial strategy.*
> *It's when a lot of my ideas, answers, or solutions come to me.*
> *Plus, it keeps me fit & makes me feel better all around.*
>
> **MICHAEL RULLO**

Reassess

You've got a goal. You've set up a plan. You've started mastering the basics. You've said *Fuhgettaboutit*, taken some breaks, got some exercise. Now what? Now it's time to go back to the plan and reassess everything! Do you need to adapt something? Make some significant changes? Or continue as is and stay on track? Reassessing is something you'll come back to repeatedly, and it needs to become instinctive. You may need to re-evaluate in response to unexpected changes when they happen. If something isn't working, you must be able to reassess and quickly figure out what else you can do to make things better. Reassess for success!

If you're not looking at what's working or not working, your chances of failing are greater than your chances of succeeding! Many companies have imploded with their inability to reassess quickly enough. Take, for example, the case of Blockbuster Video. They were valued at $8.4 billion when a pissed-off customer, Reed Hastings, sick of exorbitant late fees, founded Netflix. Blockbuster missed the online-entertainment boat and went under. Netflix is currently valued at $42 billion. The adage *Adapt or Die* applies to large enterprises and small money-making ventures alike. The same can be said for a person who has a plan to make a million dollars. If he or she doesn't reassess the plan continually, making changes where and when necessary (often on the spot!), I would make a bet that that person won't reach his or her million-dollar goal!

There will always be things you can change and things you simply can't. You'll figure out what those things are faster by asking yourself, "What is it I'm after? What can I change? Can I change my end goal? Can I change my plan?" I reassess continually, on the spot, and the goal that I eventually reach is never 100 percent the one I set out to achieve. Yes, I've exceeded some goals, but I've also come up short. However, when I cross the finish line for a goal I've set out for myself, then that becomes my definition of success. I've crossed that finish line, even if its position has changed from when I originally started. I didn't quit. I'm a winner just for having reached my goal.

Enough is a constant process of reassessment. Allow yourself the freedom to move the finish line of your goal. Don't quit, as in giving up on something you still want to achieve, but recognize that it's okay to stop when you have achieved *Enough*, and it's time to tackle What's Next.

The Path to *Enough* is Paved with Hard Work

My Dad was a paver by trade, and so I should know. It takes a lot of hard work to get to *Enough*. It's even more complicated than sitting around lamenting that you don't have it, can't get it, or can't change anything in your life but the channel on the TV. I always remind myself of this:

1. I need a goal.
2. I need a plan.
3. I need a break and to forget about the plan.
4. When it's time to focus again, I need to reassess everything, adapt, and keep myself moving forward!
5. I need to repeat steps one to four, & I need to work my butt off.

When I do all of these things, I don't stress about my goals or plans or what's *Enough*. Life is good, and I'll get to *Enough* without breaking my spirit by the time I get there!

The secrets to my success were that I was always looking for money-making opportunities, always on the hunt for multiple sources of income, and always had a plan. The biggest secret that all successful individuals share is that they know that it takes hard work to achieve any worthwhile goal! There's a lot of psychobabble out there about the power of *intention* or how focusing your thoughts on something you want will make it magically appear, but that's nonsense! If you buy into that, you're kidding yourself, and you're not doing yourself any favours! Real success takes planning and *hard work*!

> *A person will sometimes devote all his life to the development of one part of his body—the wishbone.*
>
> **ROBERT FROST**

I had to do hard; tedious; repetitive; boring; and mentally, physically, and emotionally taxing things to see even the smallest successes, and you will too. You can only delegate so much, and then it's time to roll up the ol' sleeves and do the work. I don't want to sugar coat how hard it was for me, what I had to do, and what I had to give up to succeed. Success is often tedious. It's not sexy. It's dirty, hard, lonely, and filled with uncertainty and doubt the whole way through.

The sense of gratification comes later, after I've put in the time, struggled, hit the wall and got back up, and pushed forwards. It comes when I've found a path when I thought all was lost and when I've realized that I've finally reached the goal. *Enough* is something you're going to have to work for. There are no excuses, good intentions, wishes, wants, or whining that can take the place of hard work!

> *No amount of good intentions can take the place of hard work!*
>
> **MICHAEL RULLO**

I grew up in Canada, and I saw people who came from less than nothing and ended up becoming unlikely multimillionaires. There was one secret they had that others didn't. For example, I heard a story about a Russian teacher who had only been in Canada for less than eight years. He started with nothing, but within those eight years, he had already become a multimillionaire. When people asked him what the secret to his success was and how had he become so wealthy so quickly, especially when so many individuals who'd been in Canada their whole lives hadn't had such success, his response was this:

> *Russia in the seventies & early eighties was a communist country, & it didn't matter how hard I worked or how many jobs I had, we all got paid the same. There was no chance to progress there. In Canada, the more jobs I have, the more opportunities I have to make money. The harder I work here, the more I make. This country is set up for me to succeed if I am willing to work for it!*

That story struck a chord with me because it was true for me as well, and it will be true for you too. The secret to most secrets is that they are not that secret. And the secret to where money comes from? Well, it doesn't grow on trees, but if you plan(t) some seeds, put down some good solid roots, and do the work, you'll see *Enough* of the fruits of your labour to think that it does!

Not Had *Enough*? Well, Here's Some More:

- benefits of having a plan:

  https://lengstorf.com/effective-project-planning/

- how to plan when you're bad at it:

  https://hbr.org/2017/07/a-way-to-plan-if-youre-bad-at-planning

- your brain on exercise:

  https://www.eurekalert.org/pub_releases/2016-02/uoc--tiy022416.php

  https://paleoleap.com/brain-exercise/

- how Netflix originated:

  https://www.inc.com/magazine/20051201/qa-hastings.html

Chapter 3 • Takeaways:

1. Always be on the lookout for money-making opportunities, especially ones that don't seem that lucrative at first glance. Look for money that other people may be throwing away or that they may have overlooked. Also, think of where your money is going. Is there any way more money could be made or saved?

2. Always have multiple sources of income.

3. Learn how to make a plan: 1) Start with a goal and lay a foundation by mastering the basics related to that goal; 2) Determine how to get from A to B and write this plan down; 3) Start work on your plan but also try to *Fuhgettaboutit* periodically; 4) Reassess your progress by asking yourself, "What is it I'm after? What can I change? Can I change my end goal? Can I change my plan?" 5) Repeat steps one to four and work your butt off!

4. Success usually takes a lot of hard work. Your only *free* time should be when you're sleeping, exercising (or doing something to purposely *Fuhgettaboutit*), or going out with friends/family. The rest of your time is for working to realize your plan.

5. Doing more than is expected of you and working hard will help you get to *Enough*.

4

Feed the Beast or Make It Starve: Goals in the Face of Your Inner Critic

Become a Pro at something other than:
Profanity, Pro-vanity, & Procrastination!
MICHAEL RULLO

I discovered I was dyslexic when I was twenty-one. Before then, when I was in school, I had learned to get by, by being extra creative in my thoughts and actions to pass my classes. It wasn't easy because I had this inner voice always filling me with doubts, criticizing me, tempting me, and giving me reasons not to do the things I needed to do. This voice was, and still is at times, a real jolt to my self-esteem. Whenever I have a goal, and I start on a plan to realize that goal, my inner voice pipes up. The worst part is that my inner voice is Italian, so it's super loud and belligerent!

My self-doubt, as expressed by this noisy inner monster, has always been there. Sometimes, I wish I could have been one of those blissfully ignorant people who believe in themselves to the point of grand delusion. Those are the people who just go for things in life without a second thought or care in the world. My inner voice, however, is on a constant loop, and it's not kind or friendly. It always shows up when I least expect it, and it constantly tells me to quit. It's brutal! I feel like it takes pride in my setbacks and is always there to snicker and say, "Told you so," but I've learned that I can feed this inner beast or I can make it starve.

> *Going through the motions*
> *doesn't mean*
> *you're taking action!*
>
> **MICHAEL RULLO**

I imagine that your inner voice can be a monster sometimes as well, and it can undermine your efforts before even a simple goal can get off the ground. Self-doubt feeds on your fears. How can you hope to get a sense of *Enough* in your life with this self-saboteur acting as judge, jury, and dream killer rolled into one? If you let the voice of self-doubt roll on without challenging its conclusions, accusations, or assumptions, it grows steadily worse and can be paralyzing.

What shuts this inner critic down? Action! By just taking action, by the simple act of doing, the inner critic is starved of ammunition and rumination. Taking action towards realizing your goal will also cause your willpower muscles to grow, and they'll overpower the persistent critic inside your head. Letting the inner voice have free reign while dwelling on, and believing in, what it has to say without question feeds its negativity, and it will get louder, more insistent, and more persistent.

The actions it takes to get that inner voice to be quiet are not always easy, but they're doable. When I make a plan, put in the work, make it fun, and keep at it, then that critical, little inner monster can't grow stronger. I question its conclusions. I ask, "Oh really? Is that right?" Or I say to it things like, "Since when can you predict the future?" I make it work to answer me, and I don't let it off easily. I overpower it with my logic, heart, soul, mind, and action in the direction of my goal. Any action that you take, after the first spark that is the beginning of an idea or a goal, will start to silence the booming voice of your inner critic.

The voice of your inner critic is one of the biggest problems with *Enough*. It's the loud voice in your head that says you're never going to get there, that you don't deserve it, or that *Enough* is impossible and unattainable, too far away to even try to reach for it. Having concrete, measurable goals will give you that sense of accomplishment that will naturally lead you to a feeling of *Enough*. Anything that you're missing is worth aiming for. It could be *Enough* time, *Enough* money, and *Enough* adventure. It may even be the sense that who you are and what you've achieved in life is *Enough*. A goal is just something that will help you know when you're at the finish line, so it's important not to let your inner critic stop you from trying something.

Changing Lanes

There was one moment that changed my life forever; I was faced with a serious decision when I was twenty years old, which would end up shaping my entire life. If I had chosen differently, listened to my inner critic, I might still be blindly flailing around in the dark, chasing shadows in my search for *Enough*.

I was no different than any other twenty something who lusts after flashy cars, fashionable clothes, and pricey watches. I was living in the moment and didn't relate my actions to future financial success or failure. I was happy to be in the now.

From the age of ten, when George introduced me to the work-a-day world of the grocery store, until I turned twenty, I handed the majority of the money that I made over to my Mom. I knew she'd take care of it for me much better than if I did it myself. I also knew that if my parents needed help financially, they could depend on that stash. It became a habit; after all, I was a kid who had no real bills other than my old car and car insurance. I would just hand over my paycheques to her, taking twenty dollars for myself every week. Sometimes, I could even stretch out the twenty dollars for two weeks. I was pretty good with handling money after the tough-love lessons on money, credit, etc. from George and my parents. Plus, my weekly twenty dollars wasn't buying me any designer anything, anytime soon; it wasn't exactly burning a hole in my pocket.

I had been working at everything I could since the age of ten, but I had no idea how much I had accumulated by the time I was twenty. One day my Mom sat me down and showed me my bank statement. When I found out I had close to $100 thousand in my savings account, I couldn't believe it! I felt like I had won it, not worked for it! I had it spent in my mind almost instantly. I wanted a new Jeep Wrangler, a Rolex watch, and to travel the world. I had plans for that money, and I was going to have a good time spending it!

I was on my way to go Jeep shopping, my newfound riches lighting up my imagination, when my Mom stopped me at the door. With a nod and a look, she gestured me back inside. She sat me down once again and had a serious talk with me. "Your sisters bought new cars when they had some money," she said, "And what happened to them? The cars aren't even worth half of what they paid for them now! Now they're married, and they wish they could have that money today to put towards their homes or pay down their debts." I protested. I think I may have pleaded, but she wouldn't budge. "Do you want to be a big shot?" she asked, "Or do you want to make money so that when you're older, you won't have to kiss nobody's ass?"

That's a lot to think about when you're twenty, so I asked my Dad for his thoughts, and he said, "I know it's fun to have a new car and look like a big shot, but next year a new one will come out, and you'll want that one. Then you'll want to buy another one, and before you know it, you keep buying a better one, but there goes all your money!" My urge to get a new Jeep was starting to fade. "Buy a home," said Dad, "Over time it'll make you money if you take care of it and you're smart about it!"

Even my two older sisters told me, "Buy a cool used car, save your money, and purchase a home; you won't regret it!" I had imagined driving the new Jeep so vividly that I felt like it was being repossessed as I struggled with my family's advice. I knew they only had my best interests in mind, so little by little, I waved goodbye to the Jeep, and I took what they had to say to heart.

For fun, and because I was still a little down about the Jeep, we all went to look at houses that were in the price range that I could afford. I was surprised by how some people didn't show any pride in the ownership of their homes. If I was going to buy one, I had to find a good one, one that would cause me little to no stress after I bought it.

Spring and summer passed, and I bought a used VW Golf GTI with less than 10,000 kilometres on it. It was super fun to drive (Loved that GTI!). I found that I wasn't into buying new clothes, had no pressing urge to take a holiday, or even to buy myself anything else, and as time passed, I noticed I didn't seem to care about having that new Jeep anymore. The moment had passed, and frankly, I forget what I thought was so pressing about it.

One night, I got a call from our family realtor who had a property she wanted to show me. It was late on a Sunday evening, and I asked my Mom and Dad to come along and take a look. We all got in the car and drove over to see this old 1950s home that was in immaculate condition. The basement was not developed, but the sellers were the original owners, and they were proud to show it to me.

Afterwards, I hemmed and hawed to my parents. My inner critic saw only the flaws and had lots to say about it. "It's on a busy street," said the voice. "It's in front of a school, and there's a bus stop next to it." The critic was on a roll now. "There's no garage, and the basement is empty. It's not perfect; I think we should keep looking."

My parents had years of experience and a different take on what I saw as flaws. My Mom said, "It's great! It's in front of a bus stop; now if somebody doesn't have a car, this is convenient for them." I was surprised to hear such a different point of view. "It's great that it's in front of a school!" she continued. "You'll get a friendly family who will want their kids to be close to school if you go to rent it out. It's on a busy street, so lots of people will see the 'For Rent' sign, and they'll take down your number and call you!" My Dad was equally enthusiastic. "If you build a garage, then people can park their extra-big cars or trucks back there, and you could charge more money for rent. The empty basement is great! We can help you build a basement suite, and you'd double your income by renting it out."

I started to see that it was an excellent property, but when I crunched the numbers, I couldn't afford to live in it! My parents laughed out loud, and said to me, "You live with us rent free. You rent this house out until you can afford to live there. When you live in a home, it costs you money. When you rent out a house, it brings you money!"

I had to make a quick decision. I could make this work if I were to rent it out. The way I looked at it, my money was sitting in a bank somewhere collecting only a little bit of interest anyway. Heck, I didn't even know I had that much money until a few months before. If I bought the house, I could see where my money went directly, in a real, tangible way. I didn't seem to care about the money before, so either way, I just looked at buying the home as another place to park my money. My inner critic said, "Hopefully the home wouldn't go down in value." I took action. I bought my first home. My inner critic had nothing more to say.

> *A man is what he thinks about all day long.*
>
> **RALPH WALDO EMERSON**

> ### *Rullo Rules*
>
> Banks are black & white. They don't care about you or your goals. They look at cold hard assets, income, & past income statements showing that you are a small financial risk. When you approach a bank, you need to show that what you propose is beneficial for both of you. Come prepared to show them assets as collateral, proof of current and past income, & projections for future revenue. Negotiate what is required from you, & what you need from them. You *do* have leverage with banks & financial institutions, simply by knowing how the game is played.

Easy Come, Easy Go!

It was when I applied for my first mortgage that I was reminded yet again that numbers don't lie. The banking system is set up to cover its interests first and look after its clients second.

The banks are not saints; they loan money and do business to profit. They said that I had to pay 13.75 percent interest and I was told this was a good deal. It didn't feel like a fair deal when it was explained to me that I'd be paying the bank back thirty-five years' worth of accrued interest payments, which would amount to more than triple the home's asking price! (The maximum amortization period was reduced in 2008 from forty years to twenty-five years). I had learned my lesson about credit the hard way from George, my first boss, but my Dad explained that there was such a thing as good credit. "Bad credit," he explained, "takes money out of your pocket and you'll have nothing of any real value to show for it afterwards; whereas good credit is an asset that grows in value even if you factor in interest payments." My stomach was in my mouth while I was deciding to commit myself to paying for that first mortgage. My inner critic was full of doubts and worries. He wanted to stop me from doing it. He almost did!

Because of George's lessons on credit, as well as my age, I had no credit history. The banks eyed my mortgage application with skepticism. They required a cosigner. I had to ask my parents to cosign for me, and I had to show the bank I was employed for two years before they would even consider loaning me the money to get my first home. I was incensed.

"I'm putting down a lot of money, and you still need reassurances?!" The bank replied with the cold hard facts of how they protect their interests, "If you miss a payment and that leads to two or three missed payments, we need to know we can recover our money, and if not from you, it's going to be from your cosigners."

They told me what I was responsible for, explained the payment structure, and reminded me about how long I'd be committing myself to paying it all back. It seemed like a life sentence. What they didn't do was give me a plan on how I might be able to pay it off sooner. Their objective was just to get me to sign on the dotted line, locking me in for the next thirty-five years. No bank has ever told me how to pay off a mortgage and save myself possibly hundreds of thousands of dollars or more in interest payments.

My Mom, on the other hand, asked all the right questions and showed me that there are ways to navigate the system, if I were smart about it. Knowing the right questions to ask is a big part of any plan, which is where mastering the basics comes into play. With the right questions, the bank opened up about the advantages and disadvantages of closed and open mortgages.

Closed mortgages limit (often on an annual basis) how much of the mortgage balance you can pay off sooner, while open mortgages allow you to pay off any amount without any additional charges. Just explaining the various industry terms would require another book, but as an example, nowadays, there are Blanket Mortgages, Balloon Mortgages, Growing Equity Mortgages, Pledged Account Mortgages, Reverse Annuity Mortgages, and Canadian Rollover or Adjustable Rate Mortgages, and the list goes on. At the start of any goal, plan, or financial transaction, it's vital to do your homework and learn everything you need to, to get in the game.

With my Mom's knowledge and expertise, we set up two separate mortgages, one a closed mortgage with financial penalties for paying it off early, and the other an open mortgage with fewer penalties for prepayment. My Mom told me that I had five years to pay off this mortgage or I would be a loser, paying for it for the next thirty-five years. She also made me aware that in thirty-five years, the home would be old and I'd probably have to rebuild, repair, or remodel, which would mean spending a lot of money all over again.

My inner voice played on my doubts, but sometimes the inner critic can be my biggest motivator. For example, I didn't know with 100 percent certainty whether or not I could afford to buy a home. I also keenly felt the pressure of having to repay money to a bank. My inner critic asked, "What if you miss a payment?" I didn't want that to reflect poorly on my parents who would then be held responsible as my cosigners. I knew my goal, my end point, and where I was starting from, but I still had to learn the rules of how mortgages work and then break them to pay off my mortgage in less than the thirty-five years that would only serve to maximize the bank's profit.

I argued with the voice of my inner critic. I wouldn't let myself or my parents down, and I wouldn't let the banks benefit from my hard-earned money when I could keep it in my pocket. Wanting to prove my inner critic wrong motivated me to develop the goal of working my hardest to pay off my mortgage quickly.

My parents had paid off mortgages before, so that was why they encouraged me to rent out the home instead of living in it. We even interviewed potential tenants to screen for good ones before even signing the papers for the mortgage. My goal became a plan, which was that every time I came into money, I would put it towards my mortgage. I felt like I could have it paid off soon enough if I stuck to the plan. Take that inner critic!

> *If you dwell on the bad*
> *& the improbable,*
> *you'll conclude,*
> *"It's impossible!"*
>
> **MICHAEL RULLO**

I bought that home for $120 thousand. I put $70 thousand down and spent $15 thousand building a basement suite. I had spent $10 thousand on my car (Seriously loved that GTI!) only a couple of months before; I went from having $100 thousand in my bank account to now officially only having $5 thousand! Easy come, easy go—But I sure had something to show for it!

The Black Hole of Negative Energy

There's a surprising amount of negativity that comes with change and the pursuit of a goal. Some of that negativity is the self-doubt, fear, and worry that are internally generated, but some of it comes from people around you. Within three years of owning my first home, I had paid it off, which was two years ahead of the schedule that I had originally planned. I did this by not buying any new clothes or unnecessary purchases. I didn't eat out at all, not even fast food, nor did I go on any holidays. For those three years, I gave up everything. That's the motivating power of goals in the face of your inner critic. I gave myself up to loneliness, and I even lost some friends along the way who couldn't understand what I was doing.

I learned that sometimes the voice of my inner critic is repeating what people around me are saying. My friends didn't like it very much when I was suddenly so focused on paying down the mortgage. Right from the moment I told people that I was going to buy a home, they started feeding me their objections. "Do you even know what owning a home means?" they'd say, and, "Do you have any idea how much it costs? You're too young to qualify for a mortgage! You should travel, have fun, buy a car, and you shouldn't think about the purchase of a home until you're thirty something; that's what most people do!"

It doesn't matter how big or small your goals may be; there will always be detractors who dredge up worst-case scenarios, declare their personal beliefs as facts, and who focus only on the downside with the endless negativity that your inner critic is only too happy to absorb and repeat. Don't get me wrong, there are also people who say encouraging things, but the negative comments are what stick with you, and they are certainly the ones I struggle with.

When I made my last payment to the bank and they closed my mortgage early without me having to pay any penalties, the bank manager couldn't believe it. "How'd you do it?" She asked me. "I work in a bank, and we get preferential rates, and I'm still paying off my mortgage!" I was twenty-three years old, and here was a woman in her fifties asking me how she could pay off her mortgage faster! I told her what I did, what sacrifices I made, how I created extra income wherever and whenever I could, and how I put all my income towards paying the mortgage. Her reply to me was, and I'll never forget it, "Oh, I couldn't do that! That seems way too hard!"

Sometimes it can feel like there's a big black hole of negativity sucking you down as you reach for your goals, that even trying to get to *Enough* or to make the smallest improvements or steps towards a goal is just "too hard." In the same way, as I learned to handle my inner critic, I discovered that I could feed or starve this negativity. I feed it by letting the negative comments repeat and build, by dwelling on the bad and the improbable and coming up with "It's impossible!" I starve the black hole by taking action, such as making a plan, but I use the power of possible thinking. Possible thinking is even better than positive thinking because your inner critic can't argue with it.

Possible thinking directly focuses on the facts. Is reaching the goal possible? Possible thinking helps you take your power back from the doubts and fears, and failings-focused inner critic. Most of the negative comments that come your way, either internally or externally, are not based on fact at all. Possible thinking is a way of saying, "I see the negatives. I hear the concerns, and I'm aware of the many different versions of 'you can't' and 'you're not good enough' that are being tabled...but I'm doing it anyway!"

> *Start by doing what's necessary; then do what's possible, & suddenly you are doing the impossible.*
>
> **FRANCIS OF ASSISI**

To achieve a goal is a major feat in and of itself, but it's also a huge triumph to not let the negativity stop you. Achieving goals is a beautiful thing, but it's also a great feeling to believe in yourself *Enough* to progress towards a goal when others don't believe you can do it. I made it a point to get past the negative comments and doubts expressed by those I loved and respected, and I got through the gatekeeper of my inner critic to get to my desired outcome, which was to have my first house paid off, free and clear. As much as it would have been easy for me to give in and give up, it was infinitely better to say to myself, "I'm doing this no matter what!"

Must Versus Want in a Sea of Doubt

Whenever a sea of doubt succeeded in tsunami-ing me as I pursued a goal, I came to realize that I was drowning in doubt because I didn't want whatever the goal was badly enough! I didn't make it a must to achieve it. When a goal is a must, I'll find a way to keep my head above water, but if it's just something I want, it's easy to justify giving up.

> When it is obvious that the goals cannot be reached, don't adjust the goals, adjust the action steps.
>
> **CONFUCIUS**

I had to pay off that first mortgage quickly. It was a big must for me because I couldn't let my parents or myself down. I couldn't let my inner critic, my vocal friends, or the banking system get the best of me. There were no set steps or rules for how I was going to do it, but I was determined. When you start on a goal that you feel will take you closer to what *Enough* is for you, it will be helpful if you ask yourself why you need to achieve that goal. Ask yourself, "Is this a must or a want?"

Musts always push me to do something big and not to give up. They empower me to achieve accomplishments beyond my wildest imaginings. When I make something a must, it becomes a need for me to accomplish it. When I ask myself, "Why am I going for this?" and the answer makes me feel hungry inside, it's a must do. I feel eager to give it everything I have. Wanting something, by comparison, is simply not that compelling enough of a drive, and you'll likely bail on it at the first sign of trouble.

I never *want* to accomplish my goals; I only go after a goal when I feel I *must* achieve it! When I approach a goal from the viewpoint of needing to do it, then my goal becomes easier to move towards, and I'm not as fazed by my inner critic's deluges of doubt, stormy seas, or unforeseen twisters of fate bound and determined to rock my boat.

With a must goal, I can envision it, and I can see how to get there and what it will take. My inner critic is noisy in the beginning, but as I replay my vision of the end point, in a constant loop, it quiets down. I'm able to see how to achieve my goal from front to back and back to front.

I know it inside and out, and it feels real to me before I even start. A plan begins to take shape, and I take that first step, no matter how small, which creates that drive, that sense of urgency and momentum that will propel me towards my goal.

That first action towards a goal can take the form of writing the goal down in detail, starting to write out a plan, doing some research online, watching documentaries on the subject, or talking to people in the know. I obsess about how getting to the end of my goal will feel, what it'll look like, what it'll mean, what it'll take to get there, and how I'll feel as I'm accomplishing it, so that I am motivated to finish! I know inside that I *must* do this, and it isn't just a passing *want*.

> *Life is like a piano.*
> *The white keys*
> *represent happiness*
> *& the black keys*
> *represent sadness.*
> *But remember,*
> *as you go through life,*
> *the black keys*
> *make music too.*
>
> **UNKNOWN**

When I took that first step, with my parent's help, and bought a house, it changed the direction of the rest of my life. It shaped my understanding of money and goals and the hard work and sacrifice necessary to achieve *Enough*. It also put me face to face with my inner critic. We don't always see eye to eye, and he still has plenty to say. I always listen to him for a while, in case he has a point, but we have an understanding these days, and when I say, "That's enough!" he shuts up. He knows better than to get between me and my pursuit of my dreams.

Not Had *Enough*? Well, Here's Some More:

- shutting down your inner critic:

  http://www.positive-way.com/stopping%20your%20inner%20critic.htm

  https://journal.thriveglobal.com/theres-power-in-writing-down-what-your-inner-critic-is-saying-fec60b305a80

  http://www.huffingtonpost.com/2013/04/06/negative-self-talk-think-positive_n_3009832.html

- strategies to pay off your mortgage faster:

  http://www.moneysense.ca/spend/real-estate/mortgages/6-strategies-for-paying-off-your-mortgage-faster/
- understanding different mortgage types:

  http://www.mortgagebrokersottawa.com/mortgage-solutions/different-types-of-mortgages/

Chapter 4 · Takeaways

1. We all have an inner critic that voices negativity and self-doubt when we consider undertaking a new goal. Taking action, such as making a plan, is a surefire way to quiet this inner voice.

2. Real banks aren't like the bank of Mom and Dad. They don't have your best interests in mind unless your interests and theirs coincide. They look at numbers and profit. Learn everything you can about what you want from them (such as a mortgage or loan) so that your professional pitch is presented as a *win-win* strategy.

3. Not all credit is bad. Bad credit is costly, and you'll have nothing of any real value to show for it afterwards; good credit is an asset that grows in value even if you factor in interest payments.

4. The inner critic is often repeating comments others have made. Use this negativity to motivate you to work harder towards your goal.

5. Practice possible thinking by focusing on the facts and steps needed to get to your goal, and then tell your inner critic you're doing it anyway!

6. Make sure the goals you select to get you from now to *Enough* are something you feel you must do or must have. Wants are fickle and change quickly and often. If your goal is a want, you may run out of drive before you run out of road.

5

Step It Up:
The Power of Preparation to Achieve Success

*Set up your goal correctly the first time around
& you're already halfway there!*
MICHAEL RULLO

I N my home, when I was growing up, there was always bread. We didn't eat it that often though, so it would usually go stale and mouldy and I'd ask my Mom, "Why do you keep buying bread when you know nobody's going to eat it?" My Mom's reply was, "Growing up during the war, my brothers and sisters and I went to bed hungry every night. We dreamt of bread. We prayed for food. We would do anything for a piece of bread! Now I can afford food. It makes me feel good knowing it's around and that my children will never have to feel how awful it is to starve!" I came to understand that to my Mom, having bread around the home was her symbol of wealth. She didn't need fancy cars or a big, empty, showpiece home, just bread. It was then that I learned that the idea of *Enough* is relative.

Up until now I've talked a lot about money and finding your *Enough* number, of always being on the lookout for money-making opportunities and multiple sources of income, and of the value of learning how to plan. Then there's good, old-fashioned hard work, but *Enough* is relative, and arriving at it takes more than money. It takes battling your inner critic and its tendency to self-sabotage. It takes learning to sift through the negativity of others around you to see if there's anything useful. It takes figuring out what makes you feel less than, and setting some goals to help you feel like you're working on at least trying to feel like *Enough*.

Many of your goals will require money, even if your *Enough* is simply always to have bread in the house, so it will open more doors to your *Enough* if at least some of your goals involve making more money. However, since *Enough* is relative, some of your goals may revolve around health, fitness, knowledge, love, etc. I want to dissect the process of setting and realizing goals down to its bare essentials for you, to help you get better at it. Whatever goals you can imagine for yourself, the primary process looks the same:

1. Dream it: Catch the spark! Determine your purpose.
2. Envision it: Imagine the end first. Visualize the steps. Be specific.
3. Cement it: Write the goal down in detail.
4. Plan it: Make a plan (MAP) and use mentors, tools, and computer applications or apps.
5. Work it: Take baby steps, keep the momentum going, and make it fun.
6. Adapt it: Modify it. Be flexible and manage your expectations.
7. Celebrate it: Got it! Reward yourself! What's next?

The first four steps of the process are all about goal preparation, and the final three focus on goal realization. It probably won't surprise you to know that in addition to being a respected builder, author, and public speaker, I'm also an *Enough* consultant. What tends to trip people up and send them looking for such a thing as an *Enough* consultant? It's usually some version of their inability to set, work on, and realize their goals. My clients tend to get stuck somewhere in the process, often in the very beginning.

In the "Dream it" phase, they may begin to imagine a specific goal but then get derailed by the struggle to envision how to get there, or they may be stopped by the negative thinking expressed by their inner critics or those around them. Others get caught up in the planning stage, which is usually the lack-of-planning stage, while still others struggle with the motivation needed to keep them working to realize their goals. The bottom line is that to get *Enough*, something must change.

It helps to think of a goal as a change. Learning to manage the process of change is going to help you to understand which goals are worthy of your focus, how best to keep that focus as you work towards your goals, and how smaller goals can add up to *Enough*. Let's take a closer look at steps one to four, which are how to select a target goal and set it up for success. Then we'll talk about steps five to seven, how to work, adapt, and celebrate your goal, in the next chapter.

> *A goal is a dream with a deadline.*
>
> **MICHAEL RULLO**

Step 1: Dream It!

Everything starts from something. When I set a goal for myself, it starts with a spark from my imagination. Some idea, word, or image stirs something deep down inside me. I've learned to recognize that spark when I feel it and to acknowledge and cultivate it. If it's compelling enough that I can't ignore it, then that spark might become a goal. The best revelations and innovations are born from sparks, yet only the best sparks deserve to develop into full-on goals.

The Land of Good Intentions

The trick is not to let a spark die in the land of good intentions. Well-meaning people who don't ever take a step towards realizing their dreams populate the land of good intentions. Why is that? I think it's because it's easier to live small and have big dreams than it is to take that first step towards a goal. Often, people's dreams die before they even have a shot at being made real because the idea is simply not compelling enough for them to do anything about it. They may intend to do something about it someday, but intention that isn't followed by action is fantasy and fiction.

Action! The word scares the daylights out of people whose dreams never seem to inch towards reality. It's easy to be a person with good intentions who never does anything to attain his or her desire. However, it's better to be an individual who's a doer, who works for and moves towards, his or her goal. To be a doer, you need to acknowledge when the spark happens and then declare your intention by following it up with

> *It is not enough to take steps*
> *which may someday*
> *lead to a goal;*
> *each step must be itself*
> *a goal & a step likewise.*
>
> JOHANN
> WOLFGANG VON GOETHE

the action(s) of researching, or at least considering, what you'd like to have happen next from this initial spark.

Recognizing or cultivating sparks is sort of like capturing fireflies, you should be looking for them and be ready to pounce when you see one. Declaring your intention is like that pounce and it, in turn, becomes the catalyst for you to start taking further action. Your first action should be to use the energy and excitement of that initial spark to motivate you to form a goal. Remember that goals are the changes that are going to help you get to *Enough*.

Purpose

To move from a spark to a goal, you must attach a strong enough purpose to it, for example, why you need to reach your target, or why your goal is important to achieve. A purpose is a sense of resolve or determination. It's the deeper meaning behind why you're doing something that you have already attached your intention to.

Many times, when I didn't even come close to achieving one of my goals, I realized it was because I hadn't attached a strong enough purpose to the goal, a reason as to why I was deciding to try for it in the first place. It isn't good enough to dream about doing, or having, or being, something. It isn't good enough to intend to do something or even to want to do something. What reinforces your will when things get tough, is a solid sense of purpose, a deep underlying reason, which makes you passionate about moving towards your goal with absolute confidence.

A strong sense of purpose always fuels me when I have the inevitable moments when I want to give up. Often, I attach a higher purpose to what I consider to be a divine spark that spoke to my soul, something that was compelling enough to make me take action. This *higher purpose* gives my goals a deeper meaning. You'll have to find your own reasons why you're going to invest your time, energy, money, spirit, health, and life in the pursuit of a goal.

Don't just ask yourself, "Why should I do this?" This is the time to use questions to help address any underlying, potential roadblocks before they stop you from achieving your goal. Asking yourself questions costs you nothing; the process only requires a bit of time and that you be honest with yourself. The more questions, the better. I just make sure I know why I'm doing something before I start a new goal. It saves me when the times get tough, which they always seem to do. It's what will push you forwards and keep you going too!

These are some of the questions I use:

- Does this inspire and motivate me?
- How will getting to the end of this goal make my life better?
- How important is it for me to make it to the end of this goal?
- Is this goal worthwhile?
- Will this goal make me a better person if I attain it?
- Will my time/energy be better spent pursuing another goal that might get me closer to *Enough* than this one in the long run?
- What sacrifices am I willing to make to achieve my goal?
- Is this goal worth doing the hard work it will take to accomplish it?
- What limiting beliefs do I have that would need to change to motivate me to take that first step towards this goal?
- Do I have the strength to say, "I'm going for it?" even if everybody tells me I'm crazy, it's impossible, and it can't be done?
- Is this goal something that scares me? If it does, can I find the courage to do it, and push myself through when the going gets rough?
- Pursuing a goal can be isolating and require some self-sacrifices; am I willing to give myself up to loneliness for a while to achieve this goal?

You'll have your own list of course, but the most important question you'll need to ask yourself is, "Am I committed to seeing this through?" What I tell myself at the beginning, when I haven't done the hard work yet, is almost always, "Yes!" When I hit the wall, the chips are down, and all is lost, I'll know what I'm made of by staying the course. If a goal matters to me *Enough* after I've asked the tough questions, I'll always ask myself once more, "Am I committed to seeing it through?" If I still answer, "Yes! 100 percent!" then I start, and I don't look back!

Step 2: Envision It!

The second step in the process of goal development is to jump right to the end and envision accomplishing your goal. I'm not suggesting that you get lost in a daydream-type fantasy, but rather that you work on your goal in your imagination first. Visualization is a mental rehearsal of your goal and how you'll achieve it. Successful people make good use of their imaginations. Think of this step as your Oscar-worthy movie with you as the star and your goal as the big, dramatic conclusion.

End First!

Before even contemplating aiming for a goal, I need to know what it is I'm moving towards. I need to be crystal clear as to what my end point is first! When a spark happens for me, it's the catalyst to my becoming more aware of whatever it is that's speaking inside of me. I use that catalyst to push myself to take action, to do research, and to learn all I can about my potential goal. From there, I determine my intention and attach a deeper meaning/purpose to achieving the goal, but before I go any further, I create a solid vision in my imagination of the whole journey from the start to "I did it!"

Push Replay!

I start with the end first in my mind. What will it feel like when I reach my end goal? What will it look like? In the process of envisioning my goal, I'm already mapping out how I see it happening. It's with this visualization that I create my story of how I see myself from the start to the end. This vision is constantly on my mind, and although I know that real life will throw me curve balls and that my plans will have to change as I go along, I've learned that I'll get where I'm going if I *never stop repeating my vision!*

Repeating your vision for your goal is an exercise that can be done anywhere, no matter what you're doing at that moment. It shapes and creates a story, a personal narrative that helps you focus on the journey from start to finish. Olympic athletes, top business people, actors, investors, and public speakers use the technique of visualization. It's very compelling!

Be Specific!

It will help you tremendously if the goal you envision is very detailed. Similarly to the work you've done (hopefully!) so far to figure out what *Enough* means to you and what your *Enough* number is, you'll never get to *there* if you don't know where *there* is.

Sometimes, in conversation, people will use general, non-specific statements to tell me what they want:

- I want to lose weight.
- I want to be rich.
- I want a truck.

> *We aim above the mark to hit the mark!*
>
> **RALPH WALDO EMERSON**

These aren't goals. They're not even half-formed ideas. When I listen to people saying they *want* something, they usually aren't being specific about what it is, exactly, that they *must* have. The above examples are not empowering enough to make someone tough it out and endure what's needed to reach his or her goal. These *wants* are too ambiguous, and they lack a clear description of an actual end point.

I make my endpoints very specific, like this:

- I weigh 225 lbs. on (today's date), and by (a goal date), I will be 190 lbs. by exercising, eating right, and getting plenty of rest. I describe my brief plan for how I see myself doing it. I then justify why I'm doing it, which gives me the added purpose I'll need to push me to reach the end. For example, I'm doing this to be healthier, live a better life, and look and feel better about myself.

- I currently am $28 thousand in debt on (today's date), and I'm going to have $100 thousand after I pay off 100 percent of my debt by (this date). Then I measure where I stand financially right down to the nickel, and I write down a specific amount as a goal. For example, I will make $150 thousand (I always over estimate the amount I need so that I will have more than *Enough*) by this deadline (I note a precise date). Then I think about my express purpose for making money and what my reasons are for needing to reach this goal. Why do I need to have $150 thousand by this time next year? It may be because I need to pay my current debt down to zero dollars so I'll have enough money to put a down payment on a new home.

- I will have a 2019 Ford F150 Limited, platinum white exterior, loaded with every option available, brand new with zero kilometres on it. I will buy it from my local Ford dealer. I will buy it in less than two years' time and pay no more than $65 thousand plus tax for it. I will save up for it until I have $80 thousand, so I can then detail the truck, buy a set of winter rims and tires, and still have money left over to service and insure it with no problems. This will be my everyday vehicle to drive all the time. This is my reward to myself for all the hard work I've done, and I'll share the truck with my friends and family. Also, it will be my highway vehicle and will keep me safe and sound on long road trips for work.

Remember that your *reasons why* don't have to make sense to others; they only have to make sense to you! As long as they are robust enough to get you started on your goal, and keep you going, that's all that matters.

Act On It!

When envisioning your goal, the same rules apply to money and to *Enough*. For example, if you want more money, ask yourself, "How much do I make now? How much do I *need*? How much more will I spend once I am making more than what covers my needs?" You need to know the exact amount, the amount you absolutely must have to survive, and then you'll need some idea of what you would likely spend the excess on. Will you have anything left over? Again, good preparation means being very specific. After asking yourself the tough questions, add the reasons why you must have more money and make

> *A man's character may be learned from the adjectives which he habitually uses in conversation.*
>
> **MARK TWAIN**

them big, bold, and empowering enough to propel you to take action.

Having a sense of *Enough* is tied to taking action. If you think of *Enough* as a balance of making money, having the time to enjoy it, achieving your goals, and enjoying your achievements, you'll recognize that it isn't a static state. It's a process, and knowing how to do what you want to do is vital to that process. Make your goals defined, empowering, and detailed, with reasons why you *must* reach for them. Being clear about a goal and creating a deadline, a purpose, and a personal meaning behind that goal will ensure your envisioning process will help you to succeed.

Some of your goals may seem daunting. They may appear to be so big that you struggle to envision them. If you can't envision something, you most likely won't take any action to achieve it. This is when I permit myself to be a dreamer. If it puts my mind at ease to just dream about something, then I use that as a starting point. The difference between a dreamer and a visionary is simply action. Set up a small goal that might take you closer to the *Big Dream* and act on it.

It's nice to dream, but it's lazy! Envisioning a goal is more than just dreaming. It's incorporating imagination and ideas to help plan your future. It's up to you to fill in the steps that will get you to *Enough* one goal at a time. When I envision a goal, it's always changing; it's never set in stone, but it stays with me all the time. I envision my goal when I'm reading, driving, eating, exercising, conversing, alone, watching TV, on walks, etc. It never leaves me. Yes, it can become obsessive at times, but it's a healthy obsession that I use to make my life, and myself, better!

Step 3: Cement It!

Somewhere along the way, I learned the power of language. I saw how the proper use of empowering language is a huge momentum builder, and how just choosing different words to describe a goal would leave me uninspired. Step three is to make your goal concrete by putting it down on paper so you can read it, see it, tweak it, and have it serve as a constant reminder of exactly what it is that you're going for! The language you use to define your goal can mean the difference between success and failure.

The Power of Language

There's a difference between how a winner speaks and how a loser speaks. A winner speaks with ownership, affirmation, and acknowledgement. He or she is present and accountable. Winners are invested in working towards a desired outcome. Even when they come up short, they still own the result with no excuses. They don't sugar coat, wish, want, or talk about how it could've been. They know where they went wrong and use that as something to work from so that they can change the outcome in the future. A winner doesn't blame, deflect, lie, ignore the truth, or look for anything or anyone to justify losing. Winners own a victory or loss, and they do it with dignity and strength of character.

A loser speaks with indifference or anger. Losers make excuses and will tell you that if *things* were only *different*, the outcome would have been in their favor. A loser is never accountable and blames others, circumstances, the weather, and everything and anything else. Losers justify why they can't be, won't be, and aren't where they wanted to be in life, why they don't have *Enough*. They don't own their part in anything. They have an excuse for how the universe, life, God, friends, family, coworkers, teammates, everybody is against them, and that's why they can't ever seem to get ahead. Losers are who they are, not because of the cards life has dealt them, (many of our greatest heroes and most successful entrepreneurs drew short straws in life's lottery), but because of how they speak.

When you first hear a winner speak, you get a sense that they will own up to things, good or bad. You want them to be on your team. You know they will do the work. They are proactive, and they get ahead by doing, not by intending to do. But how do you tell the winners from the losers when you don't know them yet? You can determine the winners by the language they use: the power their actions are given by the words they choose to use.

As you write your goal down to cement it, be aware of your speech patterns. Is the language you're using empowering? Do you own your role in how things are versus how you want them to be? Are you communicating positively? When you're starting a goal, you should see things in the present for what they are and not what you want or wish them to be. Focus on the fact that change will happen from where and how you are now, and that will move you forwards.

I always eliminate language that doesn't motivate me. How you describe your goal will create the momentum you'll need to see it through to the end. I don't make excuses. I always speak in the affirmative. I talk like a winner. I avoid negative talk and sounding like a victim, and I don't say I'm going to *try* to do something. As Yoda, of *Star Wars* fame, once said, "Do or do not. There is no try."

Rullo Rules

Everyone has words that work for them. However, here are some of the positive winner words I use to keep me motivated & moving forwards: Active, Advantage, Authentic, Balanced, Beyond, Can, Challenge, Consistent, Constructive, Determined, Disciplined, Do, Drive, Execute, Excellence, Fearless, Genuine, Inspired, Intense, Knowledge, Leading, Passionate, Persistent, Prosperity, Renew, Strength, & Worthy. Think of words that are meaningful to you & include them as you cement your goal.

The Power of Clarity

You must be 100 percent clear on what it is exactly you're going for before you begin to cement it. You need to go overboard with the finest details of your desired outcome. It can never be too detail oriented. Don't hold back or censor yourself at first. Just let it flow. I put everything I can think of down on paper every single time I cement a goal for myself.

Your goal will change. For example, I'll often go to sleep or be out for a run, and suddenly I'll realize I missed including something. When that happens, I just go back and add it to the goal. Your goal is for your eyes only. Revisit and revise it all the time, right up to completion!

The Power of Repetition

When I play a sport or start something new, the coaches, teachers, or instructors will always have me repeat the new skill so much that it ends up becoming second nature. For example, in martial arts, there are only a handful of moves, but the Master has me repeat the moves thousands of times so that they become automatic. You'll be exercising your imagination-into-reality muscle by envisioning, using winner language, and writing your goal in detail down on paper to cement it. You can't see this muscle, but it exists. The process of goal setting and realization becomes easier through repetition. The closer you get to *Enough*, the more worthwhile the journey becomes.

Get your goals down on paper, and you'll be well on your way!

Step 4: Plan It!

You've had that spark, set an intention, and can envision your end point. You understand the whys and some of the hows and have asked yourself all the questions you needed to, to give yourself a solid reason to go for this goal. You understand the power of language and how to use it to be a winner and tip the odds in your favour from the start, and you've put everything down on paper to cement it. However, putting a goal down on paper is not the same thing as *MAP*, so you're going to have to do some more preparation.

Some would say this is where you start your journey in a concrete, measurable way; this is the beginning! This is the time when you need to sit down and work out a plan just as you learned to do in Chapter 3. This will be your rough *MAP* directing you step by step to your end point! You'll need to start by creating a foundation, which means mastering the basics related to your goal (your pizza crust!), figuring out what's involved in accomplishing what you want to achieve, and noting any requirements or necessary tools, potential roadblocks, or constraints. Then you'll write down, in detail, the steps that you're going to take to get from (A) to (B)onus! You'll include a deadline/time frame for yourself to accomplish your goal, and you'll consider whether your steps are realistic and attainable within that time frame. You'll take breaks once you've set your plan in motion and *Fuhgettaboutit* for periods of time, and finally, you'll reassess how your plan is shaping up.

Make sure that figuring out ways to not give up, *when* not *if* adversity hits, and how you'll find the willpower to move forwards even when you've been knocked down umpteen times, are part of your written plan. Write, "When times get tough I will..." and "When I feel like quitting, my plan is to...into your plan." The solution may be to re-read the reasons why your goal is important to you, to call a supportive friend or family member, or to simply to take a break—*Fuhgettaboutit* for a while—and clear your head. It's surprising how a little time away can calm things down and give you a new take on a seemingly catastrophic issue, but it helps to plan for it!

Mentors

"No man is an island..." said the English poet John Donne. Although much of your goal must be pursued by you and you alone, which can be very lonely and isolating at times, there are other times when you'll need to find all the help you can get. When putting the foundation of your plan in place, you'll be researching and amassing strategies, initiatives, tools, and knowledge. It's a significant advantage, at this stage, to see if you can track down a mentor.

A mentor might be a teacher, a coach, an expert, or anyone willing to share his or her time, knowledge, and experience. There are mentors for every situation. It's up to you to find them and then make sure that they will be of assistance to you in reaching your goal.

Mentors are invaluable and can save you the time and trouble of working trying to figure things out as you go using books, the internet, YouTube, or trial and plenty of errors. When I have a mentor, the journey becomes like a paved highway instead of a bumpy, gravel road. Hence, the term, *he/she paved the way.* Based on their experience, mentors will show you the best way to go about something, rather than you having to discover it on your own. You don't have to invent the wheel if someone out there has already made one!

When I set out to look for a mentor, sometimes I'll find a good one right away, through a referral or by sheer luck. It's good to search for mentors with whom you feel a personal connection, someone you click with. Your gut will let you know, so trust your instincts. If I have a bad feeling, I've learned to listen to it. I understand that this feeling is a seed of doubt that always means it won't work out. Don't be afraid to interview people or ask around for recommendations or referrals. Sometimes one mentor can only take you so far before you need to find another one. Sometimes you'll need more than one at a time.

For instance, if I set a goal to lose weight by such and such a time, I could use just one personal trainer and hope that's enough. I know I'll be more successful if I also take an exercise class with an instructor, find a nutritionist to help with my diet, visit a doctor, ask friends and family for moral support, and consult a fitness expert who can do a body-measurement analysis. With a team of people who are more knowledgeable than I am, I multiply my chances of success.

You'll need to regularly assess whether your mentorship is working for you and be prepared to end a relationship that isn't helping you anymore. For example, I have a black belt in Hap-Ki-Do that I earned when I was seventeen. I started when I was fourteen, and I trained four to five times a week consistently for three-and-a-half years with no holidays or breaks. When I reached my black belt, my parents were no longer able to pay for my lessons, and it was suddenly up to me to pay if I wanted to continue. I had given up all my free time, including evenings and weekends, to achieve my black belt. I gave up dating or having any social life to complete my goal.

One week after getting my black belt, I tried to talk with my Master (A term used to address the headteacher of the club/Dojo). I wanted to let him know that I had to pay for my lessons now, and I couldn't afford it, so I needed to take a break from everything for a short while. The response I got was not what I expected; the Master lost his mind and berated me in front of the other students. He pounded my chest, slapped my shoulders, and said, "You just got to black belt, and this is where you have to teach others for the experience."

He would get his black-belt students to instruct his less-experienced students for free, so he didn't have to, yet the black-belt students still paid to be there while they taught his classes for free! Looking back now, I see how messed up that was, but it was just accepted, at the time, as normal. I learned right then and there that my mentor was not perfect and he had his own agenda! He needed the cash flow from my fees as a student, and he also needed instructors to teach for free. Having to take a break from my training taught me some valuable lessons at an early age: not to put people too high up on a pedestal, and that everyone has his or her agenda, which may or may not be transparent, and which may or may not coincide with mine.

I never went back after that night, and I never looked back. I never gave him another dollar or a moment of my free time to teach his classes. I'm still thankful for all I learned inside and outside of his studio because it helped make me the man I am today. However, my goals, hard work, choices, family, adaptability, and openness to learning also made me who I am, and my Master didn't have any part in that.

Tools

As part of your plan, you're going to need to look for what tools you might need to achieve your goal. The better the tool, the faster you'll progress! It's easier to have the proper tools at the start of your journey than to find out that you need them later on. These tools can be mental or physical.

> *Adopt the pace of nature: her secret is patience.*
>
> **RALPH WALDO EMERSON**

For example, if your goal is to be a writer, then you'll need a pen, paper, tablet, computer, printer or printing service, etc. But you should also be working on improving your vocabulary or reading the works of other great writers. If your goal is to learn a martial art, you'll need a uniform (called a Gi), a studio, an instructor, a partner, etc. But sharpening your focus, reaction times, and overall mental and physical fitness will also help. Envisioning the steps to your goal, using winner language, and constantly practicing are also powerful tools that can be used regardless of your goal. Use them throughout the day—the more often, the better.

You may have to incorporate a financial plan to acquire the tools you need if they're costly. Consider also renting, borrowing, or even bartering for them. I can be creative if I'm strapped for cash, but I know tools are a necessity and not a *want*. Get the best tools you can afford. You don't want anything making the job of reaching your goal any harder than it already is, and a crappy computer, or a dull saw, or a uniform that doesn't fit can all be time-sinkholes that make the journey to *Enough* take longer than it should. Set yourself up for success, not frustration.

Apps

There's virtually an app for everything. The good ones are worth their weight in gold, so early in your planning, start the search for an app that will help. You may need to try many different ones before you find one that works the way you'd like it to. You don't need to be a slave to your devices, but let me assure you that once you become comfortable using the platform, you'll see how much apps can be of service to you.

Apps are fantastic, and they have made my ability to keep track, make progress, and expedite my desired outcome that much quicker. I'm a tech lover, and when it's used to my benefit and not just for my amusement, I tell everybody about it. When first setting out on a new goal, one of the first things I ask is, "Is there an app for that?" If there is, I download it and try it out, and then I feel I'm already ahead of the game.

You'll have to find the apps that help you get to your particular goal. There are apps like *Digit,* an app that directly tracks your spending habits and income, then automatically deposits an amount that it calculates you can afford to your savings account. *Goodbudget* uses virtual envelopes to help you manage your cash flow according to predetermined sums that you allocate for each category, such as food or entertainment. *Wally* lets you scan receipts right into it to give you an overall, accurate picture of your expenditures. *Fitbits* and other fitness trackers can work in tandem with apps like *MyFitnessPal* to track calories consumed and burned, along with your activity levels. There are music workout apps like *Rockmyrun,* which matches the music to the cadence of your running, while *Charity Miles* gives money to charity for every mile that you bike, run, or walk.

There are language learning apps (e.g., *Duolingo, Babbel*), motivational apps (e.g., *Habitseed, Coach.me*) and apps to help you learn an instrument (e.g., *Yousician, Simply Piano*). Whatever your goal, there's most likely an app that will assist you on your way. *Enough* can be a bit of a moving target, but learning how to set up a goal for success will give you the confidence that comes from knowing you can achieve what you set your mind to. There's power in preparation! The next chapter will show you how all the preparation of steps one to four pays off as you work, adapt, and celebrate (steps five to seven) the achievement of whatever goal you've set your heart on.

Not Had *Enough*? Well, Here's Some More:

• visualization to help you get to your goals:

http://www.huffingtonpost.com/frank-niles-phd/visualization-goals
_b_878424.html

• the power of language in goal setting:

https://www.fearlessmotivation.com/2015/09/10/goal-setting-to-
success-the-language-of-goal-setting/

- setting up a goal for success:

  https://www.huffingtonpost.com/bradley-foster/how-to-set-goals_b_3226083.html

- tracking down a mentor:

  http://www.mentoring.org/program-resources/mentor-resources-and-publications/

- an app for everything:

  https://www.theverge.com/apps

Chapter 5 • Takeaways

1. If you prepare your goal correctly, you'll improve your chances of success.
2. There are four steps to the process of developing your goal: 1) Dream it, 2) Envision it, 3) Cement it, 4) Plan it.
3. There are three more steps to see your goal through to completion (detailed in the following chapter) for a total of seven steps from spark to finish: 5) Work it, 6) Adapt it, 7) Celebrate it!
4. Ask yourself questions to determine if your reasons for pursuing this goal are robust enough to carry you to the end.
5. Visualize reaching your goal and the steps you'll take to get there.
6. Write your goal down. Be specific and use the power of language, clarity, and repetition.
7. *MAP*, starting with learning everything you can pertaining to your goal so as to lay a strong foundation.
8. Use mentors, tools, and apps to help you prepare for success.
9. Each goal you complete will take you closer to feeling like you have *Enough*

6

The Road to *Enough* Is Paved With Goals!

Passion is great & even necessary, & it's something you'll need
at the beginning of any goal, but it's going to fade. It just does!
Discipline is what's going to see you through to the end.
Work on being disciplined for when the passion fades.

MICHAEL RULLO

Now that you have your *MAP* in place, it's time to keep up the excitement and the momentum you've generated and begin to work on your goal. Although you'll likely need to accomplish some goals to feel like you have *Enough*, it's important that your first goal is to learn how to achieve any goal that you set your mind to. However big or small, if you know the process of how to

1. dream it,
2. envision it,
3. cement it,
4. plan it,
5. work it,
6. adapt it, and
7. celebrate a goal into existence,

you can set yourself up to live a balanced and abundant life...a life of *Enough*.

> *Do the difficult things*
> *while they are easy*
> *& do the great things*
> *while they are small.*
> *A journey of a thousand miles*
> *must begin with a single step.*
>
> **LAO TZU**

You've already learned how to go about steps one to four to adequately prepare your goal, and that's more than half the battle! Now you'll begin the process of how to work through your goal to its end point and celebrate (steps five to seven) before selecting a new target to get you closer to what *Enough* is for you.

Step 5: Work It!

Goals take hard work and focus. Many goals fail when people struggle with the work that's needed to see them through. Others fail because they quit when they hit a roadblock or priorities change, they succumb to negativity (their own or the negativity from others), or they just can't adapt. They run out of momentum and drive; they lose sight of where they're going because it seems too far away from where they are.

If I've set a deadline for a goal that's months away, such as running a marathon, I must start training today and every day until the big day arrives. I do this by taking baby steps. This technique has also been referred to as chunking or chipping away. It's all about starting, just taking that first step, and not stopping until you reach the end.

Baby Steps with Permission to Fall

When I learned to take my first steps as a toddler, I would inevitably fall. With the patience and encouragement that my parents and family gave me, I got back up and tried again. No one expects a baby to walk the first time he or she attempts it. To work at your goal, you'll have to extend the same patient encouragement to yourself, as an adult, as was given to you in support of you taking your first steps. Permit yourself to fall, get back up, and take a couple more steps towards your goal. Be patient and forgiving with yourself and give yourself second, third, fourth, or more chances to do it again and again until you get it right.

> *Good luck having success without taking action!*
>
> **MICHAEL RULLO**

Would you give up on a child and say to him or her, "Well, you tried. Walking just isn't for you. Stick to crawling"? No, of course not! As you get older, you take fewer and fewer chances, you expect to be an expert at things you've never even tried, and you're likely far less forgiving of yourself when you fail. Whenever I didn't carefully follow all the steps necessary to achieve a goal, if I decided the detailed, labour-intensive preparations were holding me up or that I didn't need to write things down, I would find myself giving up, sometimes even before taking that first step.

I knew that my goal wasn't going to be easy, so sometimes I even sabotaged myself before I started! That sabotage could take the form of excuses such as, "This is too hard. I can't do this. I don't know how to do this. It's easy for other people but not me. I don't have time," or I could sabotage myself with negative self-talk that could undermine my will even to begin working on my goal, let alone accomplish it.

Nowadays, I anticipate that a goal will be hard, and I expect to not be very good at it, to the point of frustration. I always think of babies and how patiently their parents support them as they learn and fail and fall and get back up. Before you know it, the baby is crawling, which soon turns into walking, which becomes running, which leads to jumping, and pretty soon the tottering tot becomes the fearless child. An important part of working at your goal is managing the expectations that you have set for yourself, for others around you, and for how your goal is going to play out on the stage of your life. Be kind to yourself!

I learned a lot from contemplating those childhood days of intensive learning and accomplishment. When working on a goal, I learned I needed to take that first step and just continue getting up whenever I'm knocked down. I need to master self-discipline by first acknowledging that while I expect to fail, unlike what may have happened with previous goals, this time I plan to have the discipline to get up and keep getting up. Before I know it, it'll be effortless. I'll be making huge gains, and it will no longer be about just taking baby steps. Eventually, I will become a master at whatever it is I'm setting out to accomplish, one baby step at a time!

Momentum

Whether you recognize it or not, you have already set in motion a powerful force that will push you towards your goal. This force, which I refer to as momentum, is the sum of all the investment that you've already put into this goal. From the original spark, through your process of envisioning, to the actions you've taken towards changing your life by writing down your goal, your purpose, and your plan, you've already taken the first baby steps to make it a reality.

Getting the momentum started is huge. You're already much further ahead just by doing all the work from previous chapters. Once you've created the momentum, it's up to you and how much you feed it, to keep it going. It's fallible and not a force that can't be stopped. You'll need to pay attention to your successes, and setbacks, and never stop moving forwards.

One of the things that can help you maintain your momentum is measuring your progress. Write down what books you've read or videos you've watched, what work you've done or practice you've performed to help you get to your goal, and take the time to pat yourself on the back. Sometimes it takes reviewing where you've been to appreciate where you are.

There have been times when I've hit insurmountable roadblocks with any goal, and my momentum has just come to a screeching stop. This is the time I reassess and figure things out. I ask myself, "Am I a quitter? Can I create the momentum again to move forward?" Delays and setbacks aren't denials of my goal! They will only stop me if I don't want the goal bad enough! If I created momentum once, I know I can do it again.

These are some examples of how I've created momentum for myself:

- Black Belt: I found a martial arts studio near my home, and then I previewed a class. I went from sitting at home wondering about learning a martial art, to going out and doing something about it and taking that first baby step. I had some bad days where I thought, "Why am I doing this?" but I always made myself go to one more class. That class was usually good, and I'd be back working towards my goal again as if I had never even wanted to quit. That's the power of momentum!

• Half Marathon: I was doing my best impression of a pillow lying on the sofa when I envisioned my spark of "I could run a marathon" becoming a goal. I went out and invested in my first pair of proper running shoes, and then I trained first for a five-kilometre race and then a ten-kilometre race. Finally, I signed up for a training class for a half marathon. I went from dreaming I could maybe run, to buying a pair of shoes, to progressively training. I became a stronger runner and gradually increased my endurance. There were a million times when I and my sore muscles wanted to quit, but I had invested time and training in that first little spark, and that investment was my momentum to train for, and finally run, a half marathon.

• Construction: Building a house starts with nothing but a spark. Then you find some land and you envision what you might build there. You develop some plans and consult with people who can help with your vision. You lay a solid foundation before building everything up on top of it. You take baby steps, but in the end, you have a beautiful house that someone will be proud to call home.

I break my goals down into smaller measurable steps before I start. I give myself permission to fall and get back up, and I start taking those baby steps, one foot in front of the other, towards my goal. When I do something that will forward my goal on a regular basis, I create a forward energy. It's much easier to keep a steady momentum and stay on top of things before the task gets out of hand and too challenging!

> *If people knew how hard I worked to get my mastery, it wouldn't seem so wonderful at all.*
>
> **MICHELANGELO**

Hate to Work, Love to Play

Whenever I've considered something to be work, my natural instinct has been resistance. I have come to resent even the word *work*! Yes, I have mentioned that hard work is what it takes to succeed, but I'll let you in on another one of my secrets: I got where I am today because I shifted my idea of what work is.

Work is only a concept! It's different for everyone. You all probably know the guy that thinks digging in the garden is fun, or another that can't wait to go shovel droppings at the local zoo, or the person that just loves, loves, loves…accounting (Okay, maybe you don't know them, but trust me, they're out there!). I found that if I turn work into play, it becomes fun. It loses all the negative attachments I've come to associate with it, and I lose all my reluctance to do it!

When I take on something, anything, the first thing I do is figure out how to make it fun! I'll look for ways to make it silly, make what I'm doing lighthearted, or ways to joke around while I'm doing it. I'll find things that keep the mood light and the atmosphere less intense; I'm determined to make the work fun! When something for me is fun, I make more time to do it, and it becomes less of a struggle, if not completely effortless. The bottom line is you don't have to fight your way to *Enough*. The journey is even more important than the destination, and the journey should be enjoyable!

Work needs a certain amount of intensity, but I choose to make my energy lighthearted and filled with good spirits. I have a smile on my face, and I enjoy whatever it is I'm doing. I've come to find joy in the smallest of things, so that time passes quickly. I have a positive frame of mind while I work, which also elevates other people's moods, prompting them to want to do more, give more effort, work harder, and be positive as well. Fun versus work works for everybody! I'm not even going to devote any more attention to writing at length on the subject of work. Why? Because the less I talk about work right now, the quicker I can speak more about fun!

> *When we are no longer able to change a situation --*
> *we are challenged to change ourselves.*
>
> **VIKTOR E. FRANKL**

Fun!

I never pursue any goal if I can't find some way to make it fun. I was fortunate to grow up in a home where my Mom and Dad instilled in me, at an early age, the value of hard work. It was years later that I also realized they had instilled in me the importance of play and having fun. It didn't matter what my Dad was doing at work or home, I always remember him doing it while whistling and looking very content and happy. My Mom would tell jokes and laugh out loud at the top of her lungs. Each had a great sense of humour, an effortless instinct for being playful, and a natural, genuine lightness of heart. Whatever it was they were doing, they made sure to also have fun while they did it.

If you can't find a way to laugh about something or amuse yourself as you work to realize your goal, you're probably going to conclude that attaining your goal will be more difficult. When I trained for half marathons, I had nothing but time to think. During a two-hour run, I would sing a song, then make it silly and change the lyrics as I sang it over and over. I'd think of funny memories, hilarious old movies, and comedy television shows.

I made my mind concentrate on anything that would make me smile. I always got more out of a run if I had a smile on my face. I didn't think about how far I still had to run, the pain, the dehydration, the muscle soreness, everything else that was not positive because then it would start to feel like work! If your job doesn't feel like work, you'll get more accomplished.

When I was in construction, I encountered many things beyond my control, inclement weather, days that were too hot or too cold, natural disasters that caused the price of materials to go up, equipment failures, etc. There were always deadlines to be met, inevitable delays, and tempers flaring up. I have dealt with many different personalities, different cultures, big and small egos, and a lot of bad attitudes.

I had this one guy working on my job site who had a very short temper, and he was always blowing up for one reason or another. Nobody, including me, liked to be around him. It was always best to leave him to do his work alone. When he would see me on the job site, he would always tell me how difficult his job was, how important he was, how all the other guys working there didn't know what they were doing, how he was the best, and on and on and on. He was a good worker, but needless to say, he was also high-strung!

One day he came up to me, chain-smoking up a storm, cursing about whatever set him off that day. Once he got started, he would become even angrier and more upset. He'd go from just talking passionately about whatever it was that had set him off, to outright full-on screaming, getting right up in my face. He would even threaten me and whoever else had pissed him off!

When I first met him, he didn't know how to take me because I would always interrupt him by telling him a story that had nothing to do with what he was talking about. I would interrupt his pattern of behaviour by not giving him the response he was expecting.

One day, when he was right in my face complaining and looking like he was ready to take a swing at me, I calmly said to him, "You know, for a smoker, you have lovely breath! Almost minty fresh! How do you do that?" He looked at me puzzled. He had been thrown off his train of thought. I made him crack a smile, and then he laughed. He forgot what he was so upset about and went back to work with that smile still on his face.

My goal at that time was to build a home, and I had to deal with some different characters along the way. I couldn't build a home by myself, and I couldn't control how others behaved. I could only control my response to things, and I always did my best to make a tense situation more fun. My reputation grew to the point where people in different professions associated with residential building were hunting me down, wanting to work with me. They had learned I was a lot of fun to be around, but I still got things done and paid my bills.

When people say that the reason they work is to get a paycheque to pay the bills, and I see they are doing it without a defined end point, I know it'll never be fun for them, and they'll probably never get to *Enough*. When I say, I love to go to work because it's a fun time and that I enjoy and love what I do, I consider myself to be even more successful. There's a time to joke and a time to be serious. I get that, but if you put some of your effort and momentum into finding ways to make the pursuit of your goals (and your work!) fun, you won't regret it!

Step 6: Adapt It!

Nobody in my parents' home growing up was spoiled because all of us had to work for what we had. The only requirements were to do things with passion, make things fun, love what you do, and be grateful because it can all disappear in an instant. My Mom and Dad, who grew up during a terrible war, would say, "You have nothing to complain about because unless bombs are dropping all around you and you have nothing to eat, and no place to sleep, you don't know what real problems look like!" Whenever I thought about complaining about chores or some such, I knew my parents would bring up their childhoods, and they'd win the *who-had-it-worse-growing-up* conversation. They always kept things in perspective. You certainly can't win a pity contest against someone who's gone through a war!

Sometimes the best way to get through the tough times on your way to accomplishing a goal, is just to regain your perspective and adopt an attitude of gratitude. There will probably be plenty of pity parties on your way to *Enough*; there will be complaints and disappointments, maybe bitterness, certainly frustration. To think, for even a second, that everything will go as planned is setting yourself up for failure. Life has this way of unfolding that you just can't control or anticipate. When things don't go according to plan, you'll need to be positive and flexible!

Things that don't bend break. The more flexible you are in your thinking, your decisions, and your expected outcomes, the easier it'll be able to keep moving toward your goal. By being a flexible thinker, the obstacles that might threaten your original plan won't stop you. You'll think your way clear, make changes, adapt, keep your focus and get back on track.

If You Can't Duck, at Least Roll!

Think of yourself more as an easy come, easy go kind of person, and learn to roll with the punches! Any journey will have roadblocks, detours, distractions, delays, and out-of-left-field, blindsiding surprises. Shake it off; go for a walk and change your frame of mind to one of persistence, confidence, and optimism, and stay the course. I continue to move forwards no matter how many times I get knocked down or sidetracked. I'm always looking for a way to keep going even if it's just minute ultra-baby steps because it's better than stopping dead in my tracks!

When I reach a certain point in the pursuit of a goal, I need to Adapt, Change, Reevaluate, and do a *Gut Check* to see if this is something I still need to do, something I want to do, or something I don't want or need to do. If circumstances have changed, I'll need to adapt or crash and burn! By reexamining and reevaluating everything about my goal, my plan, and how it's progressing, I can see what's working and what's not and make changes.

A *Gut Check* is Not Necessarily a Colonoscopy

A *Gut Check* is a heart-to-heart conversation with yourself, which needs 100 percent honesty. If you can still truthfully answer that you're 100 percent committed to achieving your goal, it's time to push past the negative and just keep your momentum going. If not, it may be time for a bit of a break before reevaluating things once again. Sometimes, unexpected events can seem overwhelming. You may have to alter your end point and accept that this is okay!

You may feel a bit adrift if you find yourself having to redefine, restate, and reenergize yourself and your goal. You may have to come up with a new plan, do something, anything, different, or you may have just to wing it for a while, improvising until the crisis has past and you can get back on track. Life has a way of throwing things your way and it can feel daunting, but if you can find a way to keep things moving forwards, often the road ahead gets smoother eventually.

I Love Losing!

When you see athletes, who have trained their whole lives to compete, win a silver or bronze medal, you notice one of two reactions. They may seem disappointed, but resigned, because they had hoped for gold, or they may seem thrilled because, for them, the silver or bronze was as good as gold! The important lesson here is that you can lose and still be a champ! This is what I mean when I tell people they need to, "Think like a champ, but also love being a loser!"

For example, if your goal was to make an extra $50 thousand a year in income, I might advise you to set your goal higher, even if it seems unattainable to you, so now your goal would be to make an extra $150 thousand a year. If a year from now you have managed to make $75 thousand but did not hit your goal of $150 thousand, you would be a loser who, in reality, is a champion when compared to your original goal.

I set my goals up to go beyond my comfort zone, and I suggest you do the same. The result for me is that I usually end up figuring out how to go past my self-limiting beliefs and surpass what I once thought possible. Automaker and entrepreneur Henry Ford once said, "Whether you think you can or you think you can't, you're right!" There are times when I blow right past my wildest dreams because I no longer let my old limiting beliefs hold me back! By becoming a person who loses from setting goals that are too high, what I'm doing is setting myself up for being a champ no matter what, win or lose!

> *Thousands of candles can be lighted from a single candle, & the life of the candle will not be shortened. Happiness never decreases by being shared.*
>
> **BUDDHA**

Step 7: Celebrate It!

No matter how I may or may not have envisioned myself reaching the end point of a goal, it never turned out 100 percent the way I figured it would. I may have fallen short or shot past the mark of what I was going for. It may have taken less time or more time to accomplish, but none of that mattered—I was finally done! I always remind myself it's not about how I thought I was supposed to feel, but about acknowledging the end of that journey with a celebration. I make a point of celebrating the outcome either way.

When celebrating, it's important that you include friends, family, loved ones, coworkers, etc. When you make your success a joy for everybody, they remember. In turn, these people will be your biggest cheerleaders the next time you pursue a big goal.

It's also time to reward yourself in some way. It can be anything from something super small like a piece of chocolate or big like buying a new car! The bottom line is that you need to show yourself that you care about your efforts enough to reward them either way. You'll have gone through a lot to get to where you are, so celebrate!

Cherish the Struggle

People often say, "The journey is the reward," or "The journey was the best part." I never truly grasped what that meant until I accomplished an enormous goal! Take time to reflect on where you were before the goal compared to where you are now. I always notice how much I've changed and how I'll never approach something new the same way ever again. After going through some hard journeys, I've come to cherish the struggle. When something has been challenging, knowing I didn't give up is the best part!

It's also worth celebrating how much you've just learned. Even if you couldn't or didn't make your goal, you'll find that failure can be excellent. Failure forces you to learn even more new skills and knowledge than if you had easily succeeded with little or no effort. The knowledge and new skills that you've earned are impressive, but the self-knowledge that you pick up through a hard journey is unsurpassed. This self-knowledge is a big part of *Enough*.

> *I exist as I am,*
> *that is enough.*
>
> **WALT WHITMAN**

Some psychologists have suggested that we are naturally inclined to always want more, but that discounts the fact that most of us will say that we are happiest with simple things, time with family or friends, love, and walking in nature. When people struggle with a lack of self-esteem, a feeling that who they are is not *Enough*, they may be looking for security, identity, or affirmation, not the latest trend in clothing. Money, as they say, is not necessarily happiness, but the more you pursue your goals, the closer you'll be to finding what happiness is for you. The self-insight from dreaming, envisioning, planning, and working to achieve your goals will take you closer to *Enough*, win or lose.

I've come to love pushing myself to achieve harder and harder goals because I always see doing so as an opportunity to go through a new learning experience. I like to learn things about myself that I wouldn't have known if I hadn't gone on a journey called *my goal*.

Quitting versus Stopping

You'll notice that I talk about a goal's end point, which is not necessarily its successful, initially intended completion. There's a difference between quitting and stopping. Stopping is when a goal has a new end point, and I've gone as far as I'm going to go in pursuit of it. I've decided that this is it and I'm done with it. Comparatively, when quitting, I've never even pushed myself to go as far as I can, or to make any progress, because things got too difficult and I didn't even want to push myself to try.

By the time I reach my stopping point, I know I've done everything I possibly could, pushed myself past my comfort zone and realistically I know I can't go any further, so it's time to move on. Something may have prevented me from fully realizing a goal, such as when a runner sustains an injury. Insurmountable obstacles may have piled up, or I may have decided that it's better to devote my energies elsewhere.

For example, when I first started running I had dreams of running a marathon. I started training...hard. I learned everything I could to lay a solid, I-am-going-to-run-a-marathon foundation. I studied nutrition. I hired a personal trainer. I joined a running group and focused my entire being on training for the marathon. Finally, the day of my first half marathon race arrived, a trial run in preparation for a full marathon. It was during this half marathon that I had an epiphany: "Two hours of running is *Enough*. I don't have to do more than this." I gave that half-marathon everything I had and then some. At the finish line, I realized I was done with my goal of running a full marathon. I knew then that running a half marathon was *Enough* for me. I wanted my life back, and I was proud of what I'd already done. I no longer needed to run a marathon. I didn't quit my goal of running a full marathon, but I did decide to reset my end point and stop!

> *The hen lays the egg &
> the rooster has the sore ass.*
>
> **MARIA RULLO**

I want to further differentiate stopping from quitting. Quitting is bailing out when things get difficult, saying, "This is too much for me," when you haven't even come close to testing your limits or reaching your goal. The goal is still *outstanding* and something you still wish you could achieve. Quitters are often desperate and don't know how to move forwards at that moment, so they give up the whole journey. Quitting may even be a self-protective habit learned in childhood so that when the going gets tough, it's familiar and acceptable to take the easy way out, even when it isn't to your ultimate benefit.

Stopping, however, may simply be a matter of choosing not to continue because the goal is no longer something valuable or helpful to you. It can be better to stop one unproductive pursuit so as to start something else. If you've already achieved much of what you'd hoped to, or if you've learned that what's required to achieve a goal is more than you're willing to give, or if a goal is simply no longer something that you're passionate about, it may be time to reassess and stop.

As you progress through the plans you've laid out to achieve your goal, you may learn more about yourself and what is *Enough* for you to achieve under your circumstances. You may then decide to stop pursuing the original end point, set a new end point, or stop pursuing the goal altogether. If you're stuck in a rut, maybe it's time to stop spinning your wheels, but if you feel like stopping, make sure you're not quitting. Give it a few days and see if the reasons for stopping are still solid. Oddly enough, things do often look brighter in the morning. You'll likely regret quitting, but stopping merits a feeling of joy and a celebration of what you've achieved.

When you stop a goal, you're turning your energies in another direction, using that positive momentum to keep moving forwards to your *Enough*. When I'm celebrating the end point of a goal, the most important thing to do is to keep the momentum going towards the pursuit of more goals, even after just having reached one. While I'm still celebrating what I've just accomplished, is also the time to make use of that enthusiasm and ask myself, "What's next?"

> *You can't overcome problems by avoiding them.*
>
> **MICHAEL RULLO**

Rullo Rules

How to feel like you are Enough:

1. Avoid comparing yourself to others.

2. Don't believe in perfection. Good is good enough.

3. Exercise to beat the blues.

4. Only dwell on things you can change.

5. Shush your inner critic & quit beating yourself up.

6. Hang out with supportive people.

7. Celebrate the little things!

8. Help others.

9. Get a puppy or pet of some sort for some unconditional love.

10. Explore. Start something new!

What's Next?

"What's next?" That's the question I ask myself after everything is said and done and the energy of the last goal is still fresh. Moments from the previous goal have come and gone, but I have the opportunity to create new and different moments. I can work on myself, make money, learn more new things, and although I'm a human being, I'm never just *being*; I am a human *doing*. *Enough* doesn't mean coming to a dead stop in life.

Since you should always be on the lookout for sparks that can become goals, and since you should also have been working on your *Enough* number and what *Enough* means to you, you likely have a few goals waiting in the wings for your attention. Whatever you decide to do next, you must prepare for your success by following the same process of dreaming, envisioning, cementing, and planning. Once you've gotten into the habit of following the goal-setting process, it will become second nature. You'll also come to expect the unexpected and not be afraid when faced with another big goal that seems unreachable or impossible.

Let your imagination run wild at the beginning of any new goal. Imagination is abundant in children, so I think of myself as a child every time I start something new, and I permit myself to just play inside my head with visions of how I'll get to my end point. I create a *MAP*. I'm flexible in my thinking and my plans. I think about how children learn something new and fail but are encouraged to keep going. I feed my imagination generously with encouragement, and I remember to have fun.

Fool the Genie

Speaking of fun, there are a lot of jokes on the internet that employ some version of the genie and lamp, like this one:

> A man walking along the river's edge finds a magic lamp half buried in the sand. He gives it a rub, and in a swirl of smoke, out pops a genie who says, "I am the genie of the lamp, and for freeing me I grant you three wishes." The man thinks hard and says, "I wish I had a red Ferrari 250 GT" and poof! The car appears in front of him. He carefully ponders his second wish, "For my next wish, I want to be a billionaire," and poof! He has an account with a billion dollars at a Swiss bank. He thinks long and hard about his third wish before saying, "I want to be irresistible to women!" and poof! He's a puppy.

The three-wishes jokes work because we've all experienced wishing for something and getting it but feeling disappointed when it doesn't turn out as expected. This is because we weren't specific *Enough*. We all tend to wish on a whim instead of taking the time to plan, to think it through and go into greater detail to describe what it is, exactly, that we're after!

> *Be happy in the moment, that's enough. Each moment is all we need, not more.*
>
> **MOTHER TERESA**

The genie jokes rely on the wishes being very exact to try to avoid the possibility of being misunderstood. When you feel that first spark, and start to dream your next goal into reality, think about the genie in the lamp. Be specific about your goal as if you were trying to outwit him. Write it down, envision it from start to finish, cement it, plan it, work it, and adapt it, and when things aren't going as you initially imagined...you might as well celebrate being a puppy!

Not Had *Enough*? Well, Here's Some More:

- chunking goals and taking baby steps:

  https://www.talentedladiesclub.com/articles/how-to-chunk-big-goals-down-into-achievable-steps/

- turning work into play:

  http://www.gethppy.com/employee-engagement/10-ways-to-make-work-more-fun-and-increase-productivity

  http://www.businessinsider.com/easy-ways-to-have-more-fun-at-work-2014-10

- being more adaptable:

  https://www.happyandauthentic.com/10-powerful-ways-to-develop-adaptability/

  https://www.inc.com/kevin-daum/7-ways-to-become-a-more-adaptable-leader.html

  https://hbr.org/2013/03/to-become-more-adaptable-take

- the difference between quitting and stopping a goal:

  https://www.linkedin.com/pulse/quitting-vs-stopping-carl-prude-jr-

Chapter 6 • Takeaways:

1. The first four steps to prepare a goal, presented in the last chapter were: dream it, envision it, cement it, and plan it; to which you now have added three final steps: work it, adapt it, and celebrate it!

2. To begin working on your goal, take baby steps and give yourself permission to fail and start again.

3. Keep the momentum up from all your work preparing your goal by measuring your progress and keeping things moving forwards.

4. Find ways to make your job lighthearted and fun, so it doesn't feel like work.

5. Adapt by making necessary changes to your plan when obstacles arise and new information comes to light. Be flexible and do a *Gut-Check* periodically to see if you're still on track.

6. Manage your expectations by understanding that even if you could not reach your goal by your set deadline, you still gained from the experience of pursuing your goal. Cherish the struggle!

7. Celebrate your success with friends and family and reward yourself for reaching your end point.

8. Always include the question, "What's next?" in your celebrations to carry the momentum and energy over into your next goal!

9. Each goal that you work on will get you closer to feeling like you have, and are, *Enough*.

7

Make Opportunity Knock:
How You Do That and Let It in When It Does!

You can search throughout the entire universe for someone who is
more deserving of your love & affection than you are yourself,
& that person is not to be found anywhere. You, as much as anybody
in the entire universe, deserve your love & affection.

BUDDHA

I T'S surprising how many people row a boatload of regrets around a lake of opportunity. Stuck on past failures that their inner critic is happy to replay, opportunity knocks but they just never seem to answer the door. The missed opportunities and coulda-woulda-shouldas crowd out any sense of *Enough*, and it's tough to be open to the risk of taking on new goals and challenges when you're rowing in circles. To reach *Enough*, there are some tricks of the trade that, when cultivated, not only open the door to opportunities but invite them in for burgers and beer!

Be Selfish With Your Time!

One of the best ways to get more opportunities is to take advantage of the ones you already have. Now that you've established some goals that you feel will bring you closer to *Enough*, it's time to be selfish and use your time wisely. Champions in any sport give themselves up to their training, and nobody begrudges them for being selfish with their time as they master what they do. When I do the same as a professional athlete and devote my time to achieving a goal, people are less forgiving of me. You may find that as you try to make changes and start pursuing *Enough* with a more conscious intent, your friends and family will give you a hard time. They may complain that you don't make time for them, or they may make unsupportive comments about your goals.

Don't let others dictate your time, your goals, or your end point. More importantly, don't let others put their limitations on you! Set some boundaries with your loved ones, tell them what you're up to, and then have the strength of character to stay true to your convictions. Learn to be selfish with your time because that's what it's going to take for you to be a champion at whatever you've decided to go for. You don't need to be a professional athlete to do what you've set out to do. You just have to be a bit selfish and go for it!

Love Yourself First!

I make a tonne of sacrifices when I'm pursuing a goal, especially if the goal is a lofty one and it's outside my comfort zone. Even when goals appear small and easily attainable, the most important piece of advice I can give you is to always Love Yourself First above everything else! To give your best you need to be your best, so that's why I always focus on, "What do I need to do to make myself the best I can be right now?" When you're at your best, you'll naturally feel more confident and positive, and you'll be more likely to take advantage of opportunities when they arise. When I respect and love myself first, I am also of greater service to others. I don't ever apologize for that!

You have a better chance of reaching your goal if you cultivate a deep love and respect for yourself! If achieving goals was easy, and I'm talking about huge, super-out-of-reach goals that others think are unattainable, the world would be a happy utopia. The truth is, life beats you down sometimes, and you need to get back up and keep moving forwards. I do this by loving myself *Enough* to not give up!

It makes it so much easier to do the hard work when it's a labour of love. People, life, the weather, and many other factors along the way, can affect your journey to complete a goal, so you always need to ask yourself, "Do I love myself enough to see this through?" When you love yourself, the work you're doing becomes a labour of love, and then it doesn't feel so bad. You'll have a greater chance of success, and more opportunities will arise for you, if you take care of yourself, your interests, your goals, and your dreams.

If you go looking for excuses as to why you can't do something, you'll find some. If you look for reasons why you can do something and why you must, you'll find those too. In the face of the inevitable curveballs you'll meet on the way to *Enough*, the love you have for yourself will help you make decisions from a positive frame of mind and shape your destiny for the best. Opportunities come from these decisions as the choices you make open new doors.

So how do you cultivate self-love and let opportunities in? Self-care, such as exercising, meditating, eating healthy, and getting enough sleep, is an obvious choice. You can listen to the voice of your inner critic and replace criticism with kinder, more positive statements, but there's a lot more to self-love than Buddha, biking, and broccoli. I learned early in life that I need to make progress for myself, and the only way I'm able to do that is by realizing that I matter first. There will come a time when you have to let go of your mentors; put off the requests of your friends, family, and loved ones; and go it alone on your journey to achieving a goal. Your friends and mentors have their own goals in life, and they'll also have to go it alone at times.

Those around you may not always welcome your progress, especially if you're going after something outside of their comfort zones. This discomfort sometimes results in people attempting, knowingly or unknowingly, to sabotage or undermine you. It can be hard to believe that your friends and family would do that, but it's a real possibility, and it happens all the time! You don't have to apologize for doing something that is making you better or more fulfilled. You won't get to *Enough* by living other people's lives, agendas, goals, or wishes. Real friends will understand and support you, and certainly you'll be there for them when you can. However, when others are overly critical of you, and your dreams, it's both undeserved and unwarranted and can take the wind out of your sails and shut down goals and opportunities. That's when you need to distance yourself for a while from your critics and the negative energy they bring. Self-love is having the discipline to say no to people that can sabotage your journey to *Enough*.

> God gave us the gift of life.
> It is up to us
> to give ourselves
> the gift of living well.
>
> **VOLTAIRE**

Once I no longer tried to please everybody, I suddenly started making tremendous personal progress. By caring for myself and taking care of my interests first, I am showing others that I value myself, and they will come to respect that. I'm not suggesting you hurt people and do what you want at all costs, but I am suggesting that you don't allow yourself to be held back by other individuals who have their own agendas. Opportunities flow when you can pursue your interests and take time for yourself. Loving yourself is key to showing yourself you do matter, you are *Enough*, and you're worth your effort!

> *The money I spent buying books & audio programs, going to seminars, & taking courses that interested me was an investment in myself, in building a better me!*
>
> **MICHAEL RULLO**

Run Your Own Race

When I first started running in university, I was so out of shape! I set a goal for myself to run a ten-kilometre race for charity and to do it in less than sixty minutes. I trained half-heartedly, thinking, "I'm young. I'm strong. This should be a cake walk." Then came race day, and I had no idea how many people would be running! There were all different types of individuals: short, skinny, fat, middle-aged, seniors, teens, children, etc. I thought that I'd be leading the pack! Needless to say, that wasn't what happened.

In all the excitement, I started too fast. I burned myself out by the midway point trying to keep up with other runners who were in better shape. I pushed myself until I was in so much agony from pain and cramping that I almost didn't complete the race. I wanted to give up so badly. My time ended up being well over an hour and twenty minutes! I was beat, and I began to beat myself up as a result. I wanted to quit. That's when I had a revelation. I realized I hadn't run my race; I ran everybody else's! I had almost robbed myself of the opportunity to continue to run and race, even though I loved it. Had I quit I would never have had the pleasure of completing a half marathon!

Run your race and not somebody else's! This has been a tough lesson for me to learn. It's human nature to compete and compare yourself with others when your actual competition is with yourself. When I've used others as a motivator, it's never felt right inside. Whenever I just worked on something for myself, charting my progress while attaching a worthy enough reason/purpose as to why I needed to do it, it always felt way more satisfying.

When you run your race and not someone else's, you'll always be better off in the end. Competition is good, it's healthy, but it isn't what I use to measure my end result. Instead, I ask myself this, "Am I better than when I started, and if I were to redo it, could I do it even better next time?" It always comes down to growing from the experience. A world of opportunity awaits when you run your own race. You're less likely to quit when you strive for constant improvement instead of unattainable perfection.

> *It does not matter how slowly you go as long as you do not stop.*
>
> **CONFUCIUS**

This is not about winning or losing. When I refer to running my race, it's about grasping the concept that there's no winning or losing! It's about how I stayed with my plan and executed it in the best way I could at that moment. That's it! A loss in a sport is an outcome, but it's not an indication of a person being a loser. Many times in my life I have come up short, but I've felt like a winner for having given it my all, and I know I am always better off than before I started.

If you want better results, what do you do? You need to push yourself harder. Don't worry so much about pushing yourself to be better than the next guy. The next guy has his race to run, and it's not against you! I don't let the pressure of keeping up with someone else burn me out or rob me of my opportunities to achieve my goals. I run my race, no matter what it is I'm going after in life, and I don't let what somebody else is doing have an impact on me.

Here are a few more examples of why you need to run your own race:

- Martial Arts: I'm a bigger guy by nature, and I'm not that flexible. Some martial artists are extremely flexible, fast, and agile way beyond my abilities. When I try to train like I am one of them, while knowing I don't have their body types or abilities, I am missing out on my capacity for actual growth and self-betterment!

I tried to train like them, injured myself, made repeated mistakes, and I almost quit. If I had chosen to give up, I would have missed out, all because I tried to act like, and be, something I wasn't! There's an old saying that goes something like, "A fish that is trying to climb a tree will think that it's stupid." If you're a fish trying to climb a tree, it's going to be harder for you than the monkey you're competing against. Compete with yourself.

- Building: When I started out as a builder, I had no experience and not a lot of money. My appetite was bigger than my stomach; I always overbuilt and tried to keep up with the more prominent builders. Sometimes I was lucky. Other times, I wasn't so fortunate. Building is like gambling: it's a numbers game, and the house always wins in the end! Good times don't last forever. My ambition, coupled with trying to be something I wasn't, came close to ruining me! It wasn't until I took a step back, reevaluated, and did things my way within my means that I got out of the mess I had created for myself. I opened the door to the opportunity to be good at what I could do!

- Hiking: There's this one mountain that I like to hike in Banff called Sulphur Mountain. There's a gondola that goes from the bottom to the top, but people can also walk up if they choose. One time, I went with some guys who were ten years younger than I was. Right from the beginning they were super competitive, and they started to race up the mountain. I'll admit I got a bit caught up in the excitement of watching them sprint up the pathway, but I decided to go at my pace and just keep my speed consistent. They were way out in front of me and out of my line of sight for about the first twenty minutes. When I caught up with them, they were resting, and they were already burnt out! I didn't stop to rest. I just kept on moving forwards. Soon the crew raced past me again and disappeared. At about the forty-minute mark, I came across them all resting again. They had finished all their water, eaten all their food, and were completely spent! I still had tonnes of energy, lots of water, and two energy bars that I didn't need because I had paced myself and had only been racing my previous times. I shared my water and energy bars, and I made it to the top of the mountain where I had the opportunity to enjoy the spectacular view and relax. Over half-an-hour later, the gang arrived, ready to pass out!

Running your own race always pays off in the end because your only competition is with yourself and not with others. Running your race lets you take advantage of opportunities without worrying about where you stand in the pack, and it enables you to continue to enjoy those opportunities as you learn and improve. Whether you race like the tortoise or the hare, you'll have more opportunities come your way, and come to fruition, if you run your own race!

Learn to Engage!

I've faced what seemed to be insurmountable obstacles. I've run out of money, time, and what have you, but once I learned how to engage others, opportunities

> *What a wee little part of a person's life are his acts & his words! His real life is led in his head & is known to none but himself.*
>
> **MARK TWAIN**

opened up, and I would usually find answers to the problems that were otherwise holding me back. Day-to-day life may be mundane and boring, but when I can brighten people's day, and make them forget about their problems for just one moment, they're more likely to help me with my problem. A human connection goes a long way. It's what binds us all.

Everyone has his or her unique personality and way of doing things, but it doesn't take much to make another person feel good. Doing simple things like smiling more often; telling a joke; giving a sincere compliment; giving someone a thoughtful gift; giving your time, your advice, your help, or just listening; works wonders. Engaging with others is an important path to greater opportunities, and to your success when trying to reach *Enough*.

Sometimes I hit a wall, and I'm faced with total uncertainty; I can't seem to figure out a way to progress. This is the time when I must dig down deep, be creative and resourceful, and convince others and myself that my goal matters. As soon as you start working on engaging others more often, you'll learn that you're not the only one who has had those moments of wanting to quit. Listening to how other people handled similar challenges can help you to see potential problems as only setbacks and help you to brainstorm solutions that are outside of your normal routine or experience. Many of the most incredible opportunities I've experienced were originally recommended to me by someone else. Every person you meet is a potential opportunity!

When you're working on engaging people a little more often, I also recommend that you talk to people that you might not usually seek out. For example, a lot of individuals who graduate from university are surrounded by the same types of people they were in school with, even after they've gotten their degree. If they're doctors, they'll spend most of their time interacting with other physicians and people who work in the medical field. The same can be said about a lot of other professions: teachers, engineers, lawyers, technicians, etc.

Because I worked for myself and had to do many different things to make money, I wasn't around one particular type of person or trade. I had to be sharp and super diverse with my communication skills. It was through building multiple relationships with a wide variety of different personalities and tradespeople that I learned how to engage with people, and this was a big part of becoming a successful entrepreneur. Interacting with many different people also gave me more ideas about *Enough*, as I was exposed to different ideas, lifestyles, cultures, and beliefs. There's opportunity to be found both in improved communication skills as well as in seeking diversity!

Rullo Rules

Boost Your Social Confidence

The world is full of introverts, those wondrous deep thinkers that stand back & take it all in from the sidelines. If you're one of them, there are still things you can do to engage other people in conversation more often. You could

1. have welcoming body language by putting your phone away, uncrossing your arms, smiling, & making eye contact;
2. ignore your inner critic & focus on the other person;
3. read more news & use that to start a conversation, "Did you hear what happened?;"
4. ask someone for his or her opinion, recommendation, or advice;
5. comment on some aspect of your surroundings like the music or how crowded it is etc.;
6. if you already know the person, ask about their kids or pets.
7. memorize a short joke;
8. compliment someone: say you like his or her jewelry, clothes, shoes (pick one!), & ask where they got it;
9. don't worry—some days you won't feel like it—so just gradually try being more social; &
10. relax!

Build a Team!

Any money-related goal needs a team effort. Team building is the most important thing you can do when setting out to make your *Enough* number happen. The people I always want on my team, when I'm after a money-related goal, are accountants, lawyers, bankers, contractors, employees, suppliers, realtors, designers, tradespeople, and astronauts to name a few (Okay, maybe not the astronauts, but they are kind of cool!). I have my strengths, but the people I've mentioned all offer services that I lack, and I use their services to help me get ahead in life. I have never wanted to be a "Jack of all trades, master of none," but I know that there are people who do things better than I do, and I need them on my team for me to be successful. The better the person is at his or her given profession, the better I appear to be in the eyes of others. I call this *Success by Association*!

Success by Association will open up opportunities that seeking success by yourself simply can't. A good team brings a fountain of knowledge and a mountain of connections. I secure a good team because I respect and value what others bring to the table. I just have to be the best me I can be, know my role in whatever it is I'm pursuing, and let other people's talents shine above mine. If people are excellent at what they do, they've worked their butts off to get to where they are. I let them know just how much I respect their commitment to what they've chosen to do for a living.

It takes thousands of hours (the current scientific rumour mill has it at a minimum of ten-thousand hours of dedicated practice) to become the best at something. When I meet somebody who's always being referred to by others as *the best*, I let them know how much I admire how they got to where they are. I know that person is no stranger to giving themselves up to the loneliness needed to become who they are today. That's the kind of person I want on my team. Surround yourself with the best people, and you're going to be much closer to reaching your *Enough* number!

When I used to build homes, I would let the people who were looking to hire me, or who wanted to buy one of my homes, know that I had a reputation and a talent for attracting quality trades to work with me. I didn't build the home. I just got the best people for the job to do their parts, and thanks to their abilities, the end product was a quality home. My talent was bringing everybody together, engaging with everyone, and letting them do their parts without interference. I also let everyone know that they were part of a good team working together towards a great end product. People respected the fact that I gave credit where credit was due, and being so forthright helped me excel in my business.

> *Most people work just hard enough not to get fired & paid just enough money not to quit.*
>
> **GEORGE CARLIN**

The Price of Quality

> By working faithfully eight-hours a day, you may eventually get to be the boss & work twelve-hours a day!
>
> **ROBERT FROST**

The best people are in high demand and are already paid more than enough to do their jobs. Throwing big money at them doesn't always guarantee that I will get them to work with me or for me. Sometimes I have to tell them why they should work with me. I say how much I admire and respect them. I tell them my story—why it's important for both of us to do this project—and that working together means more than just doing another job for pay! I make it personal. They are usually open to listening when I show them that my agenda is to work together and do something great!

When I've convinced the best to work with me, payment is not just settled at the end of the job or with kind words. I always sincerely show it through my actions. It's the sum of all the little extras like bringing coffee or buying lunch or dinner that goes a long way to demonstrate that I do care about them as people. I pay these exceptional people like I pay everybody I encounter, with my dedicated passion for what I do, my sincerest compliments, my positive demeanour, and my encouraging words!

Just sitting with someone, talking with that person for a little while, and getting to know them on a one-to-one basis also goes a long way. People today are so consumed with themselves, and so focused on their phones, that they don't take the time to connect in person anymore. There's nothing to post or brag about when you're just spending time getting to know somebody over coffee. It may appear to be boring, but letting people know that you value them and care to hear their thoughts and views means a lot to them. Money just can't buy this! I've even been paid back in return with lower prices at the end of a job. I've had people put me at the front of the line for future jobs and think of me first when other opportunities came up. It pays to take the time to care for others and sincerely show it. People matter. Show them that and mean it, and you'll be opening up a world of opportunity that'll help you to attract the best to be a part of your team.

Inspirational Journaling: Clearing the Clutter to Open the Door to Opportunity

I'm a big fan of writing a couple of pages in an inspirational journal first thing in the morning, and I later came to realize that this was an excellent way to tap into my creative side. It's a daily practice, and I use it to help me think more clearly. By getting rid of all the junk that's inside my head when I first wake up, my mind is open to the sparks that will become goals and to seeing opportunities where others see problems.

My type of inspirational journaling has no restrictions. Its just stream of consciousness, and I don't read or edit what I've written. By not censoring myself when I journal, I get all my negativity out onto the page, and anything that's pent up pours out of me. I'm not writing anything of great importance or anything particularly profound. I'm also not writing anything I'll ever share with anyone else. It just allows me to start my day on a positive note. I try my best to write two pages first thing in the morning every day.

I am not advocating that you keep a diary of your life. It helps to think of it as a Zen-like practice, something you do for your peace of mind. It's for your eyes only, and it's not to be revisited, edited, or judged by anybody. I *never* go back and revisit what I've written. I know I'm not always filled with sunshine and rainbows with the way I think sometimes, and I have times of self-doubt like anybody else. After I've put it all down on the page, I don't give that negative stuff in my brain any more power over me.

Inspirational journaling isn't just used to get rid of negativity. You can also use it to plan your day or set mini goals or big goals. I use it to calculate numbers, to help me figure things out, and to help me make decisions. I use it to remind myself of things I have to do, to write about things I appreciate, and to create momentum to start my day. I use it to help take my life in the direction that I've envisioned. Putting it down on paper makes it more concrete.

Inspirational journaling lets me set my tasks for the day and vent and get things out. I use it to open myself up to new opportunities. It pretty much keeps me sane! It's a lifelong practice, a routine that frees me to keep moving forwards to *Enough*.

How to Begin Inspirational Journaling

There are no hard and fast rules regarding how to do inspirational journaling. Simply the act of writing every day will allow you to move forwards with your goals, heighten your creativity, get rid of the mental clutter and the inevitable buildup of negativity, and maximize your ability to recognize and take advantage of the opportunities that surround you. To get you started, here are my general personal preferences for how to begin inspirational journaling:

- Find a quiet space & write first thing in the morning, with no distractions, be completely open & honest, & don't censor yourself.
- Turn off all other devices & give yourself over to the silence.
- Get yourself a warm beverage & then start!
- Enter the date at the top of the page.
- Write in longhand (cursive); write as fast as you can, & never judge what's coming out; just let it all out on the page.
- Don't take any breaks. Remember that your goal is to complete two pages every day.
- Don't try to be perfect! Do your best to let go of your ego!
- Fill the page with single-spaced writing. If you have lots of stuff that needs to come out, just keep writing.
- Write *Today* to begin the first paragraph. Then write five to ten things you're going to get done that day. These don't have to be big things, they can be as straightforward & mundane as "I'm going to drink a cup of coffee." This first paragraph, & your list of stuff to do, is meant to create a positive momentum for your day. By checking off things you've already done & noting what you're going to do, you'll move forwards to your *Enough* number!
- Use the last paragraph of your journaling to acknowledge & appreciate the positive things in your life. You can do this by saying a prayer, sending good vibes to someone you care about, or mentioning something that you're grateful for. Always leave your journaling on a positive note to start your day off with some positive energy.
- Forget about what you just wrote, & leave your journal in the same spot so you can do it all over again the next morning.

> *Either write something worth reading or do something worth writing.*
>
> **BENJAMIN FRANKLIN**

Pretty much everything in life is structured and has rules, and reasons for the rules, but with inspirational journaling you're not restricted by a set of rules. You're free to express yourself and be who you truly are. You can use it to remind yourself of what you're truly meant to be doing with your life and of what *Enough* means for you. Journaling gives you permission to be yourself and unconditionally contemplate what opportunities make you the most excited. It's one of the quickest routes to *Enough* and will provide you with daily insights into what you want, what you need, and where you need to look to find it.

There's also something to be said about creating a daily ritual that's just for you. When I've completed my morning inspirational journaling, I always feel lighter. I think more clearly, and I know that whatever was bothering me before I sat down will feel less daunting afterwards. The truth is that inspirational journaling is an integral part of my morning ritual and always starts the day on a high.

Frankly, I was a lost soul before I started doing inspirational journaling. I struggled with *Enough* and battled with negativity, but journaling helped me to become a person of purpose, and I found meaning in my life because of it. Inspirational journaling has inspired me to write screenplays, to build impressive homes, and to teach myself how to design and create incredible indoor spaces, using the principles of Feng Shui, (which declutters home or work environments). It has helped me to realize my goals by keeping me on track every morning.

I may use it to remind myself to touch base with people who are on my mind or to consider a host of opportunities whereby I could put my life on a new path not bogged down with the negativity and pessimism we all typically carry around with us. When I journal consistently, without distractions, I start my day with a sense of accomplishment that carries over into the rest of my day. Give it a try!

Positive Minus Negative Equals Opportunity!

Opportunities flourish in a positive environment, so a trick I use when I feel like crap, or when I'm feeling very cynical, resentful, hurt, or any other less than positive feeling, is to ask myself, "How can I turn this negativity around into something good?" In retrospect, the times in my life that were less than bright were my opportunity to figure out what I could do to make them into something positive. Now I see any challenge as an opportunity to use negative energy as fuel. I use it to have a better workout, to sit down to write, and or to push past a hurdle that's blocking my progress.

It's in the moments when I'm feeling stuck that I remind myself that great things can happen because of an adverse situation. There are people I've come to admire who have made great music, art, or books from a place of negativity. I also admire athletes who have pushed themselves to new, unimaginable heights after coming back from a down-and-out period in their careers. It all starts from a dark place that these people conquered and a challenge that they turned into an opportunity. This opportunity, in turn, became something awe inspiring! Remind yourself when you're feeling not so positive that this is your chance to create something beautiful.

A negative feeling is not right or wrong; it's just a different way to view the world. From past experiences, I know how quickly a negative can turn into a positive and then feel completely different. You can change your state of mind by channeling that energy into something good. Feelings are temporary and temperamental little creatures. View your negative feelings as a dark place that your

> One day, when I was
> six years old,
> I returned home from
> elementary school with
> my first report card,
> & it was filled with Fs.
> I proudly showed my
> Mom & Dad my grades.
> When my parents asked me,
> "What are all these Fs,
> & what do they mean?"
> "Fantastics!"
> I responded, without hesitation.
> Now that's positivity!
>
> **MICHAEL RULLO**

> *It took me 19-years to get that 1-year that changed my life.*
>
> **MICHAEL RULLO**

mind takes you sometimes to give you the opportunity to see things from a different perspective. I've come to look at negativity with an unusual excitement because I know that this energy is encouraging me to do something, to react. That feeling is temporary, and it's up to me to turn it into an opportunity to do something great!

When I've been negative for too long, I say to myself, "I have to change this feeling for the better, *now!*" I also remind myself, "If something is fixable, then it isn't a problem!" If you stay in a negative frame of mind for too long, without doing anything to turn it around, it will take its toll on you. Use that negative feeling to remind yourself that you're not in your normal zone and you need to do what you can to get yourself back on track.

Feeling down is an opportunity to turn it around. In a very odd way, I have come to look forwards to my negativity. I now see it as a challenge for me to find out how I can turn it into something positive. I use that negative feeling and direct that energy towards something that will ultimately better my situation. I seize any opportunity to make something great from something that started out as a negative!

Risk It!

My Mom and Dad started their life together in debt. They had no job security. They made decisions that others considered risky, but they stuck it out together, and they ended up making some big things happen. Many friends and family members had the same opportunities, but they played it safe, and they didn't have as much as my parents to show for it as they aged. My parents are a good example of big risk, big reward. They were very fortunate, but when I asked them, "Why did you take so many chances?" Their answer was, "We had nothing to lose and everything to gain!" I asked, "Why didn't other people take the same chances?" To which they responded, "It's not for everybody!"

Everybody has opportunities and chances presented to them in different guises, and it's up to them to seize the moment or do nothing and let it pass them by. Nothing I did, when I started to invest in real estate, was considered to be *safe*—absolutely nothing! I had to learn the hard way that there are no guarantees, but I also learned I could influence my chances by making calculated decisions. Those decisions come from careful planning and following the goal process I had developed (1. Dream it, 2. Envision it, 3. Cement it, 4. Plan it, 5. Work it, 6. Adapt it! and 7. Celebrate it!).

Yes, there's such a thing as chance, luck, good fortune, etc. Sometimes timing is everything, and sometimes things unfold serendipitously. But while praying and hoping is great, God only helps those who help themselves! No risk, no reward!

I can't hope to win the lottery if I don't buy a ticket. That makes sense, but people play it safe by keeping the dollar in their pocket, and then they say something like, "Told you so!" when I don't win, and when I do win, they say, "Oh! I wish I had bought a ticket too!" To me, it's all about taking a chance. When you think about what *Enough* means to you, it will mean taking some chances. You won't always win big, but you have to buy a ticket!

I know that a steady job is great as a form of regular income, but what I did outside of my job is what set me up for life. Most of the people I worked with were content with just one job. They didn't want to think about doing anything else outside of that job or taking a risk, but there's no such thing as job security these days. People lose their jobs all the time for countless reasons, so working a steady *safe* job is not a guarantee.

However, there's a difference between a calculated risk versus what others consider to be a low risk. The calculated risk has the potential to yield big rewards in the end. A low risk means playing it safe, like staying in a steady job, but it perpetuates a feeling of never having *Enough*. I can't count the times people said to me, "What you're doing outside of your job sounds risky!" when I was buying and renting out properties at the time. Inevitably, my reply was, "It would only be a risk if I didn't carefully plan what I was doing and if I didn't calculate the numbers right. Numbers don't lie!" When I use numbers to make calculated decisions, I don't view that as risk! I create best- and worst-case scenarios with the figures, and I can see for myself the potential outcomes; then I go from there. I used to laugh when people would roll their eyes at me, but as Mom and Dad had pointed out, I knew what I was doing wasn't for everybody!

In 2008, I owned properties valued at over $5.5 million combined. Then U.S. President George Bush went on TV to say the banks weren't stable and they were running out of money. The world economy sank into a recession. My $5.5 million in properties wasn't worth that much anymore because suddenly people stopped buying expensive real estate! I was holding on to properties that I couldn't sell off because of a state of affairs outside of my control. When I went to the banks to weather this storm, they now valued my properties at less than half of what they were before the recession hit. Overnight, I lost over $2.75 million in value!

Instead of trying to sell the properties at a huge loss, I decided to take a risk and rent them out. I did that for a few years, and it paid my bills; it made ends meet. When the economy began to get a little better, I started to sell some of the properties, and I paid down my debt. I sold my property for nowhere near what it was originally valued at, but I had weathered the storm and survived! That situation is a perfect example of a time when others would remind me what I was doing was risky or *dangerous*. Yes, it wasn't for everybody, but I adapted. I started to profit, and I eventually came out ahead by riding it out and making some strategic, although potentially risky, choices. Ironically, years later, those same critical people told me, "You're lucky; you're smart; I wish I would have done what you did."

The truth of the matter is everybody has money come in and out of their lives, and there are no real guarantees! No matter what I do or don't do, at the end of the day, there's always a level of risk underlying everything. I just knew I had to take a chance or I'd never know. That's what has allowed me, and other people I've admired, to get ahead financially. I took a chance, emulating my heroes. If sometimes we risk-takers fail, we keep going despite all the naysayers!

By definition, the word risk means *uncertainty*. There are no guarantees in life. I've failed at doing things I didn't want to be spending my time on, so I felt, "Why not risk failing or succeeding at something I love, and I'm passionate about, instead?!" When it comes to *Enough*, there's always going to be risk involved, and that's the cold hard truth. I grew up watching my Mom and Dad work steady jobs, and I saw there were times they still had lots of uncertainty with their finances, but it didn't stop them from taking calculated risks.

To get to *Enough*, you're going to have to do something different. You're going to have to open the door when opportunity knocks. You're going to have to try new things and risk failure. You're going to have to be selfish with your time and learn to love yourself first. You're going to have to run your own race, engage more with others, and build yourself a great team that has your back. Inspirational journaling will help you dig for the buried treasure of opportunities waiting to be unearthed after you clear away some self-doubt and negativity, which you can then turn into something positive. The journey to *Enough* is full of ups and downs, and in the lottery of life, it isn't whether you win or lose so much as whether you bought yourself a ticket!

> *It is the person who knows well the dark sea of defeat who can rally with his last breath to turn the tide & win.*
>
> **MICHAEL RULLO**

Not Had *Enough*? Well, Here's Some More:

- loving yourself is the key to *Enough*:

  http://www.wikihow.com/Love-Yourself-First

- run your own race not somebody else's:

  http://herbertlui.net/you-should-only-compete-with-one-person-yourself/

+ how to engage other people in conversation:

https://www.bustle.com/articles/169621-11-ways-to-be-more-engaging -in-your-conversations-make-more-friends

https://www.nicknotas.com/blog/conversation-tips-new-people/

+ the amount of time you need to practice to become the best:

http://www.bbc.com/news/magazine-26384712

Chapter 7 • Takeaways:

1. Be selfish with your time and use it wisely to take full advantage of an opportunity to pursue a new goal.

2. Love yourself first because to give your best you need to be your best. Ask yourself, "What do I need to do to make myself the best I can be right now?"

3. You'll be open to more opportunities if you understand that it's not about winning or losing so much as running your own race. Don't use other people as a motivator. Compete with yourself instead.

4. Learn to engage others by making a concerted daily effort to make more human connections. Smile, tell a joke, give a compliment, listen, give your time, give advice, help someone.

5. Try to associate with a different group of people than you would normally. People are a primary source of new opportunities.

6. Build a team of top-level accountants, lawyers, bankers, etc. to help you. Practice *Success by Association*, and surround yourself with quality people. Opportunities that come their way may come your way too!

7. Do inspirational journaling to remove the mental clutter and negativity and make way for creativity and opportunity.

8. Practice positivity and try to turn negative situations into positives. Look for that silver lining!

9. Take a risk! Nothing ventured, nothing gained!

8

Hands in Your Pockets:
How to Keep the Money You Have
When the World Wants It Too!

Life to me is three things: you begin by striving, then you finally arrive,
& then if you've learned anything, you start to thrive!
It's important to do all three with humour, compassion,
& without hurting anybody along the way.
Make the world a little bit better!

MICHAEL RULLO

GETTING to *Enough* is a process because *Enough* isn't a static, unchanging condition. It's a feeling, wrapped in your own personal history, tied with a bow of accomplishment. Money can underwrite that feeling and allow you to do many of the things that you dream of doing, but sometimes the pursuit of money throws the rest of your life so far out of balance that *Enough* seems like a very distant horizon. A viable alternative is that you can also work on holding on to more of the money that you already have coming in. You can work on living within your means and keeping the world's hands out of your pockets. What amount it takes (remember your *Enough* number?) to live within your means and still achieve your dreams is something you'll have to figure out, but there are some things you can be mindful of that will help you keep more of the money you do make for yourself.

> *I cannot see what has been done; I only see what remains to be done.*
>
> **BUDDHA**

Smoke and Mirrors and Credit!

Credit card companies are always on the lookout for ways to get their hands into your pockets, but if you use them wisely, they can be of tremendous benefit to you. When I applied for my first credit card at twenty-nine, they rejected me. This was a surprise to me because I owned two homes that were 100 percent paid for, I had just sold another home for over $235 thousand, and I had over $250 thousand in my savings account. It turned out that the credit card companies look at secured income and not rental income. Up until that time, the only kind of credit I needed was for mortgages, and my parents would help me out by cosigning for me, although I was the one ultimately responsible for the payments.

I always paid for my purchases by cheque or cash, but when I started building houses, I discovered that the suppliers didn't accept personal cheques. The amount of money I'd need was so high that there was no way I could pay by cash. My suppliers asked me to pay by credit card, which I didn't have. I went to apply for one, and the only way they would give me one was if my Mom and Dad would again cosign for me! For people unable to have a family member or friend cosign for them, or who can't be added to a loved one's card, another effective way to build up a credit history is to apply for store credit cards or get a secured card.

Even with my parents, yet again, cosigning for me (My parents were the best!) the amount of credit the bank was willing to give me was only $500! Obviously, that wasn't going to help me build a house. I needed to develop my credit rating and increase my credit amount, bit by bit, if I was going to be doing business on a regular basis.

To increase my credit-card limit, I had to max it out and then make initial payments exceeding what I owed. The credit card companies had no problem with me overpaying my credit-card balance, and overpaying it gave me extra credit (that I prepaid for, kind of like on a secured card). For example, I had a $500 limit, so I would put $5 thousand from my chequing account towards my credit card, and this, in turn, gave me an available balance of $5.5 thousand. I did this on a regular basis when I had to make significant payments to my suppliers.

After one year of regularly overpaying, the credit card companies saw my spending pattern, that I never made a late payment, and that I always overpaid as soon as I got my bill. Suddenly my limit was increased to $2.5 thousand. I continued to overpay, and I did this for the next five years. Then other credit card companies started sending me offers and pre-approved credit cards without me having to fill out an application. I had built up a solid credit score, and I had a history of paying on time.

To this day, I thank George (Remember George? My first boss at the convenience store on the corner?) for teaching me at an early age the importance of paying off my debt sooner rather than later. However, what George taught me was incomplete when it came to business. Before I applied for a credit card, I was using my Dad's credit card, and I made sure to always pay it off on time. What I was doing was helping my Dad build his credit score and increase his limit, but I wasn't helping myself. I didn't know how much of a necessity credit cards were for business and life; all George taught me were the very basics when I was a youngster, and it didn't entirely prepare me for the future. I had to spend six years building my credit history.

> *The promises of this world are,*
> *for the most part,*
> *vain phantoms;*
> *& to confide in one's self,*
> *& become something*
> *of worth & value*
> *is the best & safest course.*
>
> **MICHELANGELO**

I only recommend getting a credit card when you know you can pay off whatever balance you incur within three months' time. If you can't adhere to that, you'll be in for a world of hurt with just how much interest you'll be paying. The trick to credit cards is to live within your means even when using them. Lots of people think it's free money; It's not, far from it! You have to pay it back and with interest! It needs to be explained early on, like it was explained to me at eleven years old, that if you don't have the money to pay back the credit, you're going to be in deep trouble sooner than you know. Use credit wisely, live within your means, and pay it back quickly to keep those hands out of your pockets.

Incentives Giveth and the Interest Taketh Away

Credit cards come with a seductive list of incentives. There are bonus reward programs, cash back, points, travel-health insurance, extended protection programs, and discounts on rental cars, travel, and hotels. If you use your card often, you'll start to see the benefits add up, but few people know how much spending it takes to make the incentives worthwhile. When I was building houses, I accumulated enough points to travel around the world, was given back thousands of dollars in cash-reward programs, and could buy anything I wanted from online points stores, but this is not the case for most people.

If you have a tonne of debt on a credit card and pay nothing towards it, the credit card companies will be coming after you for you to pay your outstanding balance, and the incentives that drew you in will be the last thing on your mind! If you don't pay off your balance in full, the interest you'll incur will far outweigh whatever supposed benefits the credit card company is offering. I've found that the points never seem to come back to most people as planned because most credit cards have all these levels you must hit to finally end up seeing any significant, noticeable advantage in the reward programs. The companies usually have lots of hoops they make a person jump through to see any of the benefits materialize.

Pay off your credit card, don't keep a balance, and then those rewards programs are worth it. Otherwise, if you can't afford something, hold off buying it until you can because you'll be paying for it in more ways than you thought imaginable! I view the reward programs as an added incentive to pay off my debt. If I'm smart, I'll get to enjoy the added benefits without inviting any more hands into my pockets!

The Devil is in the Details: Read the Fine Print!

When I see an advertisement for a credit card, I always look at the super tiny, itsy bitsy, written in legalese, fine print that nobody pays attention to. If instead it read like this in big bold print, "When you use this card and don't pay it back, we own you until you do! Pay us back, or else you're screwed! Pay us back, or you can't buy a new car! Pay us back, or you won't qualify for your mortgage! Have a nice day!" That, finally, would be truth in advertising!

The credit card industry is there to make money, and there's nothing wrong with that. What I have a problem with is that they are selling me an ideal lifestyle that presumably I could have by using their card. It's all smoke and mirrors to distract me from the cold hard reality: if I don't pay back what I've used in thirty days, interest will be charged. If I keep this up, the interest will continue to grow! The credit card companies and banks are not there to educate me on how to pay my debt down; they're there to keep me in debt, so they continue to get paid with all the extra interest that's accumulating. And the lifestyle that their advertisements promote? Forget about it! It's only real until the unmanageable bills start rolling in like waves in a hurricane.

Credit cards have served me well, but I wasn't a slave to them, nor did I live beyond my means. I have enough credit to go and buy a new car and purchase expensive things, but I don't. That's because if I don't have the money to pay back my purchases in three months' time, I know that the purchases on that credit card will own me, and I won't own what I bought. The devil is in the details. Know what you're getting into and whose hands are in your pockets!

Lines of Credit

When I needed a large sum of money to work in the construction industry, I had to have credit cards and a line of credit to do business. The only way the bank gives a person or small corporation a line of credit is if the bank is given a personal guarantee. Usually, that's in the form of a valuable hard asset like a piece of property. They will use the equity from that property to allocate an amount the bank thinks is safe for them to allow the borrower to borrow against that asset at a lower interest rate than what credit cards would typically charge.

As an example, a line of credit goes like this: if I have a property that's paid for and is worth $1 million, the bank will lend me whatever their policy allows against that $1 million. If the bank's policy is to give only 50 percent of the value of the asset (in this case the piece of property), I will get a line of credit of only $500 thousand, leaving the other $500 thousand as their guarantee. That way the banks ensure they will recover their money, even if I were to later default on the line of credit.

The bottom line with a line of credit is you must have something of value and put that up as a guarantee to secure the credit. Nowadays it's even harder to apply for a line of credit because of the new rules and regulations the banks have set up for lending. They'll need to see all your financial statements, speak with your accountant, and see the last couple of years of your tax returns. Sometimes even when you show them all of that, and you have an excellent credit rating, the bank will still deny you the line of credit, without even an explanation.

Now a line of credit is still a hand in your pocket because you'll still be paying interest every payment period, added to each installment you make to reimburse the bank for the money you've already used. This may sound simple enough, but I often hear people tell me how much of a line of credit they have, but they never say how much they have already used so far and therefore, how much of that line of credit they have available to them. A hand in your pocket is still a drain on your finances, so use lines of credit wisely and only when you need them.

Loans

The same can be said about applying for a loan, as the process is similar to applying for a line of credit. It always depends on the amount you're asking for. The bottom line is that you'll have to fill out an application form. The bank will assess whether or not they want to lend you the money based on your answers and the paperwork you've provided. If you're approved, then you agree to pay back that money, along with interest owed, to the bank. Bankers aren't there to be nice guys; they're there to make money.

People who approach the bank with nothing (i.e., no assets, no credit rating or a poor one, and no long-term employment or financial history) will be leaving the bank with what they came in with, *nothing*! If you choose to apply for a loan, be prepared to show what you have financially and what you have in assets, and be ready to pay the interest they are charging. Know what it's going to cost you and know that until you pay it off, it's another hand in your pocket.

Lease Me...Forever!

Whatever my parents owned was always *Enough* for them because they would take care of their things. They would maintain whatever it was they bought, from cars, to homes, to technology such as TVs, stereos, etc. My parents never got sucked into buying the latest and greatest like most people who never seemed to make any real progress in their lives. By keeping the things they owned for a longer time, my Mom and Dad could bank more money away and were able to reinvest it to buy more properties and pay for them in full without a mortgage and without giving any money to the bank in interest payments.

I was taught it pays to take care of your things because they'll take care of you in the end in more ways than one. I apply my parents' lesson to many areas in life, and I've found that I could reach *Enough* faster by looking for ways to save money as well as earn money. Buying an older model car instead of leasing and always wanting to have a newer model is just one example of where you can save your money and benefit in the long run.

> *I do my best to tune into my purpose & align with it, setting goals so that my vision is an expression of that purpose, & then life flows much more smoothly for me.*
>
> **MICHAEL RULLO**

Car companies loan money to buy or lease their vehicles by appealing to some people's basic need to feel significant. Their marketing targets how their product is going to make you feel. Car companies have a system of lending that is similar to the banks, but their system is even less scrupulous than the banks' because they want to keep people in debt indefinitely!

Let's say I qualify for a loan to buy a car. After a few years, when my vehicle isn't the latest and greatest any longer, I'll see an ad that'll entice me with an offer too good to be believed to get me into a newer and better model. If I keep this cycle going every few years, I will never have anything to show for it other than a new car to drive that I don't own. If I take a look at what I would be paying in interest towards a car loan and what I've paid over a ten- to twenty-year span, I would see I could have bought two or three brand-new cars in full! Leasing is a never-ending hand in your pocket.

Leasing is a system of perpetual debt. You're worth more to them by never paying off your car than if you did. Yes, there are tax benefits to leasing versus buying (i.e., Leasing costs for a vehicle used for your business are deductible, subject to limits, and you must keep meticulous travel records including dates, destinations, distance, and reasons for each trip.), but for argument's sake, I'm just speaking about going in to buy a car for your use and nothing else. When you buy a car for personal use and can't write off the payments for tax purposes, there's no point in continuing to stay in the system so that you can drive the latest and greatest model. If having lots of the latest *stuff* was *Enough*, you wouldn't see so many desperately unhappy wealthy people, but there's more to the *Enough* equation than the car ads would have you believe.

If you buy what you can afford and pay it off quickly, then in the long run, you'll come out ahead. If you lease and continue to flip the current car for a newer one every two to three years, you'll always stay in debt!

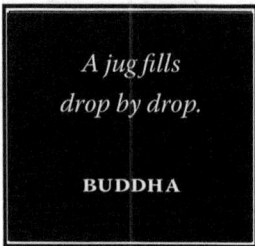

> *A jug fills drop by drop.*
>
> **BUDDHA**

I buy a vehicle only when I know I can pay it off within a few years. That's my rule for a new car purchase, but I always pay it off in full and drive it for many years after it's paid off. I don't let the car dealerships seduce me with fancy ads and endless sales, and I keep my money for things that matter to me.

Do it Right with Real Estate: Maximize Hidden Revenue!

Sometimes your financial drain is just that you're not getting the most out of what you have. Money that isn't in your pocket is in someone else's, so it pays to maximize your income. Reducing your debt and increasing your disposable income will give you more peace of mind and the freedom to focus on the goals that will take you closer to feeling like you have *Enough*. I'll use the example of real estate, but you can apply a similar magnifying glass to whatever your revenue stream is. Not only are you looking for holes in your pocket where you're losing money, but you should also be looking for ways to maximize what's coming in.

My real-estate holdings are a stronger asset when they're bringing me money through rental income, as well as when I'm doing things to increase the equity that is already established. When I'm improving a house, for example, by adding a garage or a legal rental suite in the basement, that makes my property more valuable in the bank's eyes, thereby increasing my equity and the value of my real estate.

I always try to get the most out of any property in any way I can, and at the same time, I also find ways to increase my equity. Today it's commonplace to see on television how a relatively inexpensive home renovation can enhance the value of a home, but when I started out, those TV shows didn't exist. I started with limited funds, so I had to learn to be creative with how to bring in extra income from my property for as little investment as possible. Sometimes there are unknown revenue sources with a property, and it doesn't matter if I own it outright, if I live in it, or if I bought it to be an investment property.

Here are some ways I increase the income from my properties:

- I renovate and add another rental space to the property such as a legal basement suite. It pays for itself in no time, and it pays huge dividends in the end when it's done right.
- I rent out my garage to someone who's willing to pay me for it when I'm not using it, and then I just park outside.
- I rent out an empty room or two in my home. If I can't afford to build a separate, legal suite, I get some roommates. I then act as landlord to my new roommate/tenant(s).
- I charge more if people have pets when they rent from me.
- I give a discount on rent if people do the upkeep on the property, such as cutting the grass or shoveling the snow, if it's less than I'd pay somebody else to do it.
- I do minimal landscaping, enough to add to the curb appeal of my property and make people want to come inside to see my home. (In real estate, it always starts from the outside first.) By keeping the outside clean, my tenants usually stay longer because they are happy to live in a place that shows pride of ownership.

- When my property is paid for or close to being paid off, I use the equity to buy another property, but only if I have the numbers to do it and it makes profitable financial sense.

- If I don't have a garage, but I have a big backyard with a back lane, I put up a garage. If I don't have the money for a garage, I create an economical parking pad and charge people a fee to use it. Lots of people have campers, trailers, or boats, and they need a place to park; they're willing to pay lots of money to have a place for their toys!

- Whenever I come across extra money, I put it towards the principal of the home, and that, in turn, lowers my overall interest payment because I've now shortened the amortization time. I put extra money towards the principle, and I just forget about it! My equity grows every time I do this, and my interest payments shrink so there'll be one less hand in my pocket sooner! Of course, it only makes sense to do this when you don't have other debts at higher interest rates, as those would have to be paid off first.

These are just some examples of how I created extra value and income from my properties. I used creative thinking, and I was willing to put up with some of the difficulties that come with owning a property. I was ready to get dirty and do the work myself. I learned firsthand that my property is an investment that continues to grow when I give it extra attention. Be on the lookout for ways that you can maximize your revenues in your living and work situations. Is there more that you can be doing to bring extra money in or to lighten your debt load? Remember that getting to *Enough* needs you to embrace change, so think about what hidden revenues you're letting slip away.

> *Education is what remains after one has forgotten what one has learned in school.*
>
> **ALBERT EINSTEIN**

Rullo Rules

Advantages of an Incorporated Company

- A limited company (i.e., an incorporated company) is a separate legal entity from the person(s) who owns it.
- You, as the owner, are only liable (i.e., for debts or if you're sued) up to the value of your company's shares, so any taxes or debts due are the responsibility of your company, not you as an individual.
- Banks & clients may perceive your business as more legitimate & more attractive as a corporate entity with Inc. after your business name.
- Funding the business can be done both through issuing company shares & through borrowing.
- An incorporated business, also called a Canadian Controlled Private Corporation or CCPC, pays a much lower federal tax rate on the first five hundred thousand dollars (as of 2016) due to the small business tax deduction. A corporation pays less tax than a similarly profitable sole proprietorship.

Disadvantages of an Incorporated Company

- An incorporated company is more expensive to run with high initial set-up & ongoing administrative costs.
- Incorporated companies have complex rules regarding when & how they report to the government (corporate registry annual reports), so you're going to need professional help to follow all the rules & regulations.
- Company losses can't be written off against the owner's personal income.
- An incorporated company has to pay income tax & may also have to pay Canada Pension Plan contributions & Employment Insurance premiums.
- You must file a personal tax return as well as a company return.

Sweat Equity

I'm often asked how I got ahead if I didn't have lots of money to start with. My reply is, "I did a tonne of sweat equity for free!" Yes, puzzled looks often follow. Not having any money never stopped me from pursuing things that seemed out of reach for me. If I was interested in learning something that mattered to me, I found a way to trade a service in exchange for gaining something in return; this is my version of sweat equity.

The brilliant thing about sweat equity is that it can save you a fortune in student loans from pursuing expensive courses or higher education. There's usually more than one way to get the knowledge or training you need without putting yourself in debt. Sweat equity can be money in your pocket, money that you're not giving to someone else in exchange for knowledge/education. It may also allow you to make more money or realize another type of goal in the future.

Gaining knowledge and being able to apply and execute that knowledge is incredibly valuable. With some of my mentors, I was able to gain their knowledge by offering my labour in exchange for learning from them. I can tell if someone is a poor thinker or a rich thinker by the way they value their service to another. If someone refuses to do anything for free in an exchange that could help them out in a big way, later on, they are a poor thinker. If a person is willing to work for free and exchange their time and energy for someone else's knowledge or skills, which will be of tremendous future benefit, that's rich thinking. The rich thinker knows the value of information and learning, while the poor thinker lives in the now and can't see the big picture!

I have had to give up my leisure time to accommodate my mentors' schedules, and there was no bargaining with them. They knew that what they were teaching me was important, and while I was the protégé, their time was more valuable than mine. When I was unable to pay my way for something, I understood that my sweat equity took a back seat to those who ponied up the money. The balance of power is never 50:50, but I don't let myself get bogged down with what I don't have at any given moment. The money works itself out in the end, and I always work my butt off.

If you focus on what you don't have, you'll find yourself stuck not having *Enough*. Of course, you'll have to make money elsewhere while you offer up your sweat equity for knowledge, but make sure your mentor knows that you're not providing a free service, but rather a fair exchange. You're offering your sweat equity to get ahead in life. It's not altruistic. Your time is also valuable. Working for free to gain information can change your life for the better and is ultimately an incredibly valuable and rich way of thinking! It's just that sometimes the hands in your pockets are your own. To get to *Enough*, take them out and put in some sweat equity to see some amazing results!

The Taxman Cometh!

When I worked for large enterprises, I never gave my taxes much thought. Deductions were automatically taken from every paycheque, so I didn't have to think about it. At the end of the year, I would go to our family accountant, I'd give him the form my employer had given me, and my taxes were filed promptly. I soon realized that things worked differently when I went to work for myself. It doesn't matter how you're making your money; it pays to have a good understanding of taxes because the government can have a big hand in your pocket.

The Canadian tax system has different rules that apply if a company is incorporated versus if a person is only declaring that he or she is self-employed (called a sole proprietorship). The differences kick in when you exceed a certain amount of income. If your income doesn't exceed it, it's to your advantage to be simply self-employed as the sole proprietor of your business endeavours, but if you make more than the allotted amount, it's better to incorporate your business.

I didn't have to know every single tax code, but I did need to learn that there's a difference between being a small business (sole proprietorship) and a small corporation, and I had a better chance of success when I understood the difference between the two regarding taxes. Being an entrepreneur, I had to shoulder the responsibility of knowing how my business operated and how to optimize my chances of success. Understanding the basics of how the tax system worked was an important part of that success. Whichever route you choose (incorporation vs. sole proprietorship), my biggest recommendation is that you seek professional advice.

There's too much to cover regarding the tax system, but I'm going to touch on what I found valuable about my understanding of the Canadian tax code, and what I had to do to increase my chances of success in business and life. When I decided that I could keep more of the money that I earned in my pocket by incorporating my business, I also discovered the following:

- I needed a corporate accountant versus a general accountant. A corporate accountant is a specialist who can explain what you must do and what you shouldn't do. A good corporate accountant is worth all the high fees and then some. When I started to make big money in construction, my corporate accountant gave me advice on how to save tens of thousands in payments by telling me what I could and couldn't write off.
- I needed a corporate lawyer to keep my contracts legally tight and to protect my interests. He helped me with the legalities of all contracts, property sales, and the disbursements of money to other parties and the government. My attorney has helped me stay on track with all my big contracts.
- I needed a bookkeeper that knew how to file my day-to-day expenses properly and how to differentiate my personal from my business costs. Every penny counted when I worked for myself; I made sure that the accountant taught me everything I had to do, and I then confirmed how I spent my money with my bookkeeper, so we both knew I was doing it right. When the books are not kept well, it always ends up costing me more, so this is not something to skimp on.
- I needed software programs for all my business dealings. This allowed me to stay on track and to project future earnings. The right program makes filing taxes easier for all concerned: the corporation, the bookkeeper, the accountant, the lawyer, the clients, the banks, the government, and most importantly me! There are a lot of programs out there, and it takes a while to find one that's easy and fun to work with. Take a look at *FreshBooks*,

QuickBooks, or *Sage.* It makes life easier, and it saved me even more money by saving my bookkeeper and accountant time when doing my books!

• I needed to always have my books organized and up to date. Bankers always need to see my books, and it helps when I have them organized so that the banks can communicate with my accountant quickly, efficiently, and professionally. Bankers love to see that my corporation is run correctly, and I've had fewer problems with the banks because I was so organized.

• I needed to get into the habit of organizing all my receipts and paperwork to make it easier come tax time. I'm guilty of using the shoe-box filing method when I first started out, but by the time I decided to close down my corporation, I had become very proficient with how I organized all my paperwork before I handed it over to my accountant. If I'm organized, it saves the accountant time trying to figure it out, and that, in turn, means less billable hours for me and more money in my pocket!

Whether I was working for myself or a larger company, I made it a point to learn how the tax system was set up, and I suggest you do the same. I bought books about taxes, I combed the internet, and I took the time to speak to my bankers, my parents, other entrepreneurs, different accountants, lawyers, successful individuals, and people who had tried and failed at being business owners. I learned from everybody and absorbed every little piece of information on what I had to do and what not to do.

Understanding the tax code for the business I was entering into helped me succeed at a rapid rate. Knowledge was power, and it paid for itself when making important business decisions. You'll have to pay taxes, but how much you pay and how labourious it is for you to pay them is within your control.

The government is not set up to make it harder for you to succeed; it's set up to collect taxes for the collective whole and keep the country running. I never looked at the government as a combative enemy of mine like so many people do. I saw the government as doing their job, and I was focused on doing mine. I had nothing to worry about because I learned to play according to the laws, and I succeeded because I understood what had to be done. When I knew the law, I saw that the government helps my corporation and me, unlike what so many people who don't understand taxes would have you believe. The government doesn't get in the way of my success; I'm the only one that can do that!

I'm smart enough to know that it's my job to make money, the accountant's job to file my earnings, and the government's job to collect my taxable income. That's it in its most basic form, but it's also my job to have at least a basic understanding of how the system works, although I don't have to be an expert at it. For you to succeed, you'll have to know how taxes work. If you don't understand how the tax law applies to your situation, you may be handing over a lot more than you need to. Get some professional advice and learn what you need to know to keep more of your money for your goals and your journey to *Enough*.

Paying the Piper

If people don't respect how the tax system is set up, they can expect the government to penalize them for not doing their parts. I have a basic understanding of the laws, so I abide by them, and I will accept a penalty when I'm not doing my part or playing within the law. Penalties are there to keep people honest, not to hold them back. With the government keeping everyone honest, we all have a better chance at success. Just like in Las Vegas, sooner or later the house (the government) always wins and catches the cheaters.

The government is like a referee: if people don't pay on time, they get penalized. It's not the government's fault that these individuals are delinquent on their tax payments; it's their fault! There's no point in giving this topic any more energy than to only say, *be on time. Do it right, and you won't have to worry about having to pay any penalties!* This is one time in your life when being late, filing incorrectly, or showing indifference is going to cost you a lot. There's usually a fine, but in extreme cases, a person can go to jail. Avoid the penalties and the stress, and keep the government out of your pockets as much as possible by respecting the laws and the dates taxes are to be filed by. Once again, I can't stress this enough: please get a professional to help you when you need it!

Lending to Other People

It's tough to hang on to your money when the world wants it too. With all the endless seductive marketing trying to target your tastes, the misinformation, and the pressure to buy to be a better person, it's tough to keep the money you make and put it where it will do you the most good. *Enough* can seem like a distant dream with so many competing interests syphoning your savings. You can do everything you can to pinch your pennies, reduce your taxes, maximize your income, and trade sweat equity for knowledge, but you still might find there are hands in your pockets.

Friends and family will sometimes come to me instead of going to a bank and ask me to loan them some money. They're hoping they'll have a better chance asking me rather than asking a bank for a loan, and they're expecting that I won't charge any interest. People usually turn to their families first, and their friends second, when seeking a loan. A family is also more forgiving when the borrower hasn't paid the loan back as planned or can't pay it back. The bottom line is people will turn to family or friends instead of a bank because they're looking for a break.

This is a tough one, and you're going to have to decide for yourself what your boundaries are. The more money people think you have, the more likely they are to approach you with this kind of request, and there can be a lot of bad feelings on both sides as a result. It's best to consider this possibility ahead of time and think about possible answers and how you might prefer to handle it.

> *When someone does something for me, or if I do something for them, that doesn't necessarily mean that we're friends. I just think of that as 'being a nice person.' Friendship takes time to grow, to build trust & a shared history, & it goes both ways. Friendship is like marriage without the formalities, & it always comes from a place of love even if it's buried underneath some great sarcasm!*
>
> **MICHAEL RULLO**

These are my experiences with lending money to family and friends:

- Small loans up to $500 get paid back relatively quickly with no drama, and there are no hard feelings or headaches afterwards.
- Medium loans from $500 to $2,000 typically get repaid more slowly than small loans, as people often have a hard time paying the debt in full, all at once. Eventually, they usually do end up paying it back, but sometimes there are hard feelings about it for various reasons.
- Large loans, which I categorize as anything over $2,000, can be very difficult to collect on. It's usually with large loans that people tend to magically disappear. They won't return texts, phone calls, or emails, and I start to notice a reluctance to pay back any portion at all. There's resentment on both sides with large loans, and I caution against them.

> *Better the friend*
> *you can see*
> *than the money*
> *you cannot.*
>
> **GREEK PROVERB**

I have had people say to me:

- "You don't need the money back."
- "You can live without it."
- "You can get more where that came from!"

and my favourite,

- "I thought it was a gift!"

I've been burned by many people because they confused my good nature for my being a sucker, but they didn't realize that by deciding not to pay me back, their debt came at a high price—my friendship! Be careful of burning bridges with people you care about. In my opinion, it isn't worth burning a bridge over having a decent person in your life! Friendship and money are poor bedfellows because when money crosses hands and the other person agrees to pay the loan back, that's a contract, and that's business!

If someone asks me for a loan and I know they will most likely not pay me back, I sometimes decide to lend them the money anyway, but in the back of my mind what I'm thinking is that I'm gifting them these funds. I know they have come to me seeking a loan, but I don't expect them to repay me. I don't necessarily tell that person that I'm giving them the money as a gift; I just think of it that way so that I am not disappointed if they don't pay me back. If by chance they end up paying me back, that's great. I can remain friends with that person either way and expect nothing in return. When someone pays me back and does it without attitude, is grateful and tells me so, they are a true friend or a loyal family member.

To gauge whether or not a person intends to pay me back, I'll ask them one of three questions: "Do you have anything you can give me as a guarantee you'll pay me back?" or "Are you willing to sign a piece of paper saying you'll pay me back?" or "If you don't pay me back in such and such a time, will you pay interest on the money I loaned you?" Sometimes, I may also ask that person a few more questions for extra clarity about whether they went to the bank first, such as, "Did you qualify for a loan?" and "Why didn't you sign a contract with the bank and get the loan through them?" Just seeing how comfortable someone is talking about money can tell me if his or her intentions are good.

I have lots of friends and family, but I know that loaning money may damage important relationships. To me friendship is priceless; this is why I would never ask to borrow from any of my friends. It can potentially lead to trouble. How you handle loans is something that you'll have to decide for yourself, but the more money you appear to have, regardless as to what you intend to do with it, the more *friends* you'll have with their hands out. There are many tales of lottery winners who've lost friends and family even after having shared their winnings.

> *You have reached the pinnacle of success as soon as you become uninterested in money, compliments, or publicity.*
>
> **THOMAS WOLFE**

If your version of *Enough* includes friends and relatives, be delicate and discreet about who you lend your hard-earned money to. Give it some thought ahead of time and consider some responses in advance such as, "Let me look at my budget, and I'll let you know tomorrow." or "I have a strict rule about lending money. I've just ruined too many relationships that way." Remember that you can help the person in other ways as well, or you can make a gift of the cash. If I have the money to give, I'll give it to people I care about, even though it may enable other problems in their lives. My bottom line for all of this is, "Money is serious business." Get to know whose hands are in your pockets, and you'll get to your *Enough* number faster.

> *Be more concerned with your character than your reputation, because your character is what you really are, while your reputation is merely what others think you are.*
>
> **JOHN WOODEN**

Not Had *Enough*? Well, Here's Some More:

- how credit cards work:

  http://money.howstuffworks.com/personal-finance/debt-management
  /credit-card.htm

- understanding your credit score:

  https://www.canada.ca/en/financial-consumer-agency/services/credit-
  reports-score.html

- tips for getting your loan approved:

  https://www.forbes.com/sites/investopedia/2013/07/03/5-tips-for-
  getting-your-bank-loan-approved/#4df372b42a95

- understanding the language behind buying, leasing, and financing a
  vehicle:

  http://www.cosmopolitan.com/lifestyle/a52448/heres-what-all-those-
  crazy-words-in-new-car-ads-actually-mean/

- understanding the Canadian tax system:

  https://thefinancialintern.wordpress.com/2012/08/26/a-simplified-
  explanation-of-the-canadian-income-tax-system/

  https://www.thebalance.com/tax-information-4073880

- formulating boundaries for lending to friends and family:

  https://www.moneytalksnews.com/tired-loaning-money-friends-and-
  family-heres-how-stop/

  https://lifehacker.com/five-key-rules-to-follow-when-lending-money-
  to-friends-1780147903

Chapter 8 • Takeaways

1. Getting to *Enough* is a process with which you can work on getting the money you need to support your goals, or you can work to keep more of the money you already have coming in—or both!

2. Build up your credit by always paying on time, paying off your balance within three months, and paying more than you owe to avoid paying high amounts of interest.

3. Credit card rewards programs, lines of credit, loans, and leases are costly and rarely give you more than what they take. Use them judiciously and always read the fine print.

4. Buy what you can afford and pay it off quickly and you'll come out ahead.

5. Look for ways to maximize sources of revenue, such as renting out your garage or getting a roommate. Examine how you could get the most out of what you already have regarding extra income.

6. Look for opportunities to trade your labour/time (sweat equity) for knowledge that you would otherwise have to pay for.

7. Get professional advice on how to manage your taxes and whether or not you should incorporate your business. Hire a team of experts to keep your taxes organized and accurate; this will save you money in the long run.

8. Don't lend money to friends or family unless you're prepared to lose it or them! Gift it instead!

9

The Psychology of *Enough*:
The People, Power, and Politics of Money

Money brought out a lot of things in me that were already there
& amplified them. It made me even more generous. I didn't view money
as my God or my devil but rather as a source of the energy
& the value I brought to the table.

MICHAEL RULLO

I've talked a lot about goals and the role they play in getting you to *Enough*. I've introduced you to the concept of your *Enough* number and how much money is *Enough* for you to live the life you'd like to lead while feeling free and confident in pursuing your dreams. I've also mentioned that a faster way to *Enough* is through silencing your inner critic, maximizing your revenues, and controlling the bleed as money slips from your pockets in various ways. But now I want you to imagine with me that you have your money...all you need...your *Enough* number and then some! Or maybe you do already have money, lots of it, but somehow it isn't buying you balance, peace of mind, or a sense that what you have is *Enough*. What happens when you have money? How does it change you and the individuals around you? Is *Enough* enough when you have *Enough*? Maybe, before you work so hard to get there, it's a good idea to have some idea of what you may be in for. I'd like to give you a better understanding of the psychology of *Enough* and an introduction to the people, power, and politics that often come with the territory of money, so that you'll be forewarned, forearmed, and able to deal with anything that might be coming your way.

> *The reason why some people put on airs is that they have nothing else to put on.*
>
> **UNKNOWN**

Money as An Amplifier

It's been my experience that having money doesn't change people per se; what it does is amplify a person's personality to the extreme. If a good person comes into a lot of money, they become an even better person and do great things with it. However, if a bad person comes into money, they become even more of a jerk and let everybody know just how much of a selfish lout they can be. Money makes a good person better, and a bad person worse.

I've seen people, who think of themselves as *good people*, come into some serious money and appear to change for the worse. That's not what's going on. They were just better at hiding their true natures before, and the money gives them the perception of power sufficient to no longer feel the need to self-censor. I've seen people who were thought to be grumpy curmudgeons come into some money and instead of being miserable, miserly Scrooges like people would expect, they give it all away or help out as many people as they can. Just because a person might not be likable, doesn't mean he or she is a bad individual.

Tell Me What You Have, and I'll Tell You Who You Are

Some people, who want to appear to others as though they have money, have certain tells. Tells, in poker, are subtle behavioural changes that indicate a player's cards. Tells in money are ways in which the wealthy show the world their status, for example, the cars they drive, the clothes they wear, the watches and jewelry they flaunt, the fancy limited-edition shoes, and the upscale homes and neighbourhoods they live in. Then there are the phones and the expensive phone cases that surround the phones that are even more expensive than the phones themselves sometimes! Some wealthy people can also be real braggarts, so you don't even have to look for elaborate symbols of wealth or the tells that say so much more about people than they realize. Not all of it is impressive by any means.

I'm all for having nice things, driving cool cars, living in fancy homes, but I'm not about being ostentatious and bragging about it, especially to others who don't have these things. There's a lot to be said for subtlety! A person can aspire to have nice things, but a good person will work hard to get those things. A good person will share their wealth with their friends and family in his or her times of good fortune. A genuinely good person will celebrate that good fortune in a way that makes others happy for him or her.

Money can be a blessing or a burden, a comfort or a curse. As you reach your *Enough* number, watch out for the temptation to lose yourself to the worst in your nature. That darker side, which the marketers are only too happy to exploit, makes attaining things a goal, and insidiously encourages you to think that this stuff will provide a feeling of significance and status. People who have succumbed to this fickle illusion announce it to the world with their actions, their demeanours, and the words they use to describe just how important and how much of a big deal they are. These tells always tell me a lot, but mostly they say be careful of these people because they will never have *Enough*. They are the people who are constantly looking for their own reflections in your eyes as they try to undermine your journey to self-satisfaction.

Rullo Rules

If you want to try to buy the biggest happiness bang for your buck, psychology professor Dr. Elizabeth Dunn from the University of British Colombia suggests that you

1. shell out for an experience of some type such as theatre tickets or a concert.

2. spend smarter, rather than simply spending more, & think of your long-term (i.e., I'm saving for a trip) vs. temporary (i.e., I like those shoes) happiness.

3. buy your way out of doing things you don't like to do to give yourself more free time to do what you do want to do (i.e., get a maid or a lawn-care service so you can spend more time with your family).

What Do You Value?

When money amplifies people's positive qualities, they reveal what they value, and what they think is most important in their lives. They're philanthropic and try to help those less fortunate than themselves. They have more leverage to help more people by using their fortune and new-found position in life. They can bring attention to an issue by lending their name and reputation to a worthy cause. Such people may be drawn to politics or positions of power where they can affect the issues of the day.

People for whom money brings out the worst always seem to be trying to fill a void inside themselves with material possessions, and this too affects their values. They act as if they are in competition with others whom they perceive to have the same amount or more than they do. They are often seen to be doing everything but helping others. Sometimes they will throw money at a cause, but they don't care about it; they do it for how it may appear to others. They'll always let you know when they've done something charitable or what they think of as a noble act. They give so they can get recognition for their giving. Everything is done for attention or power.

They are the manipulators and the game players who will never be satisfied, and several recent studies have shown that wealthy people of this type lack empathy. An experiment at the University of Berkley in 2012 revealed that even having more Monopoly money could change a person for the worse, making him or her more aggressive, while another 2012 study at the same institution showed that drivers of expensive cars were four times less likely to stop for pedestrians than were drivers of less-expensive models. When researchers discovered a correlation between having lots of money and depression, it didn't initially seem to make much sense. I mean these people have *Enough*. Right? Shouldn't they be happy? It turns out that the endless pursuit of wealth, and the constant hunt for the latest and greatest material things to support their perceived status, might be what's making them unhappy. As you strive for *Enough*, be mindful of your values and watch out for those that don't share them. Also, watch out for changes in how you think about the concept of money and the lure of materialism in a Lamborghini world. Money may not only *not* buy you happiness but may, in fact, buy you its opposite.

Greed, Envy, and the Ballet of Balance

Believe it or not, there's such a thing as *Enough* money. Personally, I'm not someone who is committed to a lifelong pursuit of such crazy amounts of money that I'd never be able to spend it all, even if I lived ten lifetimes! I'm more interested in balance and knowing that there's such a thing as *Enough*. Psychologists call this greed for more and more money an addiction. The clergy refers to it (and its partner envy) as one of the seven deadly sins. Popular culture holds up miserly examples such as Scrooge for ridicule and reform.

Greed causes friendships and partnerships to end, as it produces an imbalance of power and may trigger envy. Greed causes people to make unhealthy choices and exhibit compulsive behaviours like what you would see in a gambling addiction. Greed also makes relationships hit rough patches. A sense of entitlement grows along with the bank account, and a person focuses all their energy on the pursuit of money, seeking the high of buying material things to the exclusion of all, and everyone, else. It consumes people, and at the end of their lives they are left wondering, "What was it all for?"

I've met some super wealthy people, financially speaking, and when they pass away, it's sad to hear how others thought of them and how they chose to live their lives pursuing money instead of anything meaningful. I just knew I never wanted to be that guy who passes away rich but socially broke!

The saying, "He who has the most toys when he dies wins!" attributed to millionaire, Malcolm Forbes, must be the stupidest sentiment ever expressed, and yet it's what we're all taught to believe. The message that *more is a must* is communicated online through advertising and via television, movies, and magazines. I know that what I'm supposed to be doing is trying to make lots of money so that I can accumulate more and more things, but my Dad was a fan of the saying, "You can't take it with you!" He taught me that life isn't about how much stuff you have when you die. If all people talk about is my stuff at my funeral, and they don't talk about me as a person, then, in my opinion, I will have died a poor soul!

In a perfect world, you can imagine that you've acquired all the money you could ever want, but what will it do for your life? Life is finite, and while you're trying to fill the emptiness inside with increasingly more money, things, and experiences, ironically, wealth itself won't ultimately make you happier. That's according to science. It turns out scientists have studied the relationship between money and happiness. In a 2010 Princeton University study, researchers found that up to approximately $75 thousand, more money does seem to buy happiness; the problem is that beyond that magic number, more money doesn't make you all that much happier. It turns out that retail therapy isn't that, well, therapeutic.

> *People often confuse the size of their paycheques with the degree of talent or the value they bring to a position of employment or a business enterprise. One is rarely indicative of the other.*
>
> **MICHAEL RULLO**

I enjoy nice things, adventure, exploring, and living life to the fullest, but I take holidays and create experiences because it makes me grow as a person, not because it will necessarily make me happier. I've also learned to be okay with just sitting still and taking in all the moments life brings. I always try to achieve a balance, I look for meaning, and I remind myself that money doesn't buy either of them.

If you find that through all your hard work money starts coming to you in abundance, there may come a point where it surpasses your *Enough* number, and that's fine, as long as you're not continuing to pursue money out of greed. I always live within my means regardless of the amount of money I have coming in! Anything I make more than my *Enough* number will not affect me either way because I always live within my *Enough* number even if I'm making more. That's what *Enough* means to me; it's knowing and understanding that I live my life and I can have nice things because I own my stuff, and it doesn't own me. I can live very comfortably because I don't need anything more than my *Enough* number for me to feel fulfilled and accomplished.

Everyone has a different *Enough* number, but if a person hasn't taken the time to figure out what that number is, they will continue to live their life never feeling like it's *Enough*. The greedy person buys the fancy car and the expensive yacht for appearances only, as proof of a narcissistic sense of entitlement and baseless superiority that ties who the greedy person is, as a human being, to their financial worth. That's the addictive and detrimental nature of greed.

Such people are earning an amount they could easily live with, but they still choose to live a lifestyle that exceeds their paycheques, and they continue the hungry pursuit of money and material goods. Greed, as with any addiction, throws the rest of a person's life wildly out of balance. Oblivious to the fact that their lifestyle is killing them, the greedy person still thinks they never have *Enough*. That's why I want you to think about your *Enough* number now, before you start to focus on making more money. If you already have money and are still struggling with *Enough*, it's time to see greed for the addiction that it is. Seek help, start to live within your means, and work on your *Enough* number to get a clear end point and to get out from under the burden of greed and envy.

I lived a greedy life for years. I didn't ever stop to think, "What's my *Enough* number?" I was greedy with my desire to always have the best, the newest, the fastest gadget, car, or phone. I had to have bigger and bigger homes that would just ultimately sit empty, and I kept thinking that when I bought this or that new thing, I'd finally have *Enough*. Deep down, however, I knew it was never going to be *Enough*. Did I want to get rich or just richer? Did I need big or biggest? I needed an end point, a freedom point. I had to change my thinking, change my life, and figure out my *Enough* number. What was *Enough* for me to feel content?

Your *Enough* number will naturally lead you to open your life to balance. It will give you more psychological *free space* in your thoughts to contemplate other goals that don't involve the pursuit of money. It will give you more *free time* to pursue those goals, spend time with loved ones and friends, or to relax and smell the expensive roses that you already bought! Finally, considering what *Enough* means to you will start to free you from the fear-based desperation of the never-ending quest for more.

The greedy way of thinking went away for me when I stopped trying to buy my happiness. I had to look within and stop being so selfish. I had a lot of nice things that most people would envy, but I just didn't care about that stuff after I acquired it. The fix for my addiction was temporary. The shift for me happened when an old cliché rang true for me. I finally stopped wanting what I didn't have and started appreciating what I did have! That's what changed me. It made an immeasurable difference in my quality of life.

The Paradox of Power

In movies, I saw a pattern where a super-rich, powerful man was often buying his way around and trying to influence things to match his way of thinking. The theme was that money buys power. I started to ponder, "What does power mean to me?" Power, for me, again comes down to what my Dad taught me. His definition of power was, "To make enough so that I don't have to kiss anybody's ass, and I can do things because I want to, not because I have to!" Now that's real power!

I know there are people in this world who have deep pockets, wheeler-dealers, trying to pull strings behind the scenes. Some may consider this to be power. My reality is that I'm not in that position, and there's nothing about that kind of life that I find appealing. I'm not impressed with the size of a person's bank account. A lot of times, the very wealthy people I've met are insensitive, manipulative, ego-driven royal pains! I'm much more impressed with someone who lives life on their terms, doesn't hurt anybody along the way, lives within their means, and doesn't brag about it!

> *Basically, there are two types of people. People who accomplish things & people who claim to have accomplished things. The first group is less crowded.*
>
> **MARK TWAIN**

Psychology says that the paradox of power is that the very skills that help people to rise to a position of influence often vanish when they get there. The scandals and corruption that follow the falls of the wealthy and powerful are the stuff of legend, or at least the stuff of the daily entertainment news and tabloids. Ironically, the powerful tend to judge other people's ethical lapses of judgment much more harshly than they judge their own moral and legal lapses. My definition of power is that I have more than *Enough* and I can relax and enjoy it if I live within my means!

My notion of power is that I don't have to answer to anybody unless I choose to (or it's my Mom). I go about life knowing that I'm in control of my situation and my future. I don't know what it's like to have huge amounts of money and then use it to buy influence, massive castles, or small countries. I will not let myself be distracted from how good I have it now by wanting something absurd that I know wouldn't make me happy in the end.

I earn money so that I can live my life on my terms, so I can pass on my good fortune by sharing my knowledge and wisdom, and so I can do something because I love it, not because I have to! Power ultimately means you're in control of your life, not necessarily that you're in control of other people's lives. Your life is always a good place to start!

Rullo Rules

Break a few rules

Once I had learned the difference between asking for forgiveness versus asking permission, I no longer put my destiny in the hands of others. I am not one for breaking laws; I'm talking about breaking the rules! Philosopher Henry David Thoreau said, "Any fool can make a rule, & any fool will mind it!" Yes, I'm okay with following rules for the most part, but there are just those moments in time when I've had to break them instead of asking for permission for an exception. People in charge of the rules are more likely to forgive than they are to give permission. In those moments when I'm faced with a dilemma after I've asked for permission & been told "No," I can live with the rules, or I can decide to break them! I'm not advocating doing anything illegal or putting others in harm's way! I'm saying that there are times in life when a rule shouldn't apply or makes no sense.

The Psychology of Sweet and Sour and Other Patterns of Persuasion

My Mom is my hero, and she always has the best sayings that are simple and to the point: "The hen lays the egg, and the rooster has a sore butt; Don't stress about things. Call yourself Easa. Easa come, Easa goes; No grass grows underneath my feet!" My favourite was, "Watch out for the people who are fake and are like a Chinese-food dish. They are sweet when you meet them for the first time, but by the end they are sour!"

My Mom will never become as renowned as Mark Twain with her insights and musings about how the world works, but she has a way of nailing things by being straightforward and matter of fact with her observations. Before I ever became a landlord myself, my Mom told me, "People never show up for the first time to rent a home without being sweet, but it doesn't take long for them to go sour, especially near the end." That always stayed with me, and I would see it first-hand when I did business, rented out homes, or after I had said, *No,* to someone who wanted me to buy something I didn't want, need, or have any use for. Politicians use this *sweet and sour* strategy to persuade voters, but they seldom make good on their campaign promises.

I have more respect for the person who is a curmudgeon from the beginning and stays that way to the end or else turns out to be a sweet soul. The person who appears to be sour at the beginning, in my experience, is kind but hides this from the world for whatever reasons. I remember my Mom saying, "He isn't a bad person. He pays the rent, doesn't complain, and is a hard worker," and, "Just because someone wears a suit and tie doesn't mean he can, or is going to, pay the rent on time. Give me a moody person who pays the rent without trying to be charming any day! I don't have time for BS!"

Growing up, I saw all kinds of characters who had applied for my parents' rental units, and my Mom didn't usually give it to the person who was the sweetest to her. She saw past appearances and looked deeper at the person standing in front of her. She didn't discriminate like so many people would do at the time. She would always talk with them to get a sense of who they were. Somehow, she had a knack for seeing through the sweet talk. Truth be told, it's hard to know what type of person you're dealing with before you reach the end of a contract or business deal, but being aware of the psychology of sweet and sour certainly helps.

My Mom also taught me, "Always be a good boy. Life's too short, but don't let them push you around!" Some people think that being nice is a sign of being an easy target, being naïve or simple minded, or they believe that friendly people are not going to stand up for themselves. Psychology says that confident people are more convincing, and this may be part of why seeming too sweet can put people off. It's rare that a rental agreement or business transaction leads to conflict. Even when there were bumps in the road with our business dealings, my Mom would always be a kind person, and I saw first-hand how much of a difference that made.

> *Good breeding consists of concealing how much we think of ourselves & how little we think of the other person.*
>
> **MARK TWAIN**

It may seem odd to say be nice, but at the same time, as you work towards your money-related goals, be suspicious of sour in sweet's clothing. Whether it's a politician or a partner, a customer or a con artist, as you accumulate the wealth you need to make your *Enough* happen, you'll meet more and more people trying to persuade you of something. It helps to be aware that when people are trying to persuade you, there are common techniques that they'll use.

You're more likely to be influenced by someone if that person

1. has authority or claims to be an expert,
2. is someone who seems likable or that you trust (that's the *sweet* my Mom had warned me about!),
3. makes you feel like you owe them something (even if what that person gave you is not that valuable, there's a social pressure to reciprocate and give back), or
4. has convinced you that what they are trying to persuade you to get or do is scarce or popular.

Business is a lot like dating; people will put their best foot forwards when they initially meet, but over time you'll see their true colours. I'm hopeful that most people truly are sweet, but I seldom know until the end of a business deal; so just be aware of the psychology of sweet and sour and the patterns of persuasion. This is a pattern my Mom brought to my attention, and now I'm bringing it to yours.

Integrity Matters

My Dad also gave me a piece of advice that stuck with me, "Your word means nothing if you don't follow through on what you say you're going to do! Integrity matters and it's the most valuable thing you'll ever have in life!" My Dad was a simple man, but people knew that if my Dad said he was going to do something, they didn't have to second guess if he'd do it. I saw, growing up, how much people respected my Dad because he always honoured his word. He was someone you always knew you could count on because his integrity shined through.

Integrity is doing the right thing even when no one is watching, and I suggest you cultivate it in yourself, in those you choose to work or do business with, and in those with whom you spend your leisure time. Feeling like you have *Enough* is more than achieving a set amount of money or certain life goals, it's about balance, sustainability, and feeling good about yourself and your life. Individuals who struggle with who they are inside, versus how they behave outside, often have a host of personal problems ranging from substance abuse to self-esteem issues. To feel like you're *Enough*, you'll need to work on being a person of integrity.

In my business dealings, I have met a lot of individuals with little integrity. For example, when I do a walk-through before returning a person's damage deposit, I always ask my tenant three questions before even entering the property: 1) Is there anything you'd like to tell me or feel I should know? 2) Is anything damaged or broken that I should be made aware of? 3) Did you leave the place the way I gave it to you? A person with integrity will answer truthfully, but that isn't usually the case. People, for the most part, just want their money returned to them even if they're responsible for having broken something that belonged to me. People with integrity will tell me up front that they've damaged something, and most times, I don't even need to do a walk-through with them because I know they're honest.

It makes life much easier when you deal with people that have integrity, and behaving with integrity is an antidote to many of the bad habits that plague the wealthy. A question I'll ask people sometimes is, "If you're driving, there's nobody around, and you know 100 percent for sure that you won't get caught, would you still slow down in a playground zone? Or would you slow down regardless because it's the law?" I'm all for bending and breaking the rules, but not the law. The playground question was asked of me in a job interview (Yes, I answered that I'd slow down even if nobody was watching by the way.), and that's how this employer weeded out potential candidates. The manager said to me, "I need to know I can trust my employees even when nobody's watching!" I found that idea to be simple yet profound! Surround yourself with that type of person and more importantly, be that person yourself, and you'll reach *Enough* faster.

When you live with integrity, you don't have to hide anything or struggle with who you are. You practice what you preach, and it's consistent with your values. It becomes easier for you to make decisions because they're based on the sense of integrity that defines you. Researchers say that more *authentic* people, people with integrity, are more successful, make more efficient leaders, are more well-liked, benefit from more social support, and have better romantic relationships. The word *integrity* is Latin for *wholeness*. When you have integrity, you are whole.

My parents met people who were sweet and sour, as well as individuals who had integrity, and they taught me to be the latter. What others do is their business, what I do is mine, and what you choose to do can make the difference between *Enough* and *stuck*. Cultivate wholeness with each decision and behavioural choice. Go through life with your eyes open to the integrity, or lack thereof, in others, and if I can give you one piece of advice to help you get to your sense of *Enough* it would be this: honour your word. Integrity does matter and you can stake your reputation on it!

> *Mastering others is a strength. Mastering yourself is true power.*
>
> **LAO TZU**

Dealing with People Who Have a History of Bankruptcy

Another type of person who will doubtless cross your path as you make your way towards your *Enough* number is the person who has, at some time or another, declared bankruptcy. I always try to give people the benefit of the doubt, but I've learned the hard way that individuals who have filed for bankruptcy are not worth my time in doing business with them! This is especially true if those people are wanting to start a business with me and asking me to be their partner. The banks will look at both of our previous histories, and if I have a clean history and my partner doesn't, good luck getting a bank to sign off on anything! They probably wouldn't even allow us to open an account. The banks look at anyone who has ever declared bankruptcy as bad news, and so should you!

You'll hear a lot of hard-luck stories as you try to accumulate *Enough* personal wealth to feel comfortable. Some are legitimate tragedies, but the majority follow a familiar pattern. People who have filed for bankruptcy usually tell me it's somebody else's fault and they had to do it. They say it was an ex-wife, ex-business partner, or a family member who took advantage of them and they had no other choice. I know from the minute they start pointing fingers and failing to own up to their part in it that this is someone to be avoided. You'll rarely hear someone say, "I learned my lesson, and I won't repeat that mistake again!"

Like people who lack integrity, and the sweet and sour individuals that start out gracious and change, people who have filed for bankruptcy tend to be very confident and persuasive in the beginning, but when things get difficult, they suddenly disappear. Bankruptcy is an indication that the person may not readily accept responsibility for their mistakes. When they mess up, they may pass the blame onto others, the weather, somebody, anybody else. Their word means nothing, and they won't sign a legal document because they don't want to be responsible for anything later. Conversely, they will go ahead and sign a document, knowing that their word means nothing, and they have nothing to lose if anyone tries to collect! I have never had a good experience when dealing with people who thought their only option was to quit. I encourage you to be very wary of someone with a bankruptcy in his or her background who wants to either do business with you or be your business partner.

There's a saying that when someone's a millionaire, it was the first million that was the hardest to make, but it was much easier for them to make the next million. In theory, if that person were to lose it all, they could make it back again because they know the effort and time it took to make it in the first place. The same can be said about most people who've filed for bankruptcy, except once they've lost it all, chances are they'll lose it all again. They tend to repeat the same mistakes because they never took responsibility for themselves in the first place, and as a result, their story repeats as well.

> *Running away from your problems is a race you'll never WIN!*
>
> **UNKNOWN**

I'm sure there are legitimate ways in which someone goes bankrupt without it necessarily being their fault, but this is a time when you're going to have to selfishly stick to your goals to get ahead, and you don't need someone else's bad history slowing you down. As you find your way to get to your *Enough* number, you're likely not operating as a big corporation at first. If you're just a small entrepreneur who's trying your best to make it in this world, it's important not to make it any harder on yourself. The banks are tough, and if you've built up a stellar history with them, you don't need to risk it all because of someone else's previous problems.

The Psychology of Bankruptcy

When starting any business, it's good to know your outs in case things don't go as planned. While that's all well and good, know that by learning your outs, you're planting seeds of doubt and failure. So while it's always a good idea educate yourself and prepare for any eventuality, it's a better psychological technique to focus on doing whatever it takes to get ahead. It's smarter to have the mindset that failure is not an option. You'll increase your chances of success by cultivating that sheer will to succeed.

Some of the popular books I've read advise you to set up a corporation in case your business dealings go south. That way you're not personally responsible, and you'll be off the hook. It's important to know that's not necessarily the case. Frequently, the banks will still require the average person starting out to provide personal guarantees before they'll do business with them. Sure, if a big corporation goes bellyup, the owners can file for bankruptcy, but the mentality of "Let the chips fall where they may!" has many lasting consequences. For small-time business owners just starting out, they'll have no such luck. They'll be on the hook for everything, lose their reputations, and set themselves up to repeat the same mistakes!

I would recommend that anyone with a small business consult a tax expert to decide which company structure would work best for their business and what will offer the most protection should that business get into trouble; it's always best to consult with a bankruptcy lawyer. For your benefit, it's also preferable to negotiate with the banks rather than ignoring debts and being unresponsive out of fear. Although some people thrive on closing companies that are hitting financial difficulties, only to then start up again with a clean slate and minimal effort, I find this practice dishonourable and extremely harmful to others. Some prominent business people have become very successful after filing for bankruptcy (Henry Ford, Walt Disney, Milton Hershey, Henry Heinz, among others), but those are exceptions.

The psychology of bankruptcy is that past behaviour often predicts future behaviour. If your business is struggling, I recommend that you break this pattern by doing everything you can to learn how to handle your business affairs, and your money, properly. Bankruptcy discharges people from an obligation to pay a debt, but it should only be used as a last resort. There's still a moral obligation to pay a debt and a personal and psychological cost if you fail to do so. Conduct your business and your life honourably and ethically, and your reward will be *Enough*.

> *Life is about pitching & catching.*
> *I don't have time for people who just want to do one without the other!*
>
> **MICHAEL RULLO**

A Friend by Any Other Name

As you become more comfortable with money, you'll be on the lookout for how it may amplify your personality characteristics, entice you into the addiction of greed and the illusion of power, and challenge your integrity. Money can change you, but it can also alter the people around you. In the last chapter, I cautioned you about lending money to friends and family, but money can also cause people to want to be your friends only to manipulate you in some way. There are a few more red flags that I want to share, that, as I settled into enjoying *Enough*, caused me to think about what makes a friend a friend.

Here's what to watch for:

1. Someone who asks how much you have or make all the time. This level of curiosity about your financial situation is a huge red flag. A friend wouldn't snoop to find out what you have or don't have! There are ulterior motives at work here. None of them nice.
2. Someone who seeks payment for helping you out, and then makes you feel like they did you a favour. A person who gets paid to provide a service is an employee, not a friend. Make sure things are clarified before any *help* is provided.
3. Someone who uses your contacts or reputation for their personal gain without your permission is not your friend.
4. People who say things behind your back that they don't say to your face. Your reputation is one of the most valuable assets you have and will have taken you years to develop. You shouldn't have to worry about what people in your inner circle are saying about you, so be selective about who you let in.
5. People who regularly ask for things without offering something (even gratitude) in return. Some people return favours with money, gifts, a night out, a thank-you card or email, or some thoughtful gesture. A friend offers to pay from time to time. When I made it and was very generous with my money, knowing it couldn't be returned in kind, a simple thank you would go a long way! Friendship is a two-way street. You shouldn't always be in the position of the provider.

6. People who are envious of your success instead of happy for you. Watch out for people who regularly make fun of, or rib you, for your achievements. This type of behaviour is only thinly disguised jealousy, not friendship. Friends are happy for one another's successes and champion the efforts it took to make something big happen.

7. Someone who is showing up and interfering with your business or requesting regular discounts. This is a huge red flag. Friends respect each other's work and work hours. Working for free for these people won't get you money, reciprocity, respect, or gratitude. Freeloaders aren't free, and they aren't your friends!

Rullo Rules

Who signs a contract first?

My rule of thumb is never to be the first to sign a contract when someone is offering to do a service for you or buy something from you, but be the first to sign when you're the one proposing to buy something from someone else, or when you're providing a service to another.

Get It in Writing!

There's a lot to think about when you mess with money. It brings out the best and the worst in people. It can give and take power and make and break politicians faster than you could say, "Freddie Mac, Fannie Mae, or I have a bridge to sell you." It makes friends into freeloaders and strangers into fast friends and can change your personality in the blink of an I.O.U. What, other than keeping an eye out for red flags and warning signs, is a person to do to protect themselves on the road to *Enough*? Fortunately, there's a quick and easy way to see someone's real intent. If you want to know if a person is trustworthy, honourable, has integrity, and will honour their word, ask if they'd be willing to put what they're telling you or selling you in writing.

There's a world of psychology behind the act of signing your name to a document. Making something legally binding is one of the best ways to protect yourself from those who are thinking that they can take advantage of you. When people don't want to sign their names to a piece of paper

> *A man is usually more careful of his money than he is of his principles.*
>
> **RALPH WALDO EMERSON**

that'll hold them accountable for what they're offering or what they want from you, what they're telling you is they can't be trusted, and it's only a matter of time before they cheat you or try to!

I worked in construction, and in that industry, I came across many kinds of shady people. I liked doing business with the bigger companies because they would make me sign a piece of paper showing I understood I was entering a contract with them. I had no problem signing those contracts because I was always going to hold up my end of the bargain. If things didn't go as planned, I found that the people who made me sign their contract would step up and make things right because they knew they were legally responsible for their part in the deal as well. Contracts and signatures are there to keep both parties safe and honest.

For most of my building career, I did business with handshakes. I honoured my part of the bargain every time, but I can't say the same for some of the people I did business with. Handshakes used to mean something. I'm not sure why, but a handshake today feels meaningless. A handshake today is worthless unless both parties are honourable people. My thoughts on handshakes are simple: I greet people with a sports-type fist bump, and I will only shake someone's hand after I've signed a contract and completed a legitimate business deal with them. Otherwise, I avoid handshakes as a form of unwritten contract.

Very rarely would a contractor balk at signing a contract, and when they would *never* sign one, I knew right away something was off. I knew that when people were adamant that their word was their bond, it was only a matter of time before they changed their word, and then asked me for more money, time, or what have you. In the thirteen years I was in construction, I never had a contractor honour his or her word without signing a contract!

Without a contract, I was overbilled and charged for other unforeseen *extras*, such as additional materials that for some reason they never knew they'd need for the job. They had labour costs that exceeded estimates. They had changes to the expected completion dates that caused me endless complications, chronic customer complaints, and to be countless dollars over budget. I would remind them of their written quote and the conversation I had with them at the outset when I had asked, "This is the final price, taxes all in?" to which they would always answer, "Of course, I've done this a thousand times; it's the usual price. No surprises here; that's 100 percent the final price!"

What such people are failing to consider is that they can only do this so many times to so many people before it catches up to them. The bad karma they put out in the world allows them to profit once, maybe even twice from someone, but they are missing out on repeat business and good word-of-mouth references. When a person gets a bad impression of someone or something a company or contractor did, that person is sure to tell others about it. They will put complaints online or post negative comments on social media that spread like wildfire. When a company or contractor does a good thing for someone, people talk about that too, and they'll want to hire that person again. Companies and their representatives that won't put their word on paper only think about the now and the quick score; they never think about the long game!

These are the same people who, if they're working for someone else, may do other morally miserable things. For example, they may steal from the company by 1) Taking material that isn't theirs, 2) Charging for more working hours when they're taking smoke and coffee breaks while still claiming to be working, and 3) Taking and making personal calls on their phones, and trying to pass it off as official business. If the writing isn't on paper, then it's on the wall. A shady person foreshadows

> *It's always chaotic
> & crowded at the beginning
> of your journey to success,
> but the longer you go,
> & the harder it gets,
> the fewer people you'll find
> are there with you.
> After you're successful...
> it gets chaotic &
> crowded again.*
>
> **MICHAEL RULLO**

what they're going to do, and it's usually when it comes time to sign the contract at the very beginning. I never go into business with someone if they don't sign a contract first. My time with them ends on the spot when it's time to sign and they choose not to.

> *My principles are more important than the money or my title.*
>
> **MUHAMMAD ALI**

There are also those people who'll sign a contract, and then say "You know, this isn't legally binding, and here's why..." immediately afterwards. They think they're smart and that I won't take them to court because it'll cost me more than they're going to be overcharging. They'll put their name on a piece of paper while knowing full well that their name is worthless, just like their word or character. They don't think of themselves as that bright when I take my business elsewhere and tell others about our work dealings, which in turn causes them to lose future business! I see it as a sign of good faith when someone signs first. This still gives me a chance to stop the proceedings if something doesn't feel right.

Perhaps that's what the psychology of *Enough* is all about. Things should feel good. The people around you, the goals you're pursuing, the money you're making, how you're making it, and what you're doing with it once you've made it, all these things have to feel right. And if they don't? Then it's back to the drawing board.

Having more money can change how you think about the people around you and how you think about the world, but more importantly, it may not change how you think about yourself when it comes to having and being *Enough*. Dr. Paul Piff at the University of California studies money's effect on people. He says that money may cause you to be self-focused, less sensitive to the well-being of others, and downright mean.

Doubtless money, power, and politics go hand in hand. Money's potentially corruptive effect is always under scrutiny in countries that boast a democratic system of government. If wealth comes with corruption, bad behaviour, depression, increased social isolation, and a decrease in social compassion and generosity, what can you do to make sure that your journey to *Enough* is smooth sailing and the waves aren't choppy once you get there?

Learn from those who have gone before you on the same journey. Benjamin Franklin didn't know that his face would one day be synonymous with money in the United States when he said, "Money never made a man happy yet, nor will it. The more a man has, the more he wants. Instead of filling a vacuum, it makes one." Understanding the people, power, and politics of money is helpful, but understanding your own psychology when it comes to money and *Enough* is vital. Maybe the real measure of *Enough* is what you'd feel about your self-worth if you were to lose all your money. Billionaire Warren Buffett had some simple advice for those looking for *Enough* in a pile of money. His words of wisdom? "Think it through."

> *Success isn't measured*
> *by money*
> *or power*
> *or social rank.*
> *Success is measured*
> *by your discipline*
> *& your*
> *inner strength.*
>
> **MIKE DITKA**

Not Had *Enough*? Well, Here's Some More:

- how money makes you lack empathy and behave more aggressively:

  https://www.scientificamerican.com/article/how-wealth-reduces-compassion/

  http://nymag.com/news/features/money-brain-2012-7/

  https://www.ted.com/talks/paul_piff_does_money_make_you_mean

- drivers of expensive cars four times less likely to stop for pedestrians:

  http://www.philly.com/philly/news/pennsylvania/Rich-peo.html

  https://wheels.blogs.nytimes.com/2013/08/12/the-rich-drive-differently-a-study-suggests/?mcubz=0

- money and depression:

  http://www.telegraph.co.uk/men/thinking-man/11836346/Can-money-and-success-make-you-depressed.html

  https://www.ncbi.nlm.nih.gov/pmc/articles/PMC1950124/

- money and happiness:

  http://content.time.com/time/magazine/article/0,9171,2019628,00.html

  http://time.com/money/4070041/angus-deaton-nobel-winner-money-happiness/

  http://wws.princeton.edu/news-and-events/news/item/two-wws-professors-release-new-study-income%E2%80%99s-influence-happiness

- the paradox of power, ethics, and hypocrisy in the affluent:

  https://www.ncbi.nlm.nih.gov/pubmed/20483854

https://www.theatlantic.com/daily-dish/archive/2010/04/how-power-increases-hypocrisy/187771/

http://www.kellogg.northwestern.edu/news_articles/2009/galinsky_research.aspx

- the psychology of persuasion:

https://www.fastcompany.com/3030173/how-to-use-10-psychological-theories-to-persuade-people

http://time.com/2941302/4-powerful-things-con-men-can-teach-you-about-persuasion/

https://www.psychologytoday.com/blog/sex-murder-and-the-meaning-life/201212/the-6-principles-persuasion

- the benefits of integrity:

https://www.authentichappiness.sas.upenn.edu/learn

- increasing your chances of success:

https://hbr.org/2005/07/when-failure-isnt-an-option

https://www.businessinsider.com/how-to-be-more-successful-at-work-2017-11

- money's effect on your behaviour:

http://www.reuters.com/article/us-money-behaviour-piff-idUSKCNoVP1QQ

- money and corruption:

http://www.fcpablog.com/blog/2017/1/5/dr-alexander-stein-the-psychology-of-integrity-and-corruptio.html

Chapter 9 • Takeaways:

1. Money is an amplifier that makes a good person better and a bad person worse.

2. The idea that buying things will lead to a feeling of *Enough* is not true.

3. Wealth is correlated with depression. Money doesn't buy happiness.

4. Greed is an addiction that causes compulsive behaviours, relationship dysfunction, and unhealthy choices. Who you are is not your financial worth.

5. Combat greed by cultivating an appreciation for what you have and calculating your *Enough* number so that you have an end point to aim for.

6. Real power is living life on your terms and having *Enough* so that you can relax and enjoy living life within your means.

7. It pays to be a good person, but watch out for individuals who are overly sweet at first, only to turn sour later, as well as for those who are trying to persuade you of something by 1) Faking authority, 2) Making you feel like you owe them, or 3) Claiming something is scarce or popular.

8. Beware of people who believe that bankruptcy is not the last resort. Integrity matters. Conduct your life honourably and ethically, and avoid the pitfall of thinking that declaring bankruptcy for yourself is a good out.

9. Beware of people who are 1) Overly interested in your finances, 2) Seek payment for having *helped* you out, 3) Use your contacts or reputation for personal gain, 4) Gossip behind your back, 5) Don't reciprocate, 6) Are envious of your success, or 7) Don't respect your work or your time.

10. Whatever you choose to do to get to *Enough*, and whomever you decide to do business with, remember to always get things in writing!

10

The Philosophy of Money: Change Your Thinking, Change Your Result, Change in Your Pocket

It became clear to me that goals, money, & spirit are all intertwined
& connected. When they're in sync,
my life started to have more purpose & meaning.
MICHAEL RULLO

THE word *philosophy* comes from a Greek word meaning the *love of wisdom*, but how do you go about studying the love of money? How do you figure out what money means to you so that you can change that meaning and finally have *Enough*? My takeaway from acquiring a lot of money is that it doesn't have any meaning, philosophical or otherwise, outside of the meaning you attach to it.

Money is a chameleon, changing colour from friend to foe, from good to evil, from promise to problem, depending on whatever it is you want/need to purchase at the moment. Money is power only when you understand the power it has over you. Its power derives from its metamorphosis from a means to an end to an end in and of itself, but money can't buy anything of real importance (beyond the basics of food, shelter, and medical care) because it doesn't work that way. It won't buy you a meaningful life or give that life purpose. It doesn't love you, give you hope, or care for you. Money can buy stuff, trips, and experiences, but not emotions. Love and happiness are beyond its reach, and as is often noted but regularly doubted, you can't take it with you.

Money is a commodity and currency, but it's also a philosophy, something that can be examined, questioned, and understood. If you can get under its skin and reexamine your relationship to it, you'll be one step closer to *Enough*.

The History and Misery of Money

In the beginning, there was barter. Barter is goods and services exchanged for other goods and services and relying on what came to be termed a *coincidence of wants.* Of course, if what you wanted didn't coincide with what someone was willing to offer in exchange, the bartered agreement would fail. For example, if you wanted a goat in exchange for your cow, but people only wanted to trade sheep, you'd be in trouble. Around 1200 B.C., people started using seashells, and shortly after that, metal coins, initially metal copies of shells, to get around the problem of, "You have what I want, but I don't have what you want."

Money as a means of exchange opened a Pandora's box of limitless desires and endless trade. Suddenly a seller could choose where and when to become a buyer. The advent of credit (Credit the Romans and the Greeks for perfecting that concept in the fourth century B.C.) allowed the customer to become a buyer without ever having to be a seller.

The Latin word for money is *pecunia* and comes from the word for cattle. The problem with carrying around a pocket full of portable cattle is that they're easily stolen, so banks became a heck of a grand idea, but it also was the beginning of the concept that money itself was the treasure, rather than what treasures it could buy. People could hoard money, where hoarding a herd of cattle was a lot more work. Money began its transformation from cattle to currency. The word *money* also came with its cautionary note, derived from the Roman goddess Moneta whose name meant "to remind, warn, or instruct."

Despite the goddess' warning, freedom from bartering cattle for sheep didn't bring the promised blessings. Instead, it made money the gatekeeper to all possible goals. The value of something is usually related to its scarcity, as well as the time, effort, and difficulty one must go through to get it, yet now what had value was a concept represented by a coin. Any object of desire was now only a matter of the metric of money, an abstraction, rather than a live cow, so people began the obsessive pursuit of money for money's sake.

> *Money often costs too much.*
>
> **RALPH WALDO EMERSON**

This pursuit was first acknowledged on Chinese coins, which bore the foreboding threat, "all counterfeiters will be decapitated." An old Greek proverb cautions, "A miser and a liar bargain quickly," while a Polynesian proverb advises, "Do not be like a miser who saves for those who will bury him." Another says, "A miser is always in want," and still another proclaims, "The devil lies brooding in the miser's chest." Those that became obsessed with the pursuit of money were not well thought of in any culture, and while we've progressed from Chinese coins to bitcoins, the wisdom of the ages hasn't improved one bit. People have doubtless had occasion to cry over cattle, but it's money that can make you really miserable.

I've personally met a lot of people who are money obsessed (and I was one of them not so long ago), and I've often asked them, "Do you think money makes you happy?" They always give me a philosophical answer, which includes phrases like, "It doesn't hurt," or "It allows me to pick my misery!" My next question for them is the one that reveals the real link between money and happiness, "If I gave you $10 million, would that make you happy?" They always answer me with a resounding, "Yes!" to which I add, "I'm not finished! You can only have the money; you can't spend it; you can't leverage against it. All you can do is visit it, and look at it, and be in a room alone with it. Now, will money make you happy?" Remember, multiple scientific studies have shown no correlation between income and happiness and that people are terrible at predicting how happy money, or the ability to buy an item, will make them.

At the peak of his power, one of the richest criminals in history, Pablo Escobar, was losing $2.1 billion a year to rats. Not the dirty, double-dealing, tattletale kind, but the kind that nibbled away at his stacks of expensive paper as they sat in storage. The idea of getting $10 million, and not being able to spend it, (or having it sit in storage as pricey rat food) illustrates that money is only as good as what it does. If it isn't doing what you want it to do, if it isn't making you happy, if it isn't *Enough*, it's time to rethink your philosophy of money. If money itself won't make you fulfilled, what will? We're told that spending it does, yet if you recall from the last chapter, it doesn't, and I know firsthand it doesn't!

Fund-amentally: Changing What Money Means to You

So now you're starting to get that money, by itself, is just a concept. It's a cow made convenient, a trade made transportable. So if money isn't the problem what is? It's your philosophy of money: the sum total of all you think and believe about it, multiplied by the influence of media, as well as your habits, culture, and personal history. Think for a moment about what money meant to you growing up. Did your family fight about money when you were a child? Did your parents buy things for you to show love? Did they donate money? What were you taught about money and the idea of *Enough*? How do you decide when to spend your money and what to spend it on? Determine your philosophy of money and what it means to you, and you'll regain control. Master money or money's your master.

Researchers point out that consumers spend an average of $1.10 for every $1.00 that they earn. An average of 97 percent of after-tax income is already devoted to basic necessities before considering entertainment, additional medical costs, gifts, etc. The average Canadian shoulders a debt load of over $22 thousand (as of 2016, not including mortgages), and owes $1.67 for every $1.00 of disposable income. Albertans have the highest consumer debt in Canada. Money does seem to be the answer, but only because no one is looking closely enough at the question.

I'm no longer obsessed with the game of making excess amounts of money. I've changed my money philosophy. When I stopped buying into the idea that I had to keep spending money on what was fashionable, updated, brand-new, improved, faster, better, and cooler, I just started appreciating what I did have. Money began to pile up for me because I was no longer spending it the second it came in! Sooner or later, by living within your means and not living the way our

> *It doesn't matter whether you're an entrepreneur or an employee.*
> *If your view of your vocation feels like it's a vacation, then you'll understand, & will have found, what it means to have Enough.*
>
> **MICHAEL RULLO**

society's principles of ultra-consumerism say you're supposed to be living, you'll see money become more readily available to you. You won't be spending it frivolously and going into debt to buy stuff you don't need. Ironically, by not buying things, you'll start to notice that you're becoming happier in the long run because you'll

> *If you would know the value of money, go & try to borrow some.*
>
> **BENJAMIN FRANKLIN**

have *Enough* to spend on anything you do want or need, thanks to the money you've banked away. You'll no longer be as stressed out about not having *Enough*, and you'll be happier buying things when you can afford them.

I started to change my way of thinking about money and consumerism. I saw I had power over my situation, and money no longer controlled me. I loved that with just a shift in my thinking, making the same amount of money but buying less stuff, I was okay and still happy. I became powerful when I saw money as only a concept and when I stopped my habit of buying into buying.

Start to shift your relationship to money. Examine when you're most tempted to spend and what causes you the most stress, and you'll begin to see that your buying habits are part of what's driving your endless need for more. By changing how you think about money from viewing it as a scarce treasure to seeing it as a tool that you control, you can have more. If you still feel that you need even more to get to *Enough*, consider for a moment that more doesn't necessarily have to mean more money. Your sense of *Enough* might be satisfied by more of the other things you want such as more time to spend on things you enjoy, more control, more security, or more tranquility in your money and your spending habits. Change what money means to you and *Enough* gets that much closer.

Rullo Rules

How to Stop Impulse Buying:

1. Don't go where you'll be tempted such as online stores or the mall.
2. Challenge yourself to buy only necessities for one month.
3. Change where you shop.
4. Monitor yourself to see what triggers your urge to splurge.
5. Make lists for what you need & stick to them.
6. Write down what you're spending money on.
7. Use cash & leave the cards at home.
8. Make a list of alternatives that cost less. For example, you could list free things you could do instead of going to a movie.
9. When shopping, avoid surprises & reduce impulsive purchases by using a calculator or app to add up your spending as you go.
10. Don't shop when you're hungry, upset, or stressed.
11. Think of how you usually justify your spending & call BS on it!
12. When tempted, take a deep breath & walk away, even briefly. Take a moment to focus on your values, on what you want to achieve in getting to Enough, & what's important to you. Recognize that the urge will pass & you can choose to do something different.
13. Make a "What was I even thinking?" list of purchases you've already made & regretted.
14. Declutter & make a deal with yourself to throw something out before you can buy something new.
15. Shop less often!

What is it Worth to You?

In 2014, *Forbes* figured out that Warren Buffett's net worth was near $58 billion, while the average yearly Canadian income was around the $49 thousand mark. One hundred dollars to Warren Buffett just doesn't have the same meaning as it would to the man on the street collecting pop cans to get money to buy food. It's the same amount of money. The value of money, and what it means to you, can change from one day to the next, from one car ad or cellphone commercial to another, as well as according to any change in your circumstance, but should it determine your self-worth?

When I built and sold my first big home, I made what I thought was a lot of money. The money made me feel like a million bucks, and I took myself for a big shot for about a second! I had just deposited the cheque from the sale, and I wanted to share the news with my parents. I imagined they were going to think I was a big deal now that I had money. They were going to see how I'd changed, and that I was more important because of the money I had made.

I entered my Mom's kitchen. I told her my good news and saw she was excited for me. I thought to myself, "I've made it!" but my triumph was shortlived. Without skipping a beat, my Mom asked me to take the garbage out before we ate dinner and to then set the table. My Dad told me to cut the grass after dinner was over. Did Warren Buffet have to take the garbage out? Set the table? Cut the grass? (He didn't have to, but he did, whenever he wasn't playing his ukulele that is, and he still lives in the five-bedroom home he bought in 1957 for only $31.5 thousand!)

That was not how I thought my parents would treat me after hearing about my wealth. Don't get me wrong, they were proud of what I had done, but I learned that the amount of money I made or lost didn't matter one bit to them. They accepted me for who I was, not how much I made. To those I loved and who I knew truly loved me, my worth wasn't related to how much money I had or didn't have. Whether I was wealthy or broke was not important to them, and I realized that it was becoming less important to me too.

> *A wise man should have money in his head but not in his heart.*
>
> **JONATHAN SWIFT**

When I was younger, I was impressionable, and I read about the super rich. When I read books written by billionaires bragging about all the money they had made, that just didn't resonate with me. However, these ultra-rich authors all said that having money did all these great things and made them a big deal in a roundabout way. They seemed to agree that their money determined their worth as individuals.

As an adult, I've gotten to know some very wealthy people, and I can tell you first hand that the friends and family in their inner circles, who are, in my opinion, the most important individuals in anyone's life, seldom talk about them in terms of their money. I never heard their friends or family refer to those people as more significant or as a big deal because they happened to be rich. They weren't any more or less important to their loved ones than they had been before they achieved great wealth. My parents taught me that a person's worth isn't directly correlated with how much money he or she has. When I'm not rigid in my thinking, then I'm teachable, and if I can learn, I always see myself as rich! View your self-worth as separate from your money. It's worth it!

Your True Financial Worth!

"All well and good," you say, "But money makes the world go around, and I don't have *Enough!*" What you want to talk about is not how your loved ones see you because your loved ones aren't necessarily the ones paying your mortgage, but rather how to determine and improve your financial worth. I get it. Let's talk about your financial worth.

The smartest, most well-rounded people, the individuals who have *Enough* (And you can sense it when you're speaking with them!), are people who know their real financial worth. They didn't wake up with *Enough* one morning. They went through a world of ups and downs and developed it bit by bit. Maybe you think that what you're worth financially, as in what you're capable of earning, will never get you to *Enough*, or that *Enough* is so difficult to reach that it's reserved for only a special, chosen few, but that's not the case. I've always thought that if someone is content, and has *Enough* to live the life they are comfortable living, they're the richest people I know!

Banks have formulas to figure out a person's net financial worth when they apply for a loan or mortgage. There are accounting programs that will allow banks to input data into a spreadsheet, and a number will pop out that is supposed to be what a person's net worth is. The banks will make their decisions based on those figures. When someone goes for a job interview and the employer tells the applicant what the job pays, that's another way of telling someone what he or she is worth to the company for that job. When I refer to worth, I'm not talking about just what someone sees on a spreadsheet; I'm also talking about the value that's not quantified on a piece of paper.

Whenever I had a job and was given the pay that my employer deemed fit for the service I was providing, I used to think, "This may not be enough." I felt I was worth more than what they were paying me. No matter what I thought, I didn't control the purse strings, so I had to go along with somebody else's determination of what they felt the job should pay. Finally, I reasoned it out. It's not my worth they're paying me for, it's the service or the job that they feel is only worth so much. It's not about me. When I started to see that it was the job that was only worth so much, while I still knew inside that I was worth more, I experienced a significant shift in my thinking.

If you allow others to pay only what they feel you should be given for the service they've hired you to do, then you'll always be a servant to someone else's definition of your financial worth. You won't be able to break free and find out how much you're genuinely worth. Your financial worth doesn't stop at your paycheque, your savings, the home you live in, or the cars and things you own. Your worth isn't just measured in dollars and cents; it's also measured in potential, energy, and the spirit you bring to whatever you choose to do. You're also worth whatever it is you decide to achieve on your own, outside of the amount that your job is currently paying you.

> *Success is not final;*
> *failure is not fatal;*
> *it is the courage to*
> *continue that counts.*
>
> **WINSTON CHURCHILL**

If you do decide to go the entrepreneurial route, you'll need to be prepared to take some lumps along the way, but most people who have *Enough* have learned to endure, adapt, change, execute, and engage, through defeat and despair to thrive in the end. Be prepared to be beaten down and to get back up. You'll see what your spirit is truly made of as an entrepreneur. You'll start to understand the real value you bring to the table, as dictated by the market and your abilities and insights, not as determined by former employers, banks, friends, or even family.

Not everybody's goal is the pursuit of lots of money, and the money a bank considers you to be worth doesn't define you. You may not have the sexy numbers a banker can input into a spreadsheet, but it doesn't mean you won't get there sooner or later and on your terms! You are whatever you allow yourself to be, and money is a manifestation of your self-determination. How's that for a philosophical approach to money? Your journey to *Enough* is not solely based on numbers, but more importantly, it's based on how you think.

How Not to Fail at Failure

Just as money is a mindset, so too, failure is a philosophy. Bill Gates wasn't born rich (he was listed as the world's richest man in 2015). He was born brilliant, but that didn't stop him from failing big time. His first company was called Traf-o-Data and was intended to count traffic, but when demonstration time came, the product he and a partner came up with didn't work. The company was a failure. Shortly after that the business folded. A few years later, Bill founded Microsoft and the rest, as they say, is history.

Failure is a part of every success story. J.K. Rowling's famous novel, *Harry Potter* was rejected twelve times. The degreaser and universal lubricant whose tagline was, "If it moves and shouldn't, use duct tape; if it doesn't move and should, use WD-40," was the product of thirty-nine previous failed attempts. Walt Disney was fired for not being creative enough, while the founder of *Hershey*'s chocolate, Milton Hershey, floundered in three previous failed companies before becoming the king of the candy kisses. A key component of getting you to feel like you have *Enough* and are *Enough* involves changing your philosophy of failure. If you want to get to *Enough*, you're going to have to start to view failure as feedback and not as an assault on your self-worth.

> *I never charged people by the hour.*
> *I charged people by the amount of value I brought to the job!*
>
> **MICHAEL RULLO**

I wish I could tell people that it's easy to make money, retire at thirty-seven, but I'd be lying. When I first made the decision that I was going to be a builder, everything that could go wrong went wrong. I barely had a clue about what I was doing. I ran out of money. I made rookie mistakes that cost me dearly, and the homes I built were grossly over budget because of those mistakes. Then life happened, and events like 9/11 happened. The real estate market suddenly stopped growing, and nobody was buying homes. It broke my spirit. I felt defeated.

Then I began to change my philosophy of making money and my perception of failure. I started to make changes regarding how I marketed my home. I listened to the people who came to my open houses, and then I would make little tweaks based on the comments they had made. I learned what was working and what wasn't. I lowered my price. I stayed flexible. I slowly got myself back up and said, "I'm going to sell this home, no matter what!" It took over a year and a half before the market picked up again, and if I had given up, I would have been a loser in the end, instead of making my first big sale. All those failures were the momentum I needed to create my future company. My experience with that first home became the basis for the quality, style, and design behind the many homes I built later on.

I wasn't the only builder who had it rough when 9/11 happened, but I was one of a few small independents that survived that rough patch and then thrived! I paid the price for my success, and when I learned how others had succeeded as well, I saw they also had paid the price for their achievements. The reoccurring lesson from the people I admired and chose to be inspired by, was that those people also endured. They learned from their mistakes, and they kept on moving forwards even with insurmountable odds stacked against them.

Whenever I set a goal of making X amount of money by a certain date, I'm going to fail most of the time! When you work a steady job, your pay corresponds to the number of hours you put in for your employer, or you may receive a regular salary regardless of the hours you work. Conversely, when you work for yourself, it'll always be somewhat of an exercise in trial and error. When you work for yourself, it's going to be either feast or famine! I was always either making a lot or nothing at all!

Not everybody is cut out to take the plunge and go for something on their own. The uncertainty can be too much to handle at times. I've had mentors in the past who helped me out, but that still didn't protect me from making mistakes, and things never seemed to go as I planned. I'd say I failed 90 percent of the time and made up for it with the victories that made up the other 10 percent.

> *Knowing yourself is the beginning of all wisdom.*
>
> **ARISTOTLE**

Life has an unpredictable way of unfolding, and it isn't always glamorous or easy. It was in my hard times that I learned what I was made of and what direction I needed to take next. If you expect and accept failure as a necessary part of success, you won't be surprised, upset, or derailed by it, and a failure won't cause you to think less of yourself or your abilities. Put simply, failure doesn't mean you're not good enough.

Show me someone who has made it, and I'll show you someone who didn't let their failures stop them from achieving success. Einstein was kicked out of school. Oprah was fired from her first television job. The Wright brothers certainly didn't get it right the first time. I see successful people, not as these great success stories, but rather as personal stories of individuals who endured failures, hardships, setbacks, and disasters, and kept moving forwards. Successful people know there's no such thing as playing it safe! They, for the most part, just keep playing, learning, failing, and adapting, and sooner or later they have success, thanks to the lessons they've learned from their past mistakes.

Failure is going to happen, and that is the only thing I can bank on when working for myself. Life will never unfold exactly as I planned or wished it to, but it will unfold regardless. Learning to accept failures, setbacks, and roadblocks isn't just about having a positive attitude, it's about being stubborn as a bull and completely hard-headed. It's about saying, "I'm doing this no matter what!" To keep failing at something and still deciding to keep going forwards is considered idiotic by many, but I tell them, "No, it's idiotic to repeat the same mistake over and over again, but I'm failing at *new* things all the time. I've learned from my past mistakes, and I don't repeat those anymore!"

Failures are lessons in disguise, and it comes down to how you choose to look at things. Keeping a positive perspective is more important than keeping a positive attitude. Give me a strong-willed person who can channel their energy like a laser beam over someone who's cheery and positive all the time. You need to know what is and isn't working. I always do my best to stay upbeat most of the time, but in those moments that I do get angry or frustrated, I decide right then to use that anger as energy to push past my roadblocks.

If you do decide to give up what's safe and comfortable for a chance at something great, there's going to be a long hard journey ahead. Failure is just going to be a part of that trip. The last thing I'm going to say about my philosophy of failure comes from my personal experience with failing many times. Looking back with 20/20 hindsight, my failures mean more to me than my successes! My failures are priceless to me! My failures are what shaped me into the man I am today. All the times I got back up, only to move forwards when I didn't think I could do it, made me better, stronger, and smarter. My failures are what made me, not my successes. My successes were a result of learning from past failures. Success was the outcome of discovering ways around failures.

Success may appear easy, but it's not. Some people can make things look easy, but it's because they've already paid the price to become masters of their trades by putting in their time, gaining experience, and applying the lessons learned from their failures. Success is the icing on the cake, but the actual cake is all the times

> *My great concern is not whether you have failed, but whether you are content with your failure.*
>
> **ABRAHAM LINCOLN**

they've failed. People notice the icing, but the cake underneath is what leads to success. Failing at something should produce a goal, which is to find a way to learn from the setback and use it as an example of what not to do next time. To have your cake and eat it too, look at your failures as priceless blessings in disguise!

Rullo Rules

How Not to Fail at Failure:

1. Accept that failure is a lesson in disguise. Look for the lesson.
2. Do the work. A quick buck is not usually made but lost. Don't trust get-rich-quick schemes.
3. Open as many avenues to success as you can.
4. Pursue your passion, and you're more likely to keep going after setbacks.
5. Be open to constructive criticism but know that innovating is a lonely game that only draws a crowd after you're successful.
6. Failure isn't an end. It's a beginning. View it as an opportunity.
7. Get a partner. Sometimes it helps to share the burden of failure & the joy of success.
8. Focus your energies on your best ideas first & be persistent!
9. Begin.
10. Begin again.

My Philosophy of Investing at the Speed of Speculation

As you change your view of money and embrace a new philosophy of failure, you're going to be changing other things in a domino effect. One of the first to fall may be your aversion towards speculation. What speculation is, in simple terms, is the hope of financial gain paired with the potential for financial loss.

Of course, the numbers that you calculate using spreadsheets to decide if an investment or asset purchase is a real risk are only as good as the data you input. If you fudge the numbers, you'll still get an answer, but the more honest you are when creating a spreadsheet, the better the chances of reaching your end goal. Speculation, based on calculating the numbers involved, can either encourage you to go ahead with an investment, purchase, or a business decision, or make you take a step back.

It's not easy to distinguish between speculation and investment because they often merge, especially in real estate. I made the majority of my money from real estate, and all the real estate decisions I made were speculative. Realtors, homeowners, prospective homebuyers, renters, landlords, trades, pretty much all the people I dealt with on a regular basis in the arena of real estate, depended on speculation.

The people that I knew who never took a chance on real estate didn't like the information that banks, family, and friends gave them and would insist that the numbers didn't add up! If I showed them that by making little changes to my property, I could increase its value, without hesitation they would say, "You're just speculating; you don't know for sure!" They were right, I didn't know 100 percent for sure, but I did know that if I did nothing, I had no way of finding out. These were the same people who, when I had speculated successfully, would complain about how they too should have invested.

My philosophy of money as it relates to speculation is this: I expect some failures. Expecting some failures frees you to speculate, and speculating frees you to invest in things that have the potential for a big payoff. It frees you to use money as a tool to create more money or to just create, period. The bulk of my career in real estate followed this philosophy, "I create value!" How? I loved real estate because it allowed me to make something, such as a building or a suite, from nothing, to be creative and use my imagination, and to do things to increase my likelihood of success. When I was right about something in real estate, it paid off in a big way.

> *To be successful, you have to be able to control your attitude towards the times you've failed & not let it break you or make you give up.*
>
> **MICHAEL RULLO**

I wasn't always right, but when I was, it was because I didn't let how other people were interpreting the numbers stop me. Instead, I used the numbers to motivate me to do things to increase my chances of a successful outcome. Sometimes I was told, "You can't afford to do this because it costs too much." My reply was, "I can't afford not to do it!" Yes, I was sometimes burned, but even when it didn't go as planned, I still let the numbers help me figure out a way to fix my failures.

If you decide to speculate, beware of potential swindles in windfall clothing. Some people may use fictitious numbers or loose interpretations to sway you one way or another, and they can be very persuasive. For example, in the United States, Bernie Madoff's investment company successfully swindled a slew of stars and well-to-do people along with the many victims of his long-running securities scam. Included among his victims was Hollywood director Stephen Spielberg. In Alberta, in 2011 alone, more than twenty licensed property investment companies went under, resulting in losses to shareholders in the neighbourhood of $20 billion. In 2015, a class action lawsuit was green-lighted to proceed against Platinum Equities Group, an Alberta property investment company that allegedly lost investors over $200 million. In 2017, the company's attempt to block the lawsuit failed. MacLean's magazine says Alberta has become a Wild West for property investment, with investment dreams popping right along with bursting real estate bubbles. So how do you speculate but avoid the swindlers?

If I'm going into a business deal, I will have already looked at the numbers. I know which outcome is most likely. Numbers raise questions and help me make better decisions. I can't be swayed by another person's agenda, who may be motivated to bend the truth in their efforts to make a commission or a quick buck. The best investors have a solid awareness of the risks and potential benefits beforehand. I recommend that you do your homework before speculating on, or investing in, anything. Doing your research will be your best investment. This is another instance where numbers don't lie!

Having said that, my philosophy of speculation also acknowledges that a spreadsheet may not be my only reason to go for something. There are things spreadsheets don't take into consideration, but they are noticeable precursors of your chances of success that are not always quantifiable. Successful speculators make different

> *You've encountered some setbacks; don't tell me that you're going to let that defeat you! I always keep in mind that whenever I'm not getting anywhere as fast as I'd like, delays are not denials! My setbacks never defeat me!*
>
> **MICHAEL RULLO**

associations and evaluate the cost to them if they don't go for it! They bet on themselves and know that from experience, in life and business, they have what it takes to succeed. They know that failure is to be expected and that big risks mean big rewards. Numbers serve as a gauge—that's it.

> *We're so engaged in doing things to achieve purposes of outer value that we forget the inner value, the rapture that is associated with being alive, is what it is all about.*
>
> **JOSEPH CAMPBELL**

Investment in real estate, the stock market, or in other assets always comes at a high cost that is not always measured in just money. It takes time and energy to investigate a property and figure out whether it might be a worthwhile investment as a rental property, or if it might represent an undeveloped area likely to see a building boom or population growth that will push its price up. It's expensive to hold on to land while awaiting economic or population growth, and the capital and research needed to find and keep abreast of these opportunities may be more than you want to take on. Complications such as government permits and zoning status can shut down the possibility of future development, and should your property go down in price, there's no tax allowance wherein you can write off your losses.

As with any goal, when I speculate I always ask myself, "What is the amount of effort, creativity, imagination, and time required by me going to be? What am I willing to give up to attain my goal?" These questions are just as important as the numbers I use to see if something's viable. My time, effort, creativity, imagination, and what I'm willing to give up for it all come at a cost that banks and spreadsheets don't use when making their calculations. I know that even though these factors can't be calculated, they're going to come at a high cost regarding my quality of life; I take that into consideration before deciding either way.

My philosophy of money is that there's so much more to money than money alone, and my view of speculation is that there are costs, beyond money, to any investment, and costs, beyond keeping your money, to any decision not to invest. There's also nothing wrong with making money, even lots of money, as long as you follow your ABCs.

ABC (Always Be Caring!)

He twirls his handlebar moustache, and his evil grin fills the film's frame as he counts his coins while the newly homeless family clings to each other and sobs. Many movies feature ruthless people who manipulate, deceive, lie, cheat, and show how crazy a person's level of greed can be in a sad game of winners and losers. Such extreme levels of greed play well onscreen, but in my opinion, that's merely because that ridiculous level of greed is not common among your average Joes. There are, however, those who watch those greedy characters cruelly crushing their opponents in their craving for cash, and use them as their role models, wanting to emulate them and live a life of excess.

> *Two things define you:*
> *your patience*
> *when you have nothing*
> *&*
> *your attitude*
> *when you have everything.*
>
> GEORGE BERNARD SHAW

Those characters are larger than life, and it's undeniable that they can represent all the trappings of what success typically looks like. The mottos of these characters are usually something along the lines of, *Greed is good*, and in a business where the art of closing the deal is king, A*lways Be Closing!* When I see films with those kinds of characters, I wonder why there are so few characters with the motto, A*lways Be Caring?* Can making money be a game of winners and winners instead of winners and losers?

Film studios exploit that extreme kind of greed, but like most, I find it disgusting when I read some Wall Street news story about Madoff scamming people out of billions of dollars or Martin Shkreli's unconscionable decision to change the price of a life-saving drug from $13.50 a pill to $750 each. I choose to believe that most people wouldn't stoop to that level of greed, callously ruining so many lives along the way.

For those who don't have a lot of money, nobody warns them that their chance at crazy big money might come at the expense of someone else's loss, but that possibility is not unimportant. Outside of the realm of the silver screen, extreme greed is usually considered abhorrent and is often punished (Madoff was sentenced to 150 years in prison, and the FBI arrested Shkreli in late 2015.) My philosophy is this: there's nothing wrong with making money, even more money than you need, if it's done ethically, nobody cheats or gets cheated on, and all parties can say it's a win/win all the way around when it's over! That's what I strive for, but even I know that sometimes things can happen that are simply out of my control.

I've sold homes that have later quadrupled in value. I've sold others at a loss of 10 percent of their value in the short term, but then the home rebounded back to the same price, if not more, years later. When someone tries to sell when the market isn't at its best, and they lose value from their original purchase price, most people understand that's the market, and it's beyond their control, but some people just need somebody to blame. There's only so much I can do to please someone, but I try to treat everyone fairly.

I've lost millions in real estate transactions because of greedy realtors, the market taking a dive, and the economy tanking. My thinking is, I can only control my attitude and my actions, but I must own, and live with, my decisions either way. I know that I've put myself in situations where the individual on the other side just wanted to close the deal and didn't care at all about me. I choose to live my life by taking an interest in the person I'm doing business with. There's such a thing as closing a deal and still caring about the person you're doing business with at the same time! My point is this: Even though it's not typical to talk about caring in the context of a business deal, it's the right thing to do!

Not everybody is going to care; I know we don't live in a utopian society where everyone has other people's best interests in mind. My point is that I don't choose to take part in a world where I don't care about my actions. Instead, I handle myself with integrity and always have respect for my fellow human beings! What others do is their business; what you choose to do is yours. Even when a person I don't like closes a sale with me, I will still say please and thank you all the time and stay respectful. I'm suggesting you do the same.

Choosing to care about your actions, your decisions, the products you're associating yourself with, or the product your selling, is your choice, but it's an important one. Caring comes in many guises, but at the end of the day, if you don't always make it about closing the sale, you'll feel better about it and may close many future sales by being a person of integrity. We're all on this journey of life where we have a beginning, and an end, but it's that tricky middle part I'm encouraging you to get right by choosing to care versus close all the time.

> *Money...is a really excellent servant, but a terrible master.*
>
> **P.T. BARNUM**

I see people on a one-to-one, more personal level, and because of this, making money isn't always a win/lose game against others. For me, making money is about creating the freedom to live my life on my terms, as well as making life better for my family and friends. My philosophy of money is all about making a life for myself that improves the lives of all those around me. It's not about me making more, or accumulating more, than the next guy or twirling my moustache as I gaze lovingly at my banking app. My money motto is *Always Be Caring*.

I think about money as the more I make, the more I can affect other people's lives around me for the better. If you can do anything to change your philosophy about money, failure, speculation, or how you conduct yourself in your business affairs, *Enough* will be within your grasp. When money is thought of as a win/lose kind of game, there are no winners, no matter how much anybody makes. Like P.T. Barnum, the famed circus showman, once said, "Money...is a very excellent servant but a terrible master." Make sure you know whether you are money's servant or its master.

Not Had *Enough*? Well, Here's Some More:

• the history of money:

http://www.pbs.org/wgbh/nova/ancient/history-money.html

https://www.thoughtco.com/history-of-money-1992150

• consumer debt load:

https://psychcentral.com/library/id295.html

http://www.cbc.ca/news/business/equifax-debt-loads-1.3884993

http://www.cbc.ca/news/business/national-balance-sheet-q1-2017
-1.4159851

http://globalnews.ca/news/2375223/alberta-still-has-the-highest-
consumer-debt-in-canada/

- the science of success and failure:

https://blog.bufferapp.com/why-highly-successful-people-crave-
failure-and-mistakes

https://www.wired.com/2009/12/fail_accept_defeat/

http://www.smithsonianmag.com/innovation/why-the-best-success-
stories-often-begin-with-failure-3851517/

- the Bernie Madoff swindle:

http://archive.fortune.com/2009/04/24/news/newsmakers/madoff.
fortune/index.htm

- Alberta investment losses:

http://www.macleans.ca/economy/business/nearly-2-billion-lost/

- Platinum Equities lawsuit over swindled investors:

http://calgaryherald.com/business/local-business/platinum-equities-
lawsuit-survives-appeal-but-elderly-investor-wonders-if-hell-
survive-the-case

- speculative real estate investment:

https://www.linkedin.com/pulse/speculative-real-estate-investing-
what-you-need-know-deanne-bennett

- extreme greed and the case of Martin Shkrelli:

https://www.newyorker.com/culture/cultural-comment/everyone-
hates-martin-shkreli-everyone-is-missing-the-point

Chapter 10 • Takeaways

1 Money is a philosophy, a concept invented to solve the bartering conundrum of the "coincidence of wants," but it has become a goal unto itself.

2 Money is only as good as what it does, and if it isn't working to get you to *Enough*, examine your beliefs about what money means to you.

3 Live within your means by not buying into the buying habit. Buying only what you can afford will make you happier. View money as a tool that you control.

4 Think of your value as a person separate from your money. Money won't change your worth to your friends and loved ones.

5 Could you be an entrepreneur? You won't know until you try!

6 Failure doesn't mean you're not good enough. Failure is feedback.

7 Accepting that failure is a normal part of success may change your attitude towards speculation and investments.

8 Do your research and crunch your numbers before you invest in anything, but also consider what you might be giving up, besides money, to do so.

9 *Always Be Caring* and make your money ethically. Making money doesn't have to create winners and losers. Getting to *Enough* can be a winning proposition for everyone.

11

Go With the Flow:
That's the *Spirit*!

I know a big part of my success is that I love whatever it is I'm doing at
the time, & I always find a way to make it fun!

MICHAEL RULLO

WHEN I was little, I remember that time felt like it flew by whenever I was playing. Maybe it was because I was doing something I loved. My energy would change when playtime was over, and time would feel like it was dragging if I was doing something I didn't like. As an adult, I got caught up in everyday life and working to make money, and I just forgot about the feeling I had when I was in the *Spirit* of my childhood.

It took my father having a near-death experience for me to start contemplating that *Spirit* yet again. On December 15, 2007, my world came crashing down. It was about eight months before the global economic crisis hit, when my dad hit his head on the pavement and suffered a massive brain injury. He was in a deep coma, and the doctors told my family to brace ourselves for his passing. Then, on December 25, Christmas day, a miracle happened.

Dad, who wasn't expected ever to open his eyes again, came out of his coma. He had some memory loss and couldn't recognize anyone at first, but that was the day I no longer cared for material things. I understood what a blessing it was to have my Dad still around, and the seed was planted for my transformation.

Six out of seven
dwarves
are not Happy.

SNOW WHITE

When my Dad had his accident, I had four full-time employees, a couple of part-time employees, various job sites on the go, and two of my homes had just been appraised at a combined value of over $5.5 million. I also owned several other properties destined for future building projects, and I was miserable. I was over-leveraged, and I was starting to question what I was doing and what I had built. I remembered my Dad always saying, "Don't bite off more than you can chew!"

When the world economic crash of 2008 happened, I had to let go of almost all my employees. My gross worth went from over $5.5 million to less than $2.75 million overnight! The banks were breathing down my neck, and I was struggling to stay afloat. I went from being a new-home builder to being a high-end, executive landlord renting out the properties that I just couldn't sell. Not only didn't I have a chewable mouthful, I had no choice but to swallow my pride.

I learned the hardest way possible that making lots of money wasn't enough to make me happy. The more I made, the more stress I had, and the more depressed I became. It took some hard falls, along with watching my father struggle to regain his health, to make me finally get that there's more to *Enough* than money. By being flexible, adaptable, and changing my goals, I was able to weather that economic storm, but as I weathered, I also noticed that my stress level had begun to drop. Dad's accident finally put it all together for me. Money wasn't the answer if the question was "Got Enough?"

I knew I had to look elsewhere. I started with what made me feel better. What made me happy? I determined that these were the times when I was happiest:

1. I have the freedom to do the things I love.
2. I do things that put me in a positive frame of mind.
3. I'm with family and friends.
4. I'm lost in the joy of an experience.
5. I'm in the zone and I'm fully immersed in whatever it is I'm doing.

Psychologists call this zone, or positive, immersive state, *Flow*, but in a nod to those carefree days of childhood, I like to think of it as *Spirit.*

The *Spirit* of Flow

During the latter part of the 20th century, psychologists started to study the phenomena of *Spirit* (which they called *Flow* or *Optimal Experience*) while looking into what made people happy. They noticed that many artists would often forget to eat, drink, or even sleep for long periods when they were working. They defined this state as being one of intense concentration, where a person is so completely focused on a challenging, though rewarding activity, that all worries seem to fall away, and he or she may lose or transcend, a sense of time. The person experiencing a state of *Spirit* is mostly emotionless during the activity but afterwards describes a feeling of exhilaration and profound happiness. It's a state of hyperawareness where the mind, body, and senses are all performing at their peak.

Mountain climbers, in a state of *Spirit*, report having seen every minute detail of the rock face as they climbed. Musicians tell of a sense of having been transported by the music and enjoying their performance, almost as if from afar. Athletes relate how they have been fully immersed in their sport, as each moment seemed to stretch to infinity.

Spirit/Flow has been linked to long-term, overall life satisfaction, a sense of success and achievement, and that elusive sense of *Enough*. Although you can achieve a *Spirit* state doing almost any activity, there are a few things you can do that make it more likely to occur. Here are some ways a state of *Spirit* is most likely to occur:

1. you enjoy an activity,
2. you have the skills to do the activity (you know what to do and how to go about doing it),
3. you find the activity at least slightly challenging (although not too difficult, as you must perceive it as doable), and
4. you can perform the action relatively free from distractions.

If you're bored, uninterested, frustrated, or anxious about an exercise, you're less likely to experience Flow. *Spirit*/Flow states have not only been associated with sports, exercise, music, and art but also

> *We make a living by what we get,*
>
> *but we make a life by what we give.*
>
> WINSTON CHURCHILL

with education, gaming (computer, video), planning, and problem-solving activities.

Let me share my experience with *Spirit*. When I go for a run, it takes me a few minutes to get into a groove, but then I focus on my breathing. Then once I hit that groove, I notice I'm not thinking about whatever was bothering me before I began. Eventually, I'm not thinking about anything at all. I'm just enjoying running. That's when time seems to evaporate, and I know I'm in a state of *Spirit*.

At the end of my run, whatever was on my mind before I started is now a lot clearer, and I can often come up with answers to problems that had stumped me beforehand. My whole state of being, at least for a little while, is on this temporary high (And not just from the endogenous morphine released during intense exercise, because remember, *Spirit* can happen while you're sitting down, quietly painting!). Sometimes I have eureka moments, and I often come away loving what just happened to me and how I'm feeling!

Once I discovered *Spirit*, I started to take notice of the patterns and activities that put me into that state and to analyze them. I also noticed how, if I calmed my mind, I could make the most mundane things fun. I looked for more opportunities to tap into the state of *Spirit*, and I began to feel like I could use it to give myself a short mental holiday whenever I needed it. *Spirit* always made me feel refreshed, with more energy, and I would take that energy and channel it towards my goals. When I focused on my money problems, and I didn't give myself time to forget about them, the problems persisted. However, when I did activities that put me into a state of *Spirit*, I could come back and look at my money concerns from a new point of view.

I decided to do something daily that put me in *Spirit*. I began my inspirational journaling and wrote at least two pages a day. Time would pass, and I'd realize that the cathartic act of pouring out my mental clutter also often put me in *Spirit*. As I cultivated activities that put me into that state, I had this new momentum that brought only the best kind of abundance into my life. I was less stressed, more confident, and less pessimistic. I started to feel like I had *Enough*.

What Makes Life Worth Living?

One of the founding experts on the psychology of *Spirit*/Flow, Dr. Mihaly Csikszentmihályi, pondered, "What makes life worth living?" Certainly, a part of you personally getting to your sense of *Enough* will involve you finding your *Enough* number, and learning how to realize any goal you set your mind to, but a significant component will also have to be figuring out what makes your life worth living. Getting to *Enough* may involve changing your perceptions and philosophies around money, spending, speculation, failure, and friends, but the idea all along was to be able to do more of the activities you love, and ultimately, to live a more purposeful and meaningful life. I'd like you to consider adding, "Cultivate activities that cause me to experience *Spirit*," to your list of things to do to get to *Enough*.

Spirit: How to Find Your Zone

Psychologists who study happiness recommend that to achieve *Spirit*/Flow, you should have a goal for the activity. You'll also need immediate feedback as to whether you're achieving it or not so that you stay motivated to continue. They also recommend that the goal be slightly challenging (but not too difficult), and you see it as something you can achieve, and you believe it's within your ability (which psychologists term the balance between opportunity and capacity). The activity must be enjoyable, and voluntary, and you must be in control. Finally, they acknowledge that some traditional spiritual practices such as meditation possibly use the ability of the mind to hyperfocus to achieve a *Spirit*/Flow state.

Whenever I've examined, for myself, what it means for me to be happy, I've concluded that being happy all the time doesn't seem realistic to me. Real happiness, for me, only lasts for moments at a time, as does *Spirit*. When I'm involved in an activity, I'm not thinking to myself, "I'm happy doing this activity!" No, I'm just doing it! What I'm feeling may very well be a form of happiness, but I'm focusing more on being present in the moment. I can go for a sixty-minute run, and I can honestly say that sometimes I may only feel a state of *Spirit* for a brief ten seconds, but for me, that sixty-minute run was worth those awesome ten seconds!

Both happiness and being in a state of *Spirit* are unique precisely because they only last for a few magical moments, but their aftereffects persist for much longer. It's unlikely that you'll be happy all the time, but being content is a different matter. The more you can introduce *Spirit* into your life, the more content you'll be overall, and the more you'll feel like you have *Enough*.

Spirit is when I have a magical moment of inner peace, where it feels like all is right with the world. It's the most wonderful feeling, and I know I'm different after it happens. I'm in a state of wonder. I've been fortunate to have that inner peace and wonder in my life, but I reached them by discovering that my goals, money, and *Spirit* are all intertwined. After my father's accident, I learned that *Spirit* moments would happen more often if I did the activities that made them more likely to occur. Those activities took time, and sometimes, money. It takes goals to make time, goals to make money, and goals and money to learn some of the skills needed to optimize *Spirit* states (such as learning to paint, buying a musical instrument, or training to be an athlete).

> As a single footstep will not make a path on earth,
> so a single thought will not make a pathway in the mind.
> To make a deep physical path, we walk again & again.
> To make a deep mental path, we must think over & over the kind of thoughts we wish to dominate our lives.
>
> **HENRY DAVID THOREAU**

You don't necessarily have to be a musician, a mountain climber, or an athlete to experience *Spirit*. There have even been times when I'm doing a menial task like cutting the grass, and in the middle of it, all of a sudden, I'm in *Spirit*. It's the oddest and most surreal feeling. Even repetitive activity can make the mind calm down and feel this great state of well-being. I find it's more likely to happen when I don't resist whatever it is I'm doing, and I just give myself over to the activity. I just let the action unfold naturally while I'm staying present in the moment.

To find your zone and the activities most likely to get you into a *Spirit* state, take notice of your *Spirit* moments and ask yourself, "What exactly am I doing that's giving me this *Spirit* feeling?" Think of when you're in the zone or zoned out doing something challenging that you enjoy. You can try some of the activities known to produce *Spirit* such as sports, music, learning, or art, and you can increase your ability to focus by practicing some form of meditation. Finally, if you think you don't have time for *Spirit* because you need to work, scientists say that *Spirit*/Flow states occur three times more often while working than while pursuing leisure activities.

To begin increasing the amount of *Spirit* in your life, start by thinking of what types of enjoyable things you've done in the past that made you lose track of time. What kinds of activities or thoughts do you find engaging? Think of *Spirit* as active leisure. Think hobbies, sports, intellectual pursuits, crafts, etc. Science has shown that people tend to be happier if they've spent an hour practicing a favourite hobby than if they've spent that same amount of time watching TV or socializing.

To increase the likelihood of experiencing *Spirit*, take note when you feel a sense of interest, enjoyment, and absorption during an activity. Schedule more time for these activities if you can, and if you can't think of an interest that fits the bill, try starting something that you've always wanted to do. There's no time like the present! Cutting-edge research into the applicability of *Spirit* is now being used to train elite athletes and Fortune 500 employees to encourage workplace creativity, problem-solving, and productivity.

If *Spirit* is so great, why do people collapse in front of the TV instead? Psychologists think that starting a *Spirit* activity is mentally associated with work. For example, you might have to lace up those shoes and dress for the rain to go for that run. It takes a bit of motivation to get you out the door. If you're like most people, you probably don't schedule your leisure. Recreational activities are often what happens only when all the work and demands of the day are done. Sometimes it may seem like those demands are never done, which is why you need to intentionally incorporate into your day activities that will destress you. This will help balance the *Spirit/Enough* equation.

Rullo Rules

According to the brand new science of Positive Psychology, the happiest people

1. determine their strengths (things they are good at) & use them at work, in their relationships, & to help others;
2. eat healthily & exercise regularly (regular exercise reduces depression better than medications do);
3. reduce their sugar intake (sugar has been recently linked to depression);
4. do volunteer work as members of clubs or organizations;
5. have at least one close friend;
6. cultivate family connections;
7. encourage others & actively listen to them;
8. work to think optimistically & develop an attitude of gratitude (optimism reduces chronic disease);
9. look for deeper meaning in the universe. (i.e., through religion or other forms of spirituality); &
10. engage in regular activities that put them in a state of Spirit/Flow where they do an activity because they like it.

Yoga, Meditation, Prayer, Deep Breathing, &...Naps?!

One way you can get into a *Spirit* state is through meditation, but it may take practice. As you practice, however, you'll still be increasing your ability to focus, which will help you relax, concentrate, and achieve *Spirit* in your work, play, and other activities. I used to think that meditation was only practiced in quiet, peaceful places, and then I realized that it could be practiced anywhere, whenever I'm doing whatever activity.

Meditation isn't just for yogis, Eastern mystics, martial artists, or monks in prayer, and it's thought to trigger a sense of *Spirit* precisely because it's a skill requiring focus, which must be practiced. It took me years to figure out how to meditate effectively, but once I found what worked for me, I could do it quickly and whenever I needed to. I can make myself feel at peace within minutes using meditation, deep breathing, yoga, prayer, or naps.

> *You must sleep sometime between lunch & dinner & no halfway measures.*
>
> **WINSTON CHURCHILL**

Wait a second! How did naps get in there? As with the meditative practices, I find I'm calmer, more centred, more at peace, and that I have more clarity and focus than I did before I started if I take a nap! Naps are my go-to vice when I need to recharge my mind, body, and soul. I remind myself before I lie down that whatever I was thinking about before my nap won't be that big of a deal when I wake. Knowing that I'll be better able to focus on work or running or whatever activity I've chosen to get some *Spirit* into my day makes it easier for me to get myself in the right headspace to take a moment and rest.

If you're not a regular napper, you may want to consider that many studies have shown how beneficial little relaxing nap breaks during the day can be. For example, *The Journal of Sleep Research* says naps improve reaction time and logical reasoning, and it gives you a higher tolerance for frustration. The United States even has a national nap day (March 13, the day after the switch to daylight savings time!), and some companies are even incorporating naps into their corporate cultures to enable more productivity and a less-stressed workforce. These power naps help improve alertness, reduce stress, and increase performance. A nap may not get me into a state of *Spirit*, but it will get me into the zone where I am thinking more clearly, focused, and calmly and where I can better plan my day to include more *Spirit* activities.

If I can't squeeze a nap in, a quick meditation or some yoga stretches will also do the trick. Meditation has been called the "regulation of attention from moment to moment," the "cultivation of stillness," and the "art of looking inward," but it's much simpler than that. Meditation is the act of directing your attention to whatever you'd like to focus on and keeping it there. The focus can be on your breathing, a repeated sound

> *INHALE the future,*
> *EXHALE the past.*
>
> UNKNOWN

(called a koan), a sequence of movements as in yoga, or the observation, as if from afar, of your thought processes. You can even focus mindfully on the present moment as you eat a grape or slowly walk. Scientists have found evidence that however you choose to direct your focus, meditation has a direct biological effect on the body, can improve brain function, and can boost the immune system. Many meditation techniques focus on deep breathing or breathing in certain ways or patterns.

Different breathing techniques have various effects on me, but they can make me feel at ease within minutes. Being able to modify my breathing to impact my well-being is an incredible tool for stress reduction and relaxation. Everyone should learn to focus on his or her breathing in times of stress. Since breathing becomes shallower when we are stressed, if we forcibly deepen the breaths, it fools the nervous system into relaxing the body.

Techniques like this that short circuit the stress response, or that get us to experience *Spirit*, have been called *biohacking*, and are being explored on the frontiers of science. One simple *biohack* to destress is just to count your in breaths and out breaths from one to ten. Another is to breathe out for twice as long as you breathe in, yet another is to focus on taking deeper breaths that come from your diaphragm and expand your abdomen. Once you see how focusing on your breath when you're stressed works to calm you down, you can begin to include meditation, deep breathing, or yoga in your daily routine. Regular practice will put you in the zone and help you to reach a *Spirit* state.

Prayer also works for some people, by directing their focus inwards. Prayer, or as I like to say, my *self-talk*, takes a concentrated effort for me (recall that concentration and effort are needed to achieve *Spirit* states). I have to first get over my ego and into a place of gratitude, appreciation, awe, and wonder. I become at peace when I know I play an infinitesimal role in the big scheme of life. I remind myself that, however small, I still have a part to play. I still matter.

The simple act of calming my mind takes a lot of focus, but once I'm there, it soon becomes effortless. I can practice yoga, deep breathing, meditation, or prayer, or I can take a quick nap, anywhere I am in the world, and nobody even knows I'm doing it (unless I snore!). The other commonality with these five practices is that I can do them with others around and I'm not going to draw an undue amount of attention, probably because everybody does them to one degree or another. I see people unconsciously taking deep breaths all the time to release tension; I see people napping in airports, or doing yoga-like stretching, or meditating, or praying.

As a child, I didn't have a care in the world, so it was easy to get myself in a state of being in *Spirit*. My mind wasn't weighed down with all the worries that adult life puts on a person. As an adult, I need to take the weight of worry off my mind so I can feel more at ease. Yoga, meditation, prayer, deep breathing, and naps help lift that concern. They stop my mind from being bogged down with stress. I feel lighter inside afterwards.

I consider these five peaceful practices a necessary exercise for my mind. They are my way of taking my mind to the *mind-gym* and giving it a good workout. When I'm feeling lighter inside, I know I can give more than when I don't make some meditation time in my schedule. I can work towards the goals that get me to feel like I have *Enough*, and I can pursue the other *Spirit* activities that I enjoy.

Remember that just having *Enough* money is not going to make you happy. When you think about your answer to the question "Got Enough?" there are likely a lot of things that probably come to mind, such as *Enough* time, *Enough* leisure, *Enough* energy, pleasure, joy, downtime, success, wealth, health, or wonder. Your *Enough* will be uniquely yours, but it's going to take *Spirit* to get you there.

> *Men of lofty genius, when they are doing the least work, are most active.*
>
> **LEONARDO DA VINCI**

Let the Fun Shine: *Spirit* and Play in the Everyday

I want to share with you how important being childlike is for me, and how making time for play is what got me where I am today. I stopped worrying about what others might think of me if I was acting silly. I reminded myself that children are free-spirited, and I decided to allow myself to be a kid at times and not care about anything else in the world other than what I was doing at that moment. Nowadays, I don't allow myself to get caught up in the drama of life or the problems of others anymore because when I do, I'm no longer productive. I continue to look for ways to incorporate play and a playful attitude into work and leisure activities.

Play is defined as purposeless fun. Believe it or not, there's a National Institute for Play (NIFP) in California where scientists study how important play is to human achievement. Play (and sleep!) are what they call *universal behaviours*, so the scientists at NIFP think that play is necessary for survival, in other words, mother nature has a hand in it. It looks like play may be a huge piece in the puzzle of human development. For example, recent brain studies have shown that when play generates movement, the brain's circuits light up, making new connections that encourage adaptability, innovation, and resilience. It seems that moving for the fun of it prepares us for the unexpected and encourages an exploratory mindset.

Playing in his imagination, Einstein followed a beam of light to his $E=MC^2$ conclusion. CNN notes that mega corporations are jumping on the play bandwagon, with YouTube boasting a two-story slide for its employees, Google staffers playing with scooters at work, and New York's MKG marketing offering an office photobooth, ping-pong tables, and even a petting zoo. It's not just about making work fun. Play increases productivity, which cultivates creativity, which ignites the speed-of-light imaginations critical in these changing times. These mini play breaks also allow the mind to reset and come at problems refreshed and open. Oddly enough, the downtime of play reduces downtime at work.

Even the *New York Times* is saying it's time to take play more seriously. They report that a recent study observed that 85 percent of baby seals that died off the coast of Peru were killed while playing. Their conclusion? Playing is costly regarding calories as well as calamities. So why do animals and humans do it? The play-as-preparation theory that says animals play as a rehearsal for adult life has come under fire recently, with critics claiming that there's not much science relating childhood antics to adult abilities. However, what play does seem to predict is brain growth! Play encourages more neurological connections, which equals better problem-solving skills and an improved ability to cope with change.

Children at play seem wild and free, and they appear to play instinctively. Children can play until they fall to the ground from exhaustion, and I guarantee you they never think about the stock or real estate markets, the weather, money, gossip, or any of the other grownup distractions! Children at play are the best examples of how to put yourself in *Spirit* effortlessly. By doing the things you love, just like when you were a child, not overthinking grownup life, and just allowing playtime/*Spirit* time to unfold, you'll grow your brain!

Spirit is my favourite topic because, in essence, it's all about play. I learned how to make my work fun, so I didn't have to look at it begrudgingly, and that in turn made time fly for me. I didn't realize that as a side effect it was also growing my brain, improving my creativity and problem-solving skills, and making me feel much more satisfied with life in general. Play helps me feel like I have *Enough*.

To incorporate more play into your life, start by thinking about what fun means to you. What did you like to play as a child? Is there a way to make your work more fun and include playful elements? Think of play as necessary to your cerebral development and your journey to *Enough*, rather than as a guilty pleasure or a waste of time. Play with a pet. Put on a clown nose. Build a snowman. Join a board game or role-playing group. Make something out of plasticine or clay. Colour. Try a new sport. Even if you aren't great at it, the act of playing is more important than the outcome. Play is universal, and it's instinctive for children, yet it took me many years to come back to just how important the role of play was in my work, my recreation, and my sense of *Enough*. Now I incorporate play into my life as often as possible, and I suggest you jump on the monkey bars with me!

> *I appreciate great art. That's why I spend so much time in nature drinking it in.*
>
> **MICHAEL RULLO**

> ### *Rullo Rules*
> Words of advice to live by from Kurt Vonnegut
> *'Go into the arts. I'm not kidding. The arts are not a way to make a living. They are a very human way of making a life more bearable. Practicing an art, no matter how well or badly, is a way to make your soul grow, for heaven's sake. Sing in the shower. Dance to the radio. Tell stories. Write a poem to a friend, even a lousy poem. Do it as well as you possibly can. You will not get an enormous reward. You will have created something.'*

Creativity

My earliest memories are moments when I had the freedom to, and was encouraged to, be as creative as my imagination could conceive and play with reckless abandon. I'm not sure when it was that I started to censor myself or when I decided that I had to *grow up!* and stop doing creative, playful activities. Creativity, for me, is making something from nothing, and it took time and effort for me to recognize its value and to reintroduce it into my life as an adult.

Inviting more opportunities for creativity into your life may take some work, but it's a necessary part of finding your *Enough*. Whenever you're creative, you're more likely to find moments of *Spirit*. Being in *Spirit* more often has the reciprocal effect of making you even more creative. Creativity is one of the most sought-after skills in today's job market because it's critical for problem solving, and it's the number-one requirement for top executives and CEOs.

> *Without this playing with fantasy, no creative work has ever yet come to birth. The debt we owe to the play of the imagination is incalcuable.*
>
> **CALR JUNG**

Creativity is in demand in every sector. When I see someone doing an exceptional job at whatever they're doing, straight away I consider him or her to be an artist! I can spot an artist by noticing how a person sweeps the floor or cuts hair, how a server waits on their customers or how a mechanic fixes an engine; the list is endless. *Artist* is a title for anyone who strives to be exceptional at what they do, and extraordinary people are often in *Spirit*. They are also more likely to report that they have *Enough*.

Scientists who study the neurobiology of *Spirit*/Flow and creativity (Yup, there's a scientist for everything!) define creativity as an activity that requires you to take old information and recombine it with new input. The *Spirit* state can be measured on an EEG (a machine that monitors your brain's electrical signals). Brain waves in *Spirit* slow down to a low, slow alpha rhythm (almost to a sleep-like theta wave), which indicates that a person in *Spirit* is experiencing a borderline dream state wherein information is more easily recombined. Further, they have discovered that the *Spirit* state temporarily inhibits an area of the brain called the prefrontal cortex.

The prefrontal cortex is the rational-boss area of the brain, responsible for such things as controlling impulsive behaviour. It's the seat of the sense of self but also the home of the voice of the inner critic. When we can indulge our impulses, and our inner critic can't comment, we feel much braver in imagining and trying new things (creativity!), and we feel great about it afterwards, thanks to a cascade of brain chemicals such as dopamine (pleasure/reward) and norepinephrine (focus). This jump in creativity, joy, and focus has lingering effects that leave us better able to problem solve long after the *Spirit* state has passed.

I find it ironic that in senior-citizen homes, people are encouraged to do art projects, but as regular adults, it's something society seems to frown upon because it's supposed to be for kids. Creativity is for everybody. We all still have this child inside of us that wants to be creative and play without restrictions or judgment. I've learned the importance of being creative (getting in *Spirit*) in every facet of my life and to include it as an essential part of my daily activities. I started to flourish because of it, and I got better at my work. It's a vital part of my ongoing sense of *Enough*.

> *Once & for all, there's no such thing as soy, almond, cashew, or coconut milk! Those things are all thick, white drinks or juices, but not milk!*
>
> **MICHAEL RULLO**

Creativity can be a targeted activity like drawing or writing, or it can be as simple as just asking your brain to contemplate new and exciting ways of doing something. Whenever I make something or do something challenging, and I've put my twist on it, that's me being creative. It can even come into play with how I choose to decorate my home or how I keep my office organized. Problem-solving takes creativity; composing emails and text messages often has a creative aspect to it. How I prepare my food takes creativity, and when I'm working, if I can find a way to make things fun at the same time, I can put myself into *Spirit*. I pretty much attribute everything in my life to my creativity in one fashion or another! Creativity is a constant in my life, by choice. I think of life as being like an artist's canvas, and I add to it every day, but when I'm at my very best, I know I'm in *Spirit*.

Creativity can be scheduled. When I decided to call myself a writer that was all fine and good, but like any other profession, I had to schedule a time to write. For the most part, I plan to write in the mornings, and even if I don't feel like it, I push to keep it up and sooner or later the creativity starts to come out naturally. I'll be honest, the result is not always good, but I try not to judge or do any self-edits as I go. Achieving greatness is not hit or miss. It's about showing up and doing!

When doing something creative, it's good to remind yourself not to seek approval from others. I used to feel stifled when I wanted to know if others felt that what I had created was any good or not. I might do something 1,000 times, and only 1 time out of 1,000 would I consider my creation any good, but I would never discount the other 999 attempts. Those 999 other efforts brought me to the one time where I did something truly worthwhile. I gradually lost my attachment to what people might think about my writing, my photography, the homes I design, or anything else that I did that was creative by nature. That was when being creative became a million times more enjoyable (Remember that one of the requirements of a *Spirit*-inducing activity is that it's something enjoyable!).

What will ultimately encourage a *Spirit* state? The short answer is suspending your judgment about an activity or its value, along with seeing a creative task through to completion. When you're less critical of yourself, the task at hand always becomes more enjoyable, and you'll finish it with greater ease. Don't be hard on yourself. Creativity, at its best, is effortless, and it can make you feel like time is standing still. What I mean by effortless is it doesn't have an emotional aspect to it when you're in the middle of it. It's just happening. *Spirit* feels best when it defies logic and just happens! Creativity is wonderment! If you're left in a state of wonder after you've created something, you know you've been in *Spirit*.

> *The man who does not read good books has no advantage over the man who cannot read them.*
>
> **MARK TWAIN**

As an adult, I fell victim to other people's views on how I should think and behave, what I could and couldn't do. But, I discovered that whenever I took a break to do something creative and get out of my head, it helped me to focus on something more serious afterwards, such as my goals in getting to *Enough*, making money, being an adult, and doing adult things! I did better work only after I allowed myself some creative playtime. There's no denying that creativity allows me to channel something beyond my comprehension. I know its importance and the value it brings. I don't need to have it scientifically explained to know that being creative affects my life for the better. My age and appearance are that of an adult, yet I've learned that my creative *Spirit* that shows up to play is the same as the one I knew as a child.

The *Spirit* of the Art of Storytelling

My conceptualization of the *Spirit*/Flow state differs from that of the positive psychologists who decry the influence of television and movies. My experience is that you can achieve a *Spirit* state through your creative actions but also through appreciating, and losing yourself in, someone else's original content. The creativity that captivates me the most is the art of storytelling.

I love good storytelling because I allow my conscious to suspend my reality as I'm taken away into a make-believe new world. I love how stories come to life through someone else's imagination. The stories can be in magazines, in books, or on the internet. They can be something I read, or watch on YouTube or Netflix or television or at the theatre. What's important is the story. The author creates whole new worlds where I can suspend disbelief and just allow myself to go along for the ride. I love how my imagination is ignited by the storyteller who can elicit a range of emotions. A story comes alive for me when it rings true and speaks to my heart. I'm left in wonder thinking about a good story, and I realize that when I'm in the storyteller's imaginary world, I'm in *Spirit*.

> *Here's looking at you, kid.*
>
> **RICK IN CASABLANCA**

Stories allow me to dream while I'm awake. I use the medium of a great story to daydream as I watch it unfold on a screen or as I imagine it while I read. I appreciate how stories help to quiet the noise around me so that later I can move forwards in other areas of my life. Stories give my mind a mini-holiday so I can go back to my problems refreshed. I always make time for them.

Great storytelling in movies speaks to me on another level. Great stories amplify the human experience, and then cinema presents it in a beautifully artistic way, marrying visuals, auditory sensations, and plot with actors who immerse themselves in the characters they are playing. I liken a good movie to being in *Spirit* because, while the story is playing out in front of me, I'm no longer thinking about the troubles of the day, what I'll need to do tomorrow, or what I wish had happened yesterday. I'm in the zone. The magic of movies and good storytelling connect with me on a very visceral level.

I remember my Dad once said to me, "In my twenties, I thought I knew everything. Now, in my seventies, I know nothing!" I asked him why he would watch the same movie repeatedly, and he would say, "Because I get something new from it every time!" I too can pick up new things from a film I've watched multiple times, at different times in my life. The story becomes familiar, but it's also something I want to experience again. A movie I watched as a child will mean something completely different to me when I see it again as a teen or in my twenties, thirties, and so on.

To experience a *Spirit* state, it helps to be curious, to explore and to play. A good story invites all of these activities but is drawn on the silver screen of the imagination. The art of storytelling evokes a *Spirit* state for me because, at its best, it fills me with a sense of wonder. Whether you're running, painting, playing, meditating, or being Spirited away to Casablanca, *Spirit*, just like *Enough*, is something uniquely personal that you'll have to find for yourself. And once you do find it? Play it again... Sam.

The *Spirit* of Negative Energy

A natural enemy of the *Spirit* state is negativity, especially if it goes on for too long. It can stop you from trying something new, and your inner voice may sound something like this:

1. "I won't be any good at it."
2. "It's too hard."
3. "I don't know what to do to get started."
4. "I don't have time."
5. "I'm too busy for that."
6. "I'm too tired."
7. "It's silly. I don't want to!" and
8. "I have more important things to do; I'll do it later, just not today."

> *I always felt like I could create my universe. So far so good.*
>
> **MICHAEL RULLO**

There are times when I've been filled with an incredible amount of negative energy, a bad mood that just didn't seem to take *No* for an answer, but I taught myself how to use that negativity to my advantage and turn it into something positive.

My big discovery about negativity is that energy can't be positive or negative. It's just fuel. I've learned to attach new meaning to a negative feeling, viewing it instead as an opportunity to turn it around into something positive. The fuel, or motivation and drive to take action from negative energy, is powerful if you harness it and put it towards something that's meaningful or useful to you. For example, when I start out writing from a dark place and I channel that energy into the work, I come away with some of my best writing and have a feeling of accomplishment afterwards. I ultimately feel good about what I've created from that negative energy, whether it's fueling a better workout, a better writing session, an activity or conversation that I may have been avoiding, or if it helps me to push past a hurdle that's blocking my progress.

> *The man who asks*
> *a question*
> *is a fool for a minute.*
> *The man who does not ask,*
> *is a fool for life.*
>
> **CONFUCIUS**

I am not always in a positive headspace, and that's okay. However, I'm always left feeling a sense of wonder whenever I've managed to turn a negative mindset into something active and productive. By using negative energy as fuel to push myself forwards instead of not doing anything at all and allowing myself to wallow in it, I get closer to my goals. What's the phrase? "Don't get mad. Get even"? A negative mood can be incredibly motivating, and while I'm not suggesting that you *get even* with someone else, you'll reach a calm and *even* state of mind faster if you use your negative energy to focus on a goal, activity, or task.

When you find yourself feeling negative, resentful, hurt, or any other less than positive feeling, ask yourself, "How can I turn this negativity around into something good?" In a very odd way, I have come to look forwards to my negativity because I see figuring out how I can turn it into an opportunity for action or something positive as a kind of test. I look for ways to take the negative feeling and direct that energy towards something that will ultimately better my situation. I seize any opportunity to make something great from something that started out negative, and I have experienced many *Spirit* moments that were initially motivated by negativity.

I encourage you to see negative mood states as not inherently right or wrong, but as a different way of viewing the world at that moment. These feelings are usually temporary but may serve as a mirror for your mind, showing you a different perspective, and fueling you to do something, to react. Positive or negative, there's an energy there that you can use to push yourself forwards and focus your efforts. Remember that hyperfocus also helps you to get into *Spirit*.

Adversity is Your *Spirit's* Wake-up Call

If I don't view negative energy differently than positive energy and just see it as fuel either way, why do I get fearful when I stay in a negative state for too long? Because I know the repercussions; I know how long-term negativity can affect me and none of it's good. It's also my time to forcefully give myself a wake-up call, see things as they are, and get real with myself asap before I get stuck in it.

A negative state is not something you should allow yourself to be in for too long, if you can help it. When you're feeling negative, being negative, and projecting negativity, ask yourself, "How is this negativity serving me for the better?" If it isn't working for you, that's your wake-up call to turn it around before it turns into something that will feel impossible to change.

Sometimes it'll feel like you'll need to make a Herculean effort to pull yourself out of negativity. Remind yourself that what you may have done in the past when feeling negative wasn't getting you to *Enough*. Remind yourself that life is at its most meaningful when you have moments of wonder or are in a state of *Spirit*. Take the time to do enjoyable things for yourself that have nothing to do with goals or money but do feed into *Spirit*, and they'll keep you on track with your plans to feel like you have, and are, *Enough*. It may take determination to turn negativity around, but by focusing on your goals, money, and *Spirit*, you'll find purpose, meaning, and peace of mind again.

Ask yourself, "What feels better, being negative or positive?" and "What can I do, immediately, to act on it?" The best part of having life knock you down is knowing that every time you get back up and keep moving forwards, even in the most minuscule of ways, you're making yourself a better person! Life takes its toll on me too; however, I always remind myself, "If something is fixable, then it isn't a problem."

When I'm feeling stuck in negativity, I try to remember that great things can happen because of an adverse situation. Some people have made great music or art, writers have written some of their best novels, and athletes have pushed themselves to new, unimaginable heights after they conquered a dark time in their lives. They turned a challenge into an opportunity that became something awe-inspiring!

Beethoven was suicidal when he first discovered his worsening deafness, but he learned to feel the vibrations from the piano and went on to compose some of his greatest works (including his famous ninth symphony) after he was completely deaf. Malala Yousafzai was shot in the head by extremists at age fifteen and used her near-fatal experience as a catalyst to become a global activist for education and the youngest recipient of the Nobel Peace Prize. Jean-Dominique Bauby wrote his famous memoirs, *The Diving Bell and the Butterfly* after he had had a stroke that left him so completely paralyzed he only had control of one of his eyelids. Blinking his way through the alphabet to a transcriptionist, with an average speed of one word every few minutes, inside of ten months he had written his book. The movie based on his book was nominated for four Academy Awards.

We gravitate to stories about human triumph over adversity because we hope for that same strength to emerge in our lives when negative events and feelings seem insurmountable. I am in awe of how making time for activities that put me into a *Spirit* state can take me from hopeless despair to, somehow, feeling inspiration and wonder in an instant. I know I'll never fully grasp how, but I'm in awe every time that shift happens!

> *When everything seems to be going against you, remember that an airplane takes off into the wind, not with it.*
>
> **HENRY FORD**

Making Things NEW (Next • *Enough* • Wonder)

Making things new means that you're not content with where you're at, and you're ready for some changes. You know you're ready for NEW, which stands for Next, *Enough*, and Wonder (an effect of doing more activities that put you into a state of *Spirit*), when you don't feel like you have *Enough*. Remember, back in the chapters on planning and goals, how important it was to check in with yourself and ask, "What's Next?" The future focus of "What's Next?" fans that initial spark of interest every time you start a new goal. Recall that you'd also ask yourself, "What's

Next?" at the end of a goal to keep the momentum up while you were still energized from completing your last goal. When you think of the acronym NEW think, "What do I need to do Next to get to *Enough*, so that I have more time for activities that allow me to feel a sense of Wonder (i.e., activities that you enjoy to the point where time flies and you're in a state of *Spirit* or when you feel like you're just playing)?"

When I first asked myself, "Got Enough?" I concluded that it was going to cost a lot of money to live this ambitious life I was setting out for myself. I loved to do things that put me in *Spirit*, but I knew there would be costs involved with these activities, and paying my day-to-day bills also wouldn't be cheap. I had lots of respect for the money side of my goals. Without money, the playtime that put me in *Spirit* was certainly not going to happen. I figured out how much money would suffice, which turned out to be my *Enough* number.

You'll need an idea of some of the activities that you like to do that get you into a *Spirit* state, as well as a sense of your long-term goals, to start figuring out your *Enough* number. Then you'll need to determine a plan to get to that number and select an initial (Next) goal to start you on your way there.

When I knew what my *Enough* number was, I didn't waste time trying to make even more money than that. If by chance, I did happen to make more, it was awesome, but it wasn't my objective. I always kept in mind that for me to achieve a goal, and do the things I loved doing, I needed X number of dollars. I respected money, but it never drove me.

> *I honestly don't know much about happiness.... .*
> *I was never happy because of the things I had or who I was or where I was in life.*
> *I've always been someone who had a lot going on in my head, but it always had to do with what I was going to do next, & that gave me purpose.*
> *I'm more about having a sense of purpose, & being in Spirit, than I am about figuring out what makes me happy or unhappy.*
>
> **MICHAEL RULLO**

> *Never discourage anyone who continually makes progress, no matter how slow.*
>
> **PLATO**

I needed goals to push me towards whatever was going to be the Next thing to get me to *Enough*. I needed *Enough* money to be able to pursue my goals and make them a reality. I needed *Enough* money to do things that put me in *Spirit*, and which were generally unrelated to either my goals or my money. I needed to play and do activities that took my mind away and brought me back refreshed, not stressing about whatever I was focused on beforehand (usually goals or money). I knew I needed *Enough* so that I could do more of the activities that made life fun and let me feel a sense of Wonder. Knowing which activities you can do to put yourself into a beautiful state of *Spirit* more often will help push the whole NEW wheel forwards.

NEW let me accomplish my goals and make money for myself by letting me take time out just for me so that I was in *Spirit* often. There are times when I would go for a run, read a book, take a walk in nature, or have a laugh with friends where I'd have mini-epiphanies that allowed me to see ways around my mental roadblocks. I took notice of the importance of taking care of my *Spirit* at the same time as I was also dedicated to achieving my goals and making money. My takeaway was that taking care of my *Spirit* is probably the most important thing I can do for myself when I set out to accomplish a new goal, as well as when making money. Those *Spirit* moments, doing the things I love doing, give me the most clarity (and Wonder!) afterwards.

NEW Final Thoughts

I had a life-altering experience when my Dad had his near-death accident. It made me take a step back from the life I was living and take some time for myself to put my life into proper perspective. I didn't like how I was living and the day-to-day stress I was putting myself through. I asked myself, "When am I at my best?" and "When am I happiest?" My answer to both questions was, "When I'm in *Spirit*!" My Dad's accident caused me to make a conscious decision to live a NEW life where I would have less stress and more time in *Spirit*!

Don't wait for some life-threatening event to befall you or your loved ones before you decide that NEW is the right path for you. Life is short and living it burdened by the feeling that you don't have *Enough* makes it harder. If you're ready for NEW, ask yourself, "How can I live a life free to pursue activities I love to do that put me in *Spirit*, and how much is this lifestyle going to cost?" Come up with an end number. Ask yourself, "What's Next?" so you can start to figure out how to achieve that number, and then begin living your NEW, more purposeful, active, and meaningful life.

> *The human spirit is more powerful than any drug - & that is what needs to be nurished: with work, play, friendship, & family. These are the things that matter.*
>
> **ROBIN WILLIAMS**

Not Had *Enough*? Well, Here's Some More:

• understanding *Spirit*/Flow and the science behind happiness:

  http://www.pursuit-of-happiness.org/history-of-happiness/mihaly-csikszentmihalyi/

  https://www.ted.com/talks/mihaly_csikszentmihalyi_on_flow

• the field of positive psychology:

  http://harvardmagazine.com/2007/01/the-science-of-happiness.html

  http://positivepsychology.org.uk/living-in-flow/

• the habits of the world's happiest people:

  https://www.psychologytoday.com/blog/happy-trails/201507/5-lessons-the-world-s-happiest-people

  http://time.com/2933943/the-8-things-the-happiest-people-do-every-day/

  http://www.sparringmind.com/be-happy/

• meditating your way to *Enough*:

  https://www.psychologytoday.com/blog/feeling-it/201309/20-scientific-reasons-start-meditating-today

• the science of play:

  http://www.nifplay.org/science/overview/

  http://www.npr.org/sections/ed/2014/08/06/336361277/scientists-say-childs-play-helps-build-a-better-brain

  http://www.parentingscience.com/benefits-of-play.html

• playing at work to get more work done:

  http://www.cnn.com/2013/03/29/living/play-at-work-irpt/

- time to take play more seriously:

  http://www.nytimes.com/2008/02/17/magazine/17play.html?mcubz=0

- the science behind flow and creativity:

  https://blogs.scientificamerican.com/beautiful-minds/the-real-neuroscience-of-creativity/

  http://time.com/56809/the-science-of-peak-human-performance/

  https://www.psychologytoday.com/blog/the-playing-field/201402/flow-states-and-creativity

Chapter 11 • Takeaways:

1. Money isn't the answer if the question is "Got Enough?"
2. Scientists say happiness involves doing enjoyable activities that produce a positive brain state called *Spirit* (or Flow) wherein time seems to stand still.
3. People who often engage in *Spirit* activities such as sports, music, or art, report higher overall life satisfaction and a sense of having *Enough*.
4. To find what activities produce a *Spirit* state for you, look for things that you find interesting, enjoyable, and absorbing, that have a goal, but are at the same time challenging but achievable.
5. Take naps! They improve your focus, reaction time, and logical reasoning, plus they give you a higher tolerance for frustration.
6. Do meditation, yoga, or deep, focused breathing to lead to a *Spirit* state, or use deep breathing to *biohack* the stress response.
7. Play (at purposeless fun) or do something creative to enter *Spirit* effortlessly.
8. Don't think of emotional energy as negative or positive; think of it as fuel for an opportunity to take action. When adversity happens, make time for more *Spirit* activities to reach a more positive frame of mind quickly.
9. Conceptualize your *Enough* number as, "How can I live my life free to pursue the activities I love to do (that put me in *Spirit*), and how much is this lifestyle going to cost?"
10. Make things NEW by asking yourself, "What's Next, that will get me closer to *Enough*, so I can experience more Wonder?"

12

Finding Your Balance:
On the Edge of *Enough*

I never let making a living prevent me from creating a life!
MICHAEL RULLO

THE most successful workaholics know all about balance. Richard Branson, the billionaire owner of *Virgin Enterprises*, regularly schedules getaways to optimize his productivity. According to Branson, a vacation is more than just a chance to rest: it's an interruption in the brain's normal routine. This break exposes the mind to new people and places, and all that novelty doesn't go to waste. The brain integrates the new information and is inspired to create new ideas or come at old problems with a fresh perspective (*Spirit* anyone?).

This new perspective kickstarts Branson into a higher gear of productivity when he returns to work. He's not alone in recognizing the need for balance. Website superstar, Jeff Weiner, CEO of LinkedIn, schedules daily downtime. His reasoning? CEOs who rush from meeting to meeting scarcely have time to process or prepare, let alone to just think. So just how important is empty *think* time?

Consider the case of airline pilot Chesley Sullenberger (Captain *Sully*) and his copilot Jeffrey Skiles, who famously landed a packed airplane, with more than 150 passengers on board, on the Hudson River. The National Transportation Safety Board ran flight simulations afterwards that showed the pilots could have made it to nearby LaGuardia airport, but the simulation runs had left out an important part: the time needed after a duel-engine failure for the pilots to think about their options and decide what to do. When *think* time was factored in, all simulations failed and Captain *Sully* had made the only decision (landing on a busy

> *The secret of change is to focus all of your energy, not on fighting the old, but on building the new.*
>
> SOCRATES

river) that would have, and did, save the lives of all aboard.

Taking time off to be more productive with your time *on* may seem unlikely, impossible, or counterintuitive when you have immersed yourself in the "work till you drop" idea of what will make you *Enough*. But you've probably had your fill of what isn't working and are ready to give what will work a go. What will work is balance.

When I was younger, I didn't think about balance. It was usually balls to the wall, and I filled my life with excess. My Dad's accident, coma, and incredible recovery threw my world off-balance; it changed me. He fought hard to recover, and I moved back in with my parents to help with his care. He went from not recognizing anyone in the family to being sharp as a tack and then some. I got my Dad back, but it took me a long time to get my balance back.

Balance is a big part of *Enough*, because living the life that you've dreamed of for yourself is easy...only in your dreams. Real life, however, can throw all sorts of things your way, such as duel-engine failures, illness, or unforeseen life events, that are going to upset that balance and send your sense of *Enough* careening into the abyss. The more ducks you have in a row, the quicker you'll get that balance back. Those ducks include

1. simplifying by single-tasking, all-right sizing, and living within your means;
2. viewing health as wealth and making it your number one priority;
3. experiencing the splendour of nature more often; and
4. connecting to a community.

It's tricky, but you need to create that balance all while pursuing your *Enough* number, working on your plan and the goals that you want to realize, and getting into *Spirit* as much as possible. That's a lot of ducks to line up, but it's a lot easier than landing an airplane on a river.

Simplifying: How to Live Happily Within Your Means

As my Dad struggled to recover from his accident, it was the simple things that became important. Sometimes he'd just need me to sit and watch TV with him. As he continued to recover, we'd go out for pizza once a week. It was a massive change for me to move from my expensive home back into my childhood bedroom.

I began to realize that something had happened when I started to make lots of money: my life became very complicated! I had people who worked for me. I had massive financial obligations, contracts to sign, trades to deal with, the government calling regarding my taxes, and the list goes on. In my pursuit of making more and more money, I had made my life a big old ball of stress. It took a recession, and almost losing my Dad, to give me a much-needed wake-up call and to realize the life I was living was not good!

I'm all for progress and success, but I was not able to create balance in my life while I had to make so many sacrifices to get to where I was perceived as *successful* by others. The problem was, the more money I made, the more contracts I signed to build for other people, the more my life spun out of control, and the more complexities and problems I had to deal with to get things done. When my plate was full, my satisfaction with my life progressively decreased. The idea of simplifying my life to be happier was a foreign concept to me at the time. If I wasn't super busy and over-stressed, I obviously wasn't doing enough.

The Misery of Multitasking

Instead, I was the king of multitasking, the lord of information overload, but the technology that was supposed to simplify my life caused endless complications. Problems came to me in the form of emails, posts, text messages, daily website updates, constant replies to email inquiries, and nonstop voice messages. The curse of constant communication, of being continually plugged in, is constant stress.

A 2015 study at the University of London showed that IQ temporarily drops while multitasking, while another at the University of Sussex showed that multitasking makes stress hormones rise and may be damaging the brain in the areas of emotional control, empathy, and other cognitive functions. Not only is multitasking making us stupid and stressed, it simultaneously decreases our abilities to cope with that stress!

Multitasking is also a surprising time-waster. A better name for it would be task-switching, as science has demonstrated that, despite our perception, the brain is only capable of focusing on one thing at a time. Studies have shown that it takes an average of twenty-three minutes for the brain to get fully back on task after an interruption. Additional research has revealed that multitasking impairs short-term memory function, ruins the ability to concentrate, and tanks productivity (by over 40 percent), even as it offers us the illusion that we are productive.

I once saw a musician who was so hooked on checking his Facebook every few minutes that he would check it in between each song he played on stage. He was missing the moments when he could have connected with the people who had paid to see him play. He probably thought he was multitasking, but he was just missing out.

What is the opposite of multitasking? Is it single-tasking? Yes, it is! A component of simplifying things is giving yourself permission to do one thing at a time and giving that one thing your entire focus. Simplifying also means that you intentionally schedule balance into your day with many breaks of at least fifteen minutes. Breaks don't have to be coffee and donut downtime, but can instead be used as an opportunity to sneak in some meditation or yoga, or some of the other activities that put you in a state of *Spirit*. Alternatively, take time in the day to just think and do nothing.

Simplifying means starting to take back control of the devices whose pings, beeps, and other alerts demand your immediate attention. Mute them until you're ready to give them your undistracted focus, but don't leave them until bedtime. A 2012 Harvard University study has shown that the blue light emitted by cellphones, tablets, TVs, and the like, interferes with sleep (by suppressing the sleep hormone melatonin) and may contribute to cancer, depression, diabetes, and obesity. They recommend using blue-blocking glasses, if you must use your electronics within two to three hours of bedtime, or installing an app that can block blue-green wavelengths (such as F.lux, or Twilight). They also suggest exposing yourself to more bright light during the day to improve your mood, your level of alertness, and to ultimately boost a better night's sleep.

Alright-Size Instead of Downsize to Live Within Your Means

Simplifying, to achieve more balance on your way to *Enough*, doesn't just mean the end of multitasking, it may also mean taking your spending habits to task and living within your means. Living within your means refers to spending less, every month, consistently, than you are bringing in. Surprisingly, living within one's means doesn't usually make people as unhappy or deprived as they think it's going to. In fact, it usually has the opposite effect. There have been times in my life where, on paper, I was worth X amount of dollars, but that never correlated with the amount of happiness I was feeling. Eventually, I learned that when my life was at its simplest was when I felt most content.

After much evaluation, I started to get rid of lots of the things I had accumulated. The term these days is downsizing, but I wasn't after smaller per se, but rather less. I decided to alright-size. As I got rid of things, I felt a sense of balance returning to my life. I sold properties at a huge loss because they were causing me lots of stress. I got rid of a sports car and an SUV that I regularly parked for eight months out of the year. I sold off everything I didn't need. I had been working my butt off just to keep things around I rarely even used. I was always trying to keep up with the payments while simultaneously getting ready to buy something new that wouldn't even be the latest model almost as soon as I got it home! It was a never-ending cycle. These things owned me instead of me owning them.

I love having the best things in life, and I make no apologies for that, but I also learned over time that I don't need to keep buying the latest and greatest things to be happy. I went from a mindset and lifestyle based on accumulation, which never felt like it was going to be *Enough*, to alright-sizing. Alright-sizing meant having less stuff, making less money, understanding what my *Enough* number was, and living within my means.

> *A different version of you exists in the minds of everyone who knows you.*
>
> **UNKNOWN**

Living within your means is a huge step in simplifying your life and will go a long way towards helping you find the balance that will take you to *Enough*. Living within your means necessitates that you know what your means are. Once you have a good handle on how much you make, the tough part is reducing your spending to fit that income. If you find budgeting difficult, try a technique called *backwards budgeting* wherein you start with a figure that is your monthly income and subtract each expense to see what, if anything, is left.

Not relying on credit cards, borrowing, or overdraft is also a smart strategy, since part of simplifying, and getting to *Enough*, is taking back control of your life. Credit card companies can raise your rates, cut your limits, or close your cards as they please, so they are remarkably unreliable as a financial strategy for making ends that don't meet temporarily stretch. The interest you pay to service credit card debt is just wasted money. Learn to distinguish between your wants and your needs. Save to make a bigger purchase, and you'll be amazed at how happy you feel when you can afford to buy it outright!

Living within my means meant that I could get ahead when more came in, and when I had less, I still had *Enough* to ride it out. I planned for life's emergencies, so I wasn't caught out in the cold when something unexpected happened. Stress went away when there was sufficient money to take care of my financial obligations and when I wasn't frivolously throwing it away on the unnecessary things that we are all brainwashed to want.

I started to chip away at my credit card debt. I hated knowing that I was still paying for all those times I went out to eat, the stuff I bought months ago, and the materials I needed for my job sites when the job was long since done. When I didn't have those financial distractions in my life any longer, I saw that I could focus my energy on other things that didn't necessarily make me money, but made me (1) healthier (e.g., exercise), (2) more creative (e.g., writing, photography, designing), and (3) put me in a state of *Spirit* (e.g., being in nature, going for a run or hike, etc.).

> *Simplicity is the ultimate sophistication.*
>
> **LEONARDO DA VINCI**

Alright-sizing won't make you feel deprived as long as you don't focus on everything you don't have. Whether or not you choose to simplify your life and live within your means, even as you do what you can to reach your *Enough* number, focusing on what you don't have won't ever make you a happy camper. Accumulating things and living a life with the sole purpose of always striving to want more led me to a downward spiral of discontent, bad health, depression, and isolation. I felt like nobody would understand. I was trapped in this vicious circle with no foreseeable end point until I began to change my views about money and contemplate what *Enough* meant for me.

I set my *Enough* number goal by asking myself, "How much money do I need to have so that I can live the simpler lifestyle that I'm after? How can I manage this new lifestyle financially and still live comfortably after I attain it?" I followed up with this last question, "Will living within the means afforded by my *Enough* number make my life better and less stressful?" Having more, making more, and living for more were mental traps stopping me from ever reaching a vague and undefined sense of *Enough*. I had to stop that way of thinking before I could evolve to a place where my life was simpler again and easily manageable.

I calculated my *Enough* number and found that I needed to live within that figure, or else nothing was ever going to change. I had to be the one to change because I knew the system that encourages endless consumption wasn't going to. Even though I had what many would consider to be lots of cool things, in my heart I knew that this stuff didn't make me happy, so I felt like it was time to rid myself of the possessions that were holding me back. I simplified. I alright-sized. I started living within my means. When I did that, a shift happened. I learned that not only could I live within my *Enough* number, I was happier because of it.

Simplify Your Stress

I learned the hardest way possible that making lots of money wasn't *Enough* to make me happy. The more I made, the more stress I had. I didn't grasp the concept or even consider what living within my means was. I just felt that I needed more *means,* and this caused me to be under constant pressure. You'll have to decide whether to look for more *means* in your life, or whether to simplify, single-task, and alright-size to get to *Enough.*

More money entails more problems because it comes with a lot more responsibility and stress and demands more of your time. Simplifying, single-tasking, and alright-sizing take some effort, practice, and some getting used to but will give you a better long-term shot at financial security and a happy and thriving life. A life where you have *Enough* probably requires less shopping, less stress, and more balance.

When I started to look for my balance, I began to take note of when I was stressed and what was causing me to feel that way. Little by little, I began to make changes that reduced my stress. Back in the day, before a person could block unwanted calls, I had changed my phone number so that certain people, who had been a primary cause of my stress, couldn't get a hold of me anymore. I focused more on sustainable living. I decluttered and put more of my energy into things I enjoyed doing. I stopped working on everything suboptimally and practiced focusing on the present and what I was doing and experiencing in that moment. I did a cleanse, so to speak, and saw how, by simplifying my life, I was automatically less stressed. I recommend that you note in a daily journal your stress levels and what type of events or thought patterns cause them to rise. Then, go after the root cause of your stress, and if money is it, you can either live with less or make more or both. Doing a bit of both is the beauty of balancing on the edge of *Enough.*

I'm all for making lots of money, but I will never go back to making my life more complicated than it should be. My money goals these days are also simple. I test a money goal by asking "By doing X, will my life be better, less stressful, and can I manage this without going into debt?" If the answer is *Yes,* then I'm going to go for it with 100 percent effort. I won't look back! It's that simple.

Health Is Wealth

When I was only ten years old and I got that first job in George's grocery store, I started my working life. I quickly realized I was going to have to give up a lot of things to make money, such as sports and doing things other people my age were doing. Day after working day, I gave up my youth to get ahead financially. I was willing to give up everything to be wealthy, but as I did so, I discovered that my pursuit of wealth at any cost usually came at the expense of my health, either through exhaustion, or later in life, through wear and tear, injuries, and accumulated bad choices. When I was younger, I didn't think about my health or balance. I filled my life with excess and equated that excess with success. When I got older and wiser, I found I would give up all my wealth to have the health I had when I was younger!

> *The first wealth is health.*
>
> **RALPH WALDO EMERSON**

I often saw these young guys who worked for me in the construction business. They were total go-getters, and they thought they were invincible. Then I'd see them five to ten years later, riddled with injuries, unable to work and make money. Good health for labourers is necessary for them to be able to earn a living, so they should make health a top priority, but most don't. It's sad. If and when they do decide to make health a priority, often the damage has been done. They may have already injured themselves to the point where a safe, pain-free, healthy life is difficult or impossible.

The construction industry is only an extreme example of what failing to make your health a priority can do. We all make decisions daily that either improve our health or are detrimental to it. It's the accumulation of these decisions that tips the balance one way or another, and means we could live the lives we want to, or we could spend them wishing for the health and wealth and energy of lost youth. Wishing, wanting, and hoping are incompatible with *Enough*. Striving for balance, and viewing your health as an important part of your wealth, will get you where you want to go.

Health as a Priority

I was twenty-three and in university when I went up four flights of stairs and was completely winded. I had let my health go after high school, and I didn't notice how out of shape I was until that moment. I still looked healthy, but I wasn't. I couldn't walk a kilometre without breaking into a heavy sweat, totally out of breath. I didn't need a doctor to tell me that I was out of shape! I had put my body through countless hours of physically taxing and menial work, sleepless nights of hard partying, a fast-food diet, and years of weekend alcohol binges, and just like those aging construction workers, my feelings of youthful immortality were starting to fade. That's when I realized I had to adjust my thinking. Money means nothing if you're not healthy enough to enjoy it.

I began to make my health my number one priority, even over money. It worked out well as I started to notice a connection between feeling stronger and healthier and being able to put more energy and effort into making more money. It was a win-win decision. I didn't give up my money-related and work-related goals. I just realized that being healthier would help me in the long run (no pun intended!). The dollars and cents of being healthier simply made sense.

> To keep the body in good health is a duty...
> Otherwise,
> we shall not be able to keep our mind
> sharp & clear.
>
> **BUDDHA**

Every one of us will likely get a health-related wake-up call at some point in life; luckily, mine was early enough that I could do something about it. I didn't do anything too drastic in the beginning; I just made a conscious effort to move more. I set some fitness goals for myself and as my energy level went up, so did my motivation. My thinking seemed clearer, and I began to make smarter decisions about my future. I attribute a big part of my success to the fact that I took good care of my health and made staying fit a priority.

I also noticed that when my energy level was up, it helped others up their game as well. Energy is contagious, and it does motivate others around you. When I had little or no energy, that was an excuse for me not to give a task my all. I justified giving things little or no effort, because, I told myself, I didn't have it to give. Those around me would follow my low-energy lead, and the job site, as a whole, would suffer.

No matter what stage of life you're at, please take my advice on this. Giving up your health for wealth is a lousy trade-off, and you'll go broke in the end, and by broke, I mean it will kill you! You know you can't take your money with you when you die, and although this is one of the oldest, most obvious statements ever, that knowledge still doesn't stop people from giving up their health to try to get rich. *Enough* doesn't necessarily mean rich. It means finding the right balance of all the things that are important in life, of which money is only one.

You may think you look fine; you're at a relatively healthy weight; you walk the dog every day, and you eat right now and then, but the damage you're doing to yourself by making money rather than health your top priority may not always be apparent. For example, recent research on sedentary living has called sitting the new smoking. Sitting for more than four hours a day (i.e., in front of a TV, working on the computer, driving in your car, etc.) increases your risk of dying by 50 percent. Just by parking your butt for too long, your risk of heart disease goes up by 125 percent, and the possibility of something nasty like cancer or diabetes happening, increases. Muscle wasting, bone weakening, and organ damage are other potential consequences. Sadly, spending a few hours a week in the gym doesn't offset these risks.

Cosmetic surgery can do wonders to make one look younger, but it can't cover up the damage someone's done to their insides. Money can pay for operations, but it can't make the heart any healthier without exercise, joints any more flexible without stretching, teeth and hair any more healthy without proper diet and rest. Looks are not necessarily indicative of health, and no amount of wealth can buy good health with zero effort from the individual. Money can pay for health care, but being smart about your health early on may protect you from developing many illnesses and may prevent future health problems.

Wealth, to me, is being able to enjoy the activities I do today right up until my last days on earth! I want to be able to go for a long walk, take a great nature hike, or enjoy a bike ride and not have my body riddled with injuries. Good health lets you enjoy life to the fullest. Isn't that what *Enough* is all about?

Cumulative decisions have a cumulative effect at a cellular level. Sooner or later, you'll pay for the stress, the lack of sleep, the bad choices, and the stationary position glued to a computer screen, not to mention the damage that the constant, unbalanced pursuit of wealth has on your relationships. The quest for money is pointless without a purpose, a clear end goal in mind, a number you realize is *Enough*, and a plan to incorporate health along your journey. In the long run, it may be all the short, consistent runs that count.

Run With It

To make health a priority and include it in your balanced vision of *Enough*, start with a look back at your childhood, when healthier activity was probably automatic and fun. Whatever exercise you choose

> *In my afternoon walk,*
> *I would fain forget all my*
> *morning occupations &*
> *my obligations to society.*
>
> **HENRY DAVID THOREAU**

to do to, whether it's walking, running, aerobics, or Tae-Kwon-Do, it must be something you enjoy, or you won't do it. I remember the moments playing outside as a child, where I just loved to run more than anything else. I would keep moving until I'd fall over from exhaustion. I wasn't the fastest. I didn't like racing against others, but I always felt great joy whenever I was running. As an adult, running became something I couldn't be bothered with. It was something I thought of as work.

In that moment in university where I was completely out of breath after having to walk up four flights of stairs (because the elevator was broken), I was dripping in sweat. That's when I made the decision that I would start to run again. Later that same day, I went for a run, and not only was I totally out of shape, but I didn't even have the proper running shoes or gear. Aside from having to relearn how to run, I had to learn how to make it fun by setting some goals that would make me feel rewarded after I achieved them.

I slowly fell back in love with running all over again. It didn't happen overnight for me, but I noticed how my mood, body, and mind were changing by continually doing it. One day, I had planned to go for a long hike in the mountains, but the internet warned that bad weather was on the way. I decided to go for a quick run instead before the weather took a turn for the worse. In my haste, I didn't adhere to my regular time-consuming ritual: stretching for thirty minutes; putting on my watch, heart-rate monitor, hydration water belt, and high-tech compression running gear; and stuffing my pockets with tissues in case I needed to blow my nose. This time, I did none of that! I just put on some shorts, a T-shirt, regular sports socks, and my runners. Then I drove to one of my favourite places to go for a quick run. I ran for less than thirty minutes.

When I returned to my car, a storm was brewing, and outside it was getting dark and nasty, but oddly enough, I was in great spirits (and *Spirit!*). This time my run had felt like something new that I hadn't experienced since I was a child: it was fun! When I stopped measuring everything, and I didn't make my run feel like I was training for a race, I found running to be very relaxing and enjoyable again.

I often use running as a favourite metaphor of mine for goal setting because, just as with goal setting, there's that initial spark, an intention, followed by an understanding of where my end point will be. I know obstacles may or may not present themselves. I'll need the right gear to do it, and it's going to cost me money, but when I'm done, I'll get to celebrate (after a run, it's with a yummy protein shake or a tasty meal afterwards).

It was through running I realized I put limits on myself when pursuing a goal, without ever knowing what my real limits might be, since I had never tested them before. It was my own unproven beliefs that created my limits. When you decide to test your limits, you'll discover that you're capable of much more than you ever imagined as well. If you push yourself, in exercise as in any goal that will take you to *Enough*, you may be surprised to find that things you once thought were impossible, aren't!

Goals take commitment. Running takes commitment. With every goal, with every run, you need to follow through and just do it. You'll get better at it, and it will become easier. Goals are only achieved by giving yourself up to them, setting time aside, and then doing what it takes to realize them.

You'll set yourself up for a better outcome if you prepare for your goal. What I mean by prepare is, in the case of running, have the right clothes, shoes, fitness tracker, hydration, sunscreen, and maybe tissue to blow your nose just in case. Recognize that whatever you set out to master will take time. If you were to watch me run today, I would probably make it look easy, but that's only because of the years I spent working at mastering it. I've done shorter and longer distance running, but the five-to-ten-kilometre races are my favourites. Those runs hit the sweet spot for me, but only after years of trial and error and learning about what does and what doesn't work. I've figured out five- to ten-kilometre runs are *Enough*.

> *Writing in my inspirational journal reminds me of my goals & of the things I continue to learn about life.*
> *It offers me a place where I can hold a deliberate, thoughtful conversation with myself & figure out how to keep my life moving forwards with a positive momentum instead of reliving my past.*
>
> **MICHAEL RULLO**

Fatigue happens in the mind first and then in the body. I used to think I was physically fatigued when I had these moments where I felt like I needed to walk instead of run. I knew that I had conditioned my body to run nonstop for much longer, but suddenly I would decide to stop running and start walking. Mental fatigue is real, but it can usually be overcome by gently pushing yourself to get past it. In any goal, you'll have moments when you're tired and want to stop. I look at pushing past my fatigue as giving my mind a jump-start like someone would for a car's dead battery. My mind may be drained, but if I slow down and recharge a bit, I can keep myself running. If a goal is wearing you down, slow down until you get over the hump, and you'll find yourself in a positive groove again.

Finally, balancing all the things in life and accomplishing the goals that will make you feel like you have and are *Enough* will take time. There's only going to be so much progress that you're going to make in a given amount of time, but the key is consistency. Every time I run, I see it as another day in which I'm moving forwards. It's not okay to push myself to the point of injury. If I hurt myself, then I may have to stop training, so I can't progress if I don't listen to my body. Listen to your body.

Going for a slow run is something I intend to do until I'm old and gray. I view my life as a marathon, so I take my time. I make my runs pleasurable for myself, and I always think of the big picture with every run that I do. Your health-related goals should be part of your *Enough* planning, but it's all a marathon, not a sprint. Focus on what you need to do to feel your best and live a healthy, balanced life.

I learned to love running again, as I did when I was a child, completely by accident, and I encourage you to keep trying for your own *eureka moments*, wherein whatever healthy activities you include in your balanced *Enough* plan give you back that same childhood joy. Running is one of the earliest memories I have of being free and enjoying play, but I view it now as a necessity, not a luxury. I make a point of scheduling my runs. I always think of something funny as I run to put a smile on my face, and that makes my runs even more enjoyable. When I set aside time for my run, I know I'm also setting aside time to have some peace of mind, get into *Spirit*, bring balance to my life, make my health a priority, and feel and be *Enough*.

There's Never Enough Nature

When my family went on our traditional family picnics on Sundays, my parents always took us to the mountains in and around Banff National Park, and we would go for hikes every time. Then, as we grew up, the family picnics slowly stopped happening. I got my driver's licence, and meeting girls suddenly became more important than going for a nature walk. It wasn't until my thirties that I came back to hiking, and it was because I needed to do hill training for an upcoming half-marathon run. When I went for the hike, I was thinking of it as merely a training tool, but as I drank in my surroundings, I realized that getting out in nature was another piece in the balanced puzzle of *Enough* that I'd been missing.

Hiking puts you in touch with *Spirit* and gets you away from the chaos and nonstop, over-stimulation of city life. That constant over-stimulation, combined with the brain's inability to focus attention on more than one thing at a time, makes us increasingly likely to make mistakes when we dodge distractions. Nature calms and resets the brain, recalibrates the senses, and restores balance, plus there's hard science now backing up the feel-good effect of fresh air.

Even photographs of nature scenes improve the brain's performance. People who live near parks, whether they use them or not, experience lower rates of disease and depression and fewer deaths than their building-bound brethren. Only fifteen minutes of walking in the woods will reduce your blood pressure, decrease the stress hormones in your blood stream, and slow your heart rate. Additional research has shown that the part of the brain responsible for self-criticism (the subgenual prefrontal cortex if you must know) is suppressed after a hike. In other words, you're even nicer to yourself after communing with the environment! The National Resources Institute of Finland recommends getting your nature fix for a minimum of five hours a month. How's that for an excuse to get away from it all?

As with running, I began to draw some parallels between my mountain hikes and my efforts to achieve the goals that would get me to *Enough*. A mountain hike, for example, may seem larger than life and impossible to achieve at first sight, but it's not! The hike starts the same way as any goal I set for myself. I just need to make myself take that first step and continue taking steps until I reach my end destination. When I'm halfway up, I'll have a different perspective from where I started and likely more motivation to keep going.

Of course, there may be obstacles, as with any goal, that might cause me to reevaluate how badly I want to do it. Obstacles also decide if the preparations I've made to ensure my success were enough, if I will have to turn back with the intention of trying to do it again soon, or if I must give up altogether. When I reach the top of my hike, I've climbed one mountain, but when I look around, I'll see there are other mountains out there as well. Your goals don't stop when you reach an end point. Once you've completed one goal, others will keep presenting themselves to you like distant mountains, and they will energize you to keep moving onwards to the *next* summit!

In the right place and at the right time, a hike can have an incredible impact on my *Spirit*. There's nothing like a hike to put my life into perspective, and it lets me see how tiny I am in the whole scheme of things. Day-to-day life is stressful enough, and I sometimes have to remind myself that there's more to it all than what I'm doing at a particular moment in time. When I'm out in nature, I leave my cellphone in the car, and I have zero distractions. Nature has this powerful ability to bring a sense of calm, and I find it's easy for me to be fully present, moving, but at the same time feeling everything in my mind quieting down.

Nature also reminds me that all life matters. When I'm out in nature, I feel this positive energy, and I start to respect the part I play and how everything is intertwined. To paraphrase a famous anonymous quote, "To the world, I may be only one person, but to one person I may be the world." Even though I'm only one person, I keep in mind that I still matter; therefore, my actions need to matter as well! I'm encouraged to use nature's beauty as an inspiration to remind myself to appreciate the beautiful life I'm living and be grateful. Being out in the environment is a doorway into your own nature that will help you examine what balance of the components of money, life, goals, relationships, health, community, and nature is *Enough* for you.

> *If I follow my heart,*
> *it takes me to the fridge.*
>
> **UNKNOWN**

Food for Thought

I used to be a personal trainer. After I took charge of my health, people would hire me to teach and motivate them to improve their fitness levels, but I couldn't do the work for them. Getting healthy is just one of those things that no one can do for you. You have to do it yourself. *Enough* is like that as well. No one else knows what you want, or need, in life and what's out of balance for you that needs to be worked on. No one can work out for you, run for you, or hike for you, and no one can eat healthy foods on your behalf. No one else knows what *Enough* means to you, and you may not either, until you work out your *Enough* number.

Sometimes my personal-training clients would ask me why they didn't see the results they wanted. My response would be to ask them, "Are you doing anything else outside of our training?" They would answer, *No, pretty much all the time*, and I would point out that they still had to keep moving and be conscious of what they ate and drank outside of the gym. To commit to health, they had to see it as an investment in their overall well-being. They had to commit to a balanced life that saw health as a consideration in every area. When clients owned their health, and the part they played in it, I would see positive results and their quality of life improve. They began by making better choices.

Better choices mean getting away from an all or nothing approach to healthy eating. It means eating one vegetable is better than not eating any. It means one piece of cake isn't the end of the world. It means try, with every meal, to inch that bar, which goes from not-so-healthy choices to healthier ones, into the healthier zone.

What are these healthier options? For starters, eat breakfast. Breakfast lowers your cholesterol, stabilizes blood glucose, improves memory, reduces the risk of diabetes and heart problems, and improves weight control. A 2016 study at the University of Bath (UK) showed that breakfast eaters were also more physically active during the mornings than their I-don't-do-breakfast counterparts. Take a look at the newly revised (2016) Canada food guide. It suggests about eight servings of fruits and vegetables per day, plus six to eight servings of grains such as bread or cereal, three servings of dairy or alternatives such as almond drinks, and two to three servings of protein in the form of meat, nuts, or legumes. It also suggests making one of those vegetables an orange one and one a green one. It also recommends that we drink more water!

Eating a balanced diet has more and more science behind it. Even the experts at Harvard University have plenty to say about healthy eating. Their studies in 2012 showed that eating fresh fruits and vegetables, as well as home-cooked meals, along with limiting your consumption of sugar and refined carbohydrates (i.e., that piece of cake), reduced the likelihood of having mental health problems such as Alzheimer's, depression, stress, and anxiety among others. Other researchers caution against fad-food trends, such as the latest so-called *clean eating*, which cut out major food groups to the detriment of bone and heart health. Again, balance is food for thought.

Another healthy food habit to get the hang of is reading labels. Understanding labels and what they say, or purposely don't say, can go a long way towards improving your food choices. For example, just because some labels say the bread has twelve grains in it doesn't mean it's healthy. Whole grains should be the first ingredient on the list; if they are listed second or third, there may be only 1 percent of the product that's a whole grain. Real fruit snacks, which have all sorts of healthy-sounding claims, are just fruit sugars (such as concentrated grape juice) and water with a petite serving of the original fruit's vitamin and fibre content.

They are more like healthy-sounding candy. Even the *fortified* bottled water, sold with vitamins in it, doesn't stand up under label scrutiny. Along with the paltry few vitamins, these drinks often have 120 calories or more. Meanwhile, you're getting less vitamin C than you'd get from eating just six strawberries.

> *Food is celebratory. People who don't cook don't know how much fun they're missing.*
>
> **LEO BUSCAGLIA**

I have made mental notes of what certain foods do to me after I eat them, and I see which ones make me more productive and which ones make me want to sleep. I know that whatever fuel I put into my body, it's going to affect me in different ways, so I try to balance out my choices with foods that take me into a positive headspace versus those that give me a temporary sugar high and make me crash and burn shortly after. Do a two-week food journal of what you've eaten and how you felt to help craft your best balance.

Food is community and comfort, sustenance and sanctuary. It's a critical component of our physical (and mental) well-being, but I also look at good food as something that touches a person's *Spirit*. I say this because, while eating a healthy meal or taking a bite that just blows my mind, I'm transported, if only momentarily, to a better place. There are many components to a great meal: location, company, menu, wine, atmosphere, time of day, and the list goes on. However, when it all comes together, for a brief moment in time, I feel like I'm in *Spirit*. Some meals are like snapshots in my memory bank of good times. A great meal, with the right company, speaks to my soul and affects me on a very visceral level, unlike any other activity. All my senses dance with the sight, texture, smell, taste, and even the sound of the meal being prepared. I appreciate how a meal has a beginning, middle, and end, that, when done right, create magical moments along the way!

I try my hardest to enjoy every bite mindfully, and then afterwards I go for a walk, and with every step I manifest a deep and profound appreciation. This habit prolongs the pleasurable experience of a meal even longer. It's important to balance eating with some simple exercise, and I do them together because eating and exercise both keep my mind busy. I eat so as to treat my body right from the inside out, so I do watch my portion sizes.

Too often we turn to food to comfort us when we feel depressed, but instead of trying to savour every bite, we tend to binge out of desperation. This is dangerous and can lead the comfort-seeker into the vicious circle of feeling bad for bingeing, with accompanying health and possible weight issues, yet resulting in turning to food even more as the depression and bad feelings continue. Therefore, it's essential to take your time when eating. Enjoy the experience, couple it with exercise, and value your health above everything else!

I do believe in eating a piece of cake or having a piece of chocolate occasionally, and I don't beat myself up about it. I'll also make a conscious effort to counterbalance my indulgence by exercising afterwards. Life offers many simple pleasures; for me, I feel it's not acceptable to be a glutton, but by being healthy overall for most of my life, I can still have a treat now and then!

> *If everyone is moving forward together then success takes care of itself.*
>
> **HENRY FORD**

Coming from an Italian background, I view healthy eating as an activity that starts with preparing the food with love and finishes with eating the food with those we love. For a meal to be shared with others, it's done with some care and attention to detail, and I see a lot of heart when a great meal is presented. When a meal is prepared with love, that means something to the person who made it and to me, and the whole experience feels exceptional. Growing up, I was always surrounded by good food, and it gave me a deep appreciation for everything involved in how that food goes from preparation to plate.

Food is part of almost every celebration throughout the world. Whenever I travel or visit a friend who has a different background from mine, I see how food is used for various traditions and celebrations, and it gives me new insights into another culture. I love how the sharing and enjoyment of food is a universal experience that brings people together.

Good food nourishes our bodies, minds, and spirits. It gives us energy and strength and unites us in celebration and community. Balanced with exercise, and a knowledge of when to say *Enough!*, we can keep our cups half full until we realize we don't mind so much that they're half empty.

Counting on Community

As I mentioned before, my parents are Italian, so I grew up with a strong sense of community. I saw how my parents, uncles, and aunts would all get together and help one another. This included our family friends as well. It was just understood that we all helped each other out for us all to get ahead. Growing up in Canada, I also saw how different cultures would gather together, support, and help each other. There's something beautiful that happens when everybody pitches in and does what they can. Everybody wins, and that feeling that you have people you can count on, and you're not alone in the world, is essential for reaching *Enough*.

My Mom and Dad made a point of getting to know all our neighbours. They introduced themselves to everybody, and they would let them know that if they needed anything, to just ask. My parents would be there. I often saw my mother helping other mothers by taking care of their kids while they were away at work. I saw my father and other neighbourhood men contributing their time and services to build things that would create a better home for another guy's family. What happened because of this? Our neighbours always acted in the same way. My Dad never asked for money when he helped a fellow neighbour, and he never took advantage of a neighbour who helped him out. Everybody looked out for one another, and this built a strong sense of community, along with a sense of belonging to something bigger than themselves, a large, extended family, a neighbourhood, a country.

Today people tend to move every three to five years, and the sense of community that I experienced growing up now seems lost. My parents lived in the same neighbourhood my whole life. Most of their neighbours have also been there for over twenty years. A good neighbour is priceless! I've lived in some beautiful homes that I built myself, but I often found that my neighbours were less than friendly. I never realized how good I had it growing up until I saw for myself that people weren't communicating anymore like they used to. Nowadays, it's common for neighbours not even to know each other.

If we've lost the sense of community from yesteryear, what have we lost? When people don't help others in need, it ends up costing society more in the long run. An individual who needs help, and is too proud to ask for it, or doesn't have anyone to ask, can easily find themselves behind the eight ball in life. As a result, everybody ends up paying for that person in one way or another, through increased healthcare costs, taxes, food banks, and higher crime rates.

To live a balanced life requires simplifying by living within your means, single-tasking, and destressing. It requires sleeping well, exercising, getting out into nature, experiencing moments of *Spirit* as often as possible, and eating right. But did you know that social connections are just as vital as vegetables? Current research has shown that not having social connections is worse for your health than being overweight, smoking, or having high blood pressure. Scientists say people who can plug into a community connection

1. have stronger immune systems,
2. have a faster rate of recovery from illness,
3. have less depression and anxiety,
4. have greater self-esteem, and
5. they live longer!

A sense of community also encourages the development of empathy for other people that makes you more trusting and cooperative. Another positive effect of community connectivity is that people around you are more likely to be collaborative and trusting when you are. All these positive emotions and social supports give you both an emotional and a physical sense of well-being, both of which are necessary for a balanced life of *Enough*. "No man is an island," said writer and philosopher John Donne. We need each other as social creatures. Isolation isn't good for us in large doses, even if an island sounds like a grand idea from time to time.

Virtual Communities Versus Real-Life Friends

For better or worse, we're growing increasingly connected and disconnected at the same time. All you need to know about your friends can probably be found on Facebook, Instagram, Snapchat, or some other networking site, but is social media giving us that all-important sense of community? The short answer is yes...and no. Psychologists are just starting to get a fix on what all these online communications are doing for us and to us.

It seems that heavy Facebook users don't feel as much like they have *Enough* as those who use it less often. It can make you envious of the picture-perfect lives of others (a phenomenon called "social comparison") and make you feel that you're less cool (unless you work on creating more of your content rather than just looking at other people's). Social media can make you feel jealous of your significant other and fill your time with learning information about people you scarcely know or that you'd be better off forgetting.

Ironically, social media can also make your world smaller. Heavy social media users are often lonelier, tend to avoid problems more, and hold grudges longer. Since many sites sort what you see, they may give you a false sense of consensus, prioritizing posts from people who share your opinions, ultimately distorting your worldview. Finally, social media is addictive and takes you away from real-life interactions that may eventually be better for your health and more rewarding.

> *I have learned that to be with those I like is enough.*
>
> **WALT WHITMAN**

All I'm going to say about this is ask some of your online friends to help you move or for help working in your garden, and let them know they won't get paid for their help. Then, see how many of your *online friends* show up to help you. Real friends help without seeking payment or thinking of how they might take advantage of you. They give their free time, and they know that you would do the same for them in return.

> *I intend to live forever or die trying.*
>
> GROUCHO MARX

I'm not saying there isn't a sense of community online. Virtual communities cross geographic boundaries and bring people together as never before. Health-based, virtual communities are helping people to learn from, and connect with, others who may share a certain disease or disability, ultimately improving treatment and offering support. The speed at which opinions can be voiced through our virtual communities encourages civic participation and corporate accountability, with tremendous social and political impact. The average Facebook user has 120 friends, which is right in line with Dunbar's number. Robin Dunbar was an anthropologist who asserted that there was an upper limit (150) to the number of stable social connections one person could maintain. That's a lot of connecting.

Unquestionably, the internet has facilitated the work of charities, animal rescue groups, and many more worthy causes through the mechanism of crowdfunding. For next to nothing, thanks to this technology, that we now take for granted, every cause can be publicized and supported by a massive amount of people ready to help a stranger from across the world. I love reading a story about someone being down on their luck when someone online reaches out and makes a difference for that person. What I'd like to see is more of that reaching out taking place within our communities and with our neighbours, friends, and families.

One way of reaching out to your community is to involve yourself with a group that shares your interests and then to use your involvement with that group to raise money for a charitable cause. I have entered races for charity and have found the running community to be a very generous one. When I'm running in a race, I pay to participate in it. That's my way of giving back to the sponsoring charity. Runners will unite for a good cause through a race, but they also come together to do it in a lovely, supportive, and healthy way.

Every time I enter a race, I get a sense of real community. Unlike some people in virtual communities who criticize and complain with the freedom of anonymity, on race day, I see how nice everybody is to each other. It brings out the best in people, and I always feel proud to be a part of that community and its charitable causes.

It Takes a Village

It's just plain easier to get ahead in life when you have a community of people behind you. When people band together for the greater good of helping the other guy out when he is down on his luck, it saves everyone from having to pay for it later. Eventually, it will come back around, and they will be helped when they need it. Helping others today pays for better tomorrows.

Communities can come together over shared interests, experiences, meetup groups, friends, or neighbours, but they can also emerge phoenix-like from the ashes of tragedy. Consider Captain Sully's landing on the Hudson River in New York. Over 140 firefighters, police, ferry operators, boaters, and divers came together to help rescue the 155 stranded survivors as they stood on the wings of the precariously floating airplane. The survivors and several rescuers have reunited many times since that event to reconnect and remind themselves of the good things in life...like being alive to live it. Gathering together for yet another reunion photograph, the smiling group of survivors and saviors say, *Sully* instead of *cheese*, for the camera. Sometimes a sense of community is best seen after the worst scenes.

> *The best of the best in any field don't always love what they do, but they love themselves enough to do their best anyway!*
>
> **MICHAEL RULLO**

One survivor, who had been afraid of flying before the crash, shares the news of how he decided to get his pilot's licence, another mentions how he used the new lease on life to climb Mount Kilimanjaro with his son. One former passenger, bouncing a baby on his lap, relates how, on the third anniversary of the harrowing ordeal, he welcomed his newborn son. He says the near-fatal landing has taught him not only not to sweat the small stuff but to be grateful for it. Counting your blessings brings with it a lot of the balance that is critical to the concept of *Enough*. It turns out that it takes a village, not only to raise a child, but to be a balanced, healthy, happy adult.

When my Dad got too old to do the hard labour in his garden anymore, his neighbours stepped up and helped him out. My Dad never needed a hand when he was in good health, but when the time came to help him, people stood up, no questions asked. No one looked to get paid for helping him. They remembered the times my Dad had helped them, asking nothing in return. It took a lot of the pressure off my Mom, and it was one less financial burden to worry about. It was a beautiful thing to see. When my Dad saw so many people coming by to help him, he tried to pay them, but no one would accept it. It touched his heart so much that he became very emotional. That's the power of community.

> *We are all different.*
> *There is no such thing as a*
> *standard run-of-the-mill*
> *human being,*
> *but we share the same*
> *human spirit.*
>
> **STEPHEN HAWKING**

Rullo Rules

In 1922 Albert Einstein was in Tokyo Japan & had no money for a tip for his Bellhop. In exchange for a gratuity, he wrote in German on two pieces of stationary his theory of **happiness & possible thinking.** He told the Bellhop to save the notes they might be valuable in the future.

In 2017 at an auction those notes sold for **$1.6-Million!**

'A calm & modest life brings more happiness than the pursuit of success combined with constant restlessness.'

On the second piece of paper, he wrote

'Where there's a will there's a way.'

Not Had *Enough*? Well, Here's Some More:

- multitasking drops your IQ – research:

  http://www.smh.com.au/digital-life/digital-life-news/multitasking-makes-you-stupid-studies-find-20150520-gh5ouq.html

  http://productivitytheory.com/multitasking-lower-iq/

  http://www.apa.org/monitor/oct01/multitask.aspx

  http://discovery.ucl.ac.uk/1465496/

- multitasking damages the brain – report:

  https://www.forbes.com/sites/travisbradberry/2014/10/08/multitasking-damages-your-brain-and-career-new-studies-suggest/#1df27eb156ee

  http://business.time.com/2013/04/17/dont-multitask-your-brain-will-thank-you/

- how long it takes to get back on task after an interruption:

  https://www.yast.com/time_management/science-task-interruption-time-management/

  https://www.fastcompany.com/944128/worker-interrupted-cost-task-switching

- how multitasking impairs short-term memory:

  https://bebrainfit.com/cognitive-costs-multitasking/

  http://www.huffingtonpost.ca/entry/technology-changes-memory_n_4414778

- effect of blue light from computers, TVs, cellphones etc. on sleep:

  https://www.health.harvard.edu/staying-healthy/blue-light-has-a-dark-side

- being sedentary is the new smoking – research:

  https://beta.theglobeandmail.com/life/health-and-fitness/fitness/
  would-you-do-this-at-work/article17945720/?ref=http://www.
  theglobeandmail.com&

  http://www.mayoclinic.org/healthy-lifestyle/adult-health/expert-
  answers/sitting/faq-20058005

  https://www.health.harvard.edu/blog/much-sitting-linked-heart-
  disease-diabetes-premature-death-201501227618

  http://www.cnn.com/2017/06/22/health/sitting-exercise-davis/
- how getting out in nature affects your mental and physical health:

  https://www.sciencealert.com/just-looking-at-photos-of-nature-
  could-be-enough-to-lower-your-work-stress-levels

  https://www.pnas.org/content/112/28/8567.abstract

- how nutrition affects your brain:

  https://www.sciencedaily.com/releases/2016/02/160213075107.htm

  https://www.health.harvard.edu/mind-and-mood/boost-your-
  memory-by-eating-right

- Canada Food Guide:

  https://www.canada.ca/en/health-canada/services/canada-food-
  guides.html

- social connections and your health:

  https://www.health.harvard.edu/newsletter_article/the-health-
  benefits-of-strong-relationships

  https://blogs.scientificamerican.com/streams-of-consciousness/the-
  importance-of-being-social/

  http://ccare.stanford.edu/uncategorized/connectedness-health-the-
  science-of-social-connection-infographic/

- how social media negatively affects our self-esteem – research:

  https://www.ncbi.nlm.nih.gov/pmc/articles/PMC4183915/

  https://www.psychologytoday.com/ca/blog/nurturing-self-
  compassion/201703/mental-health-and-the-effects-social-media

Chapter 12 • Takeaways:

1. Balance your life to get to *Enough* by taking time off to just think, by simplifying, alright-sizing, living within your means, exercising, eating right, enjoying nature, and connecting to a community.
2. Focus on one thing at time and schedule regular breaks.
3. Simplify and destress by reducing the amount of stuff you own and spending less than you earn.
4. Reduce your dependence on credit and save for bigger purchases.
5. Re-examine your *Enough* number, in light of a simpler lifestyle, by asking yourself, "Will living within the means afforded by my *Enough* number make my life better and less stressful?"
6. Decide on a personal, optimal balance between making more money and simplifying your life to get to *Enough*.
7. Make your health your number one priority over money.
8. Find an exercise you'll stick with because you enjoy doing it.
9. Get out into nature regularly to improve cognition and destress.
10. Eat breakfast and eight servings of fruits and vegetables, six to eight servings of grains, three servings of dairy or alternatives, and two to three servings of protein per day.
11. Social connections are vital to a balanced life of *Enough*, so get to know your neighbours, help each other out, and create a sense of community around yourself.

13

Philanthropy and Love:
Giving Back to Get *Enough*

I live in a world where people live for today.
My parents raised me to work today for a better tomorrow!
MICHAEL RULLO

AFTER my Dad came out of his coma on Christmas Day back in 2007, he began his arduous fight back to health. He would ask me what I was going to do next with my life and career, and I'd tell him my ideas for all these bigger and better things I was planning on doing. He'd say to me, "Mike, the way you're going, it's never going to be enough!" I never understood what he meant by that, but it stuck with me.

In the summer of 2011, my Dad was experiencing lots of pain in his stomach. After an examination, he was diagnosed with terminal stage-four abdominal cancer. I'd given up everything after my Dad's 2007 accident to be by his side, to give a hand, and help my Mom take care of him. I rented out my home, gave up my business, and moved back in with my parents to be of service to them full-time, 24/7, day and night, whenever they needed me. Now they needed me more than ever.

> *The best way to find yourself*
> *is to lose yourself*
> *in the service of others.*
>
> **MAHATMA GANDHI**

I felt more real value from giving back and helping my Mom and Dad than I had in all the years I had been doing construction. Introduce *service to others*, or philanthropy (from the Greek meaning *love of humanity*), into your *Enough* planning, and you'll find it's a surprising psychological boost that will give meaning to your life. Giving back will get you feeling like you've got *Enough*.

Philanthropy is broadly defined as working for the well-being of others, and it produces a sense of benevolence, generosity, charitableness, compassion, and kindheartedness. A philanthropic act is an act on behalf of a private individual(s), versus corporations or governments, that improves the quality of life for others. This can range from pounding nails for Habitat for Humanity, to huge gifts of money such as the $225 million donated to create the Perelman School of Medicine of which Doctor Oz, of TV fame, is an alumnus. Another example is the $250 million given by Facebook's president to establish the Parker Institute for Cancer Immunotherapy.

To succeed in making you feel like you are *Enough*, a philanthropic act must connect with your deepest values, who you are at the core, and how you want to impact the world. If one person wants to make a difference, they will have more luck doing so through an organization dedicated to their cause, and so monetary donations are a common way to give. Philanthropy is responsibility, caring, and compassion with a purpose, and that purpose is, in no small part, fulfilling your potential as a human being. I didn't know that by helping my Mom and Dad, I was learning how to help myself. I was learning how to give back.

Here again, science has revealed the benefits of giving. Your brain's *pleasure centre* is understandably activated when you receive money, but recent studies have shown that it's triggered even more intensely by giving it away. In one experiment in 2006, Jorge Moll and Jordan Grafman, neuroscientists at the National Institute of Health, gave $128 to their study participants and told them that they could keep it or anonymously donate it to a variety of charitable causes. All participants gave at least some of their money away (an average of 40 percent of it), but amazingly, their brains' pleasure centres lit up more when they donated the money than when they received the money.

The benefits of giving also don't appear to be as temporary as the positive feelings that getting money brings. Philanthropy helps to improve your perception of the world around you and your active role in it. Happiness and money expert, Dr. Elizabeth Dunn, says that philanthropic people are happier and have more stable marriages. Plus a 2016 study in the *British Journal of Psychology* found that altruistic people even have better sex lives!

Generosity also reduces stress. Studies have shown that generosity may even benefit our survival as a species and is a universal trait across all human cultures, serving to improve social connections. Authors Elizabeth Dunn and Michael Norton in their book, *Happy Money: The Science of Smarter Spending,* noted that philanthropy that has a social component (such as giving on behalf of a group of friends, relatives, or a social group), will make you even happier than donating anonymously.

Volunteering

Another way to give, and at the same time get the benefits of giving, is through volunteering. A 2016 study at the London School of Economics found that people who volunteered were happier, so much more joyful, in fact, that they equated it to a person who normally has an income of $20 thousand suddenly having $100 thousand. Volunteering also connects you to your community, lowers your stress levels, and expands your circle of friends, who in turn, may one day be a support system for you as well.

Volunteering can mean doing the simplest of things for someone else. For example, helping a friend move, giving your time to listen to someone's problems, taking a loved one to a doctor's appointment, helping clean up somebody else's yard, or taking care of someone when they are ill are all volunteer efforts. I used to think that volunteering had to be done with only big organizations, but I realized that wherever a person gives their time to help others, without seeking payment or compensation of any kind, is simply another form of volunteering.

> *If you want to go fast, go alone.*
> *If you want to go far, go together.*
>
> **AFRICAN PROVERB**

After helping my parents during such difficult times, I started to make volunteering a regular part of my life. I mindfully took part in runs for charitable causes like cancer, multiple sclerosis, etc., and even though running events may not be considered *volunteering* by some people's definition, these types of races are not competitive, and their purpose is to raise money for charity. I donate my time and money to run in these events as a way to volunteer and be a part of something special. I love how the organizers take the idea of a run and turn it into something that benefits a worthy charitable cause.

> *Will it be one day or day one?*
>
> **UNKNOWN**

I also see the impact of this type of volunteering on the faces of those directly affected by the reason for a charitable race, such as cancer survivors and current cancer patients, along with their friends and families. They appear to be happy when they see the turnout, perhaps because they feel supported by this loving community of volunteers and participants. Meanwhile, I'm combining running, which is a passion of mine, with a worthwhile cause, which puts me in a state of *Spirit*, and all the while I feel uplifted with joy, awe, and wonder, both during the race and for a long time afterwards.

I've learned a lot of lessons through volunteering. When I do something voluntarily, without seeking, or even wanting, anything in return other than to be of assistance, I'm filled with a great feeling that endures far past my volunteer effort. I leave my problems behind and just focus on what needs to get done in the moment. My perceived personal problems no longer exist, time flies, and my mind is no longer caught in a constant loop examining my own life and issues.

Volunteering is something I choose to do because I love it. It's not because I have to, and I strongly recommend (if you don't already) that you give it a try. Certainly, there have been times when I've helped out despite feeling some reluctance going in, but afterwards, I always came out the better for it. I try to give myself over to loving what I'm doing, and I put the brakes on being negative. When I approach volunteering from a place of love in my heart, everybody wins in the end.

There's also something to be said for a group of people that all come together to volunteer for something. There's an instant feeling of community, a magical feeling that you get when you are surrounded by that energy, and at the same time, are a part of it. That collective energy of being a part of something that feels bigger than yourself helps you to put your life, your problems, and the role you play in this world into perspective. It will help you to destress and feel good about who you are. You'll start to feel like you are and have *Enough*, and it will frequently put you into a state of *Spirit* as well. I always feel connected to something larger than anything I can rationally explain, and it leaves me feeling great.

Volunteering also reminds me of how goals are developed one small step at a time, how small amounts of money, saved or earned, can add up, and how *Enough* is a process as much as a destination. When volunteering, my contribution alone may be perceived to be insignificant, but I always keep in mind, my small efforts may make a huge difference for someone else. The mere fact that I've helped out matters.

Sometimes, it takes a long time to make a real difference, but on other occasions it's immediate. I don't need to overthink my part. I just have to do my share! *Enough* is like that. Don't overthink it. Just make whatever efforts you can in the direction of your goals, help others when you can, and know that it all matters. For me, to be truly wealthy means giving my time to another person without seeking monetary payment. When others think and feel the same way, we're all better off. Humanity is awesome when people come together selflessly for the greater good; that's when life is at its most beautiful and people are at their best!

> *Everyone who achieves success in a great venture, solves each problem as they came to it. They helped themselves. And they were helped through powers known & unknown to them at the time they set out on their voyage. They keep going regardless of the obstacles they met.*
>
> **W. CLEMENT STONE**

Karma: You Get What You Give

By now you know that getting to *Enough* means more than just getting more; it means giving more. Try to think of it in terms of karma. Karma is an ancient Sanskrit word for *doing*, but it refers to cause and effect, the consequences of not only our actions, but the thoughts, feelings, and intentions behind them. Your plans and actions today affect your tomorrow. Getting to *Enough* is about choosing how that tomorrow will look for you.

Positive choices and decisions karmically affect not only you but those around you, and it helps to be aware of the motivations behind your actions. Buddhism lists six motivating *intentions* behind a person's actions:

1. kindness
2. generosity
3. compassion
4. cruelty
5. anger
6. greed

These karmic motivations decide more than just general character; they also influence how others see you and most importantly, because you're the only one with the inside story, how you see yourself. Seeing what you have as *Enough*, and who you are as *Enough*, involves viewing yourself, your motivations, and your actions in a positive light, so it helps to cultivate good karma.

When it comes to money, it's important to my sense of *Enough* to feel good about myself, and part of that is achieved by making decisions from a good place. Positive karma creates an extraordinary energy where marvelous things come back to me in abundance in many forms such as love, generosity, knowledge, and yes, even money! Positive karma that I've put out into the world has returned to me beyond anything I could ever have imagined; whenever I've experienced positive karmic energy coming back to me, it's an incredible feeling.

Conversely, I've experienced that if I do something wrong, where anger, cruelty, or greed are underlying my actions, sooner or later I will have to pay for that bad karmic debt! I've found that there isn't a timeline for when good or bad karma will come back to me, but it does come back, resulting in positive or negative consequences. When I'm faced with having to take action or decide something, I always think about doing it from a genuine place of kindness, generosity, and compassion. Acting from a place of good or bad karma is often a habit, but if you start to become more aware of your intentions mindfully, you can encourage a more positive approach.

All habits, good and bad, have their beginnings. Actions arise from your intentions, which come from your thoughts, which in turn result from your motivations. Where you put your intentions or inclinations becomes strengthened, and what you ignore, or don't practice, weakens. Focus on your goals and what you need to do to get to *Enough*, while cultivating good karma, and you'll produce positive habits that will help get you where you want to go. Tomorrow's successes might be today's intentions. Are your intentions empowering? What are your motivations? Think about what you may be willing to change today, so that tomorrow looks better for you and so that you can answer the question, "Got Enough?" with a big smile and a resounding "Yes!"

Good karma has happened for me in my private life and has spilled over into my business affairs because of doing the right thing. There have been times when I helped somebody out in my personal life just because I felt like being of service and assistance and just because I cared. Making someone happy was enough gratification for me. Weeks later, sometimes I would get a business contract through a referral from the person I'd helped out. It's come back full circle many times in my life. When I do great things, good things come back to me, and on occasion, they come back in the form of helping my business.

Enough is about money, but it's also about so much more. If up until now you've been prone to being an angry, entitled person who lies, cheats, and steals to get what you want, I propose you develop some new habits. Karma will catch up to you, if it hasn't already, and you'll pay a karmic debt with more than just money. Karma affects how the world sees you and how you see yourself.

When you attract good karma, you're out in the world enjoying yourself and the people around you. You live an open life, happy with who you are and with nothing to hide. Individuals who have developed the habit of bad karma tend to disappear; they screen people's calls, they don't return text messages or emails. The bad-karma person moves onto the next victim who doesn't know them and keeps doing the same things all over again to new people, burning bridges with everyone they come across. They don't have strong relationships with people. They delude themselves into thinking they won't get caught or punished for their bad behaviour, because they are so very brilliant, and it won't catch up to them. You can make money with bad karma. Many do, but it's never going to get you to that transcendent feeling of *Enough*.

If you want to live a life that has purpose and is meaningful, then giving is the way to go. *Enough* requires a balance of both getting and giving. I share this with you because your journey to *Enough* is just as important as what you do when you get there. Try to attract good karma and live your life in the open. In business and any money-related matters, karmic debt does have an impact, so be on the right side of it!

Making money shouldn't be at the expense of others. If that's how you currently roll, being greedy will bite you in the butt sooner or later! In business, I know that by caring, I'll also close (remember your ABCs of *Always Be Caring*). I can still be profitable by incorporating that thinking into my business style. Focusing on both caring and closing has always worked for me.

Earn your good reputation, and the money will follow. Be the same person on the outside as the individual on the inside, and you'll feel more like who you are is *Enough*. I don't have to hide when my actions and life are lived from a place of integrity and fairness! Even when somebody who's doing business with me doesn't care about me, that doesn't mean I have to stoop to their level; I can choose to still care on my end, even with the *sh#heads* of this world. If you want to get to the feeling that you have *Enough*, my advice is *don't be a sh#thead!* Always be caring! It's not only good business, but it's also good karma!

> *Your dreams & goals should scare you, push you, & excite you; otherwise, they aren't big ENOUGH!!!*
>
> **MICHAEL RULLO**

The Gift of Laughter, Family, Friends, and Pets

When I refer to family, friends, pets, and laughter and how they relate to *Enough*, it's because I've noticed that something wonderful happens when I'm in another's company (including a beloved pet); our thoughts and minds feel connected, and we just click. I feel an undeniable bond that I just can't explain. Even if it's a complete stranger, if we share a laugh together, for that brief moment, I feel in tune with that person. I compare it to those moments when I'm doing my solo activities, and I experience the flow state of *Spirit*. Recall that *Spirit* is a state where you're intensely concentrating, entirely focused on a rewarding but challenging activity, so much so that you lose your sense of time.

Rullo Rules

Look for laughter wherever you can. Here's a laugh to get you started: **The World's Funniest Joke**

In 2002, Dr. Richard Wiseman, a psychologist at the University of Hertfordshire, went looking for the world's funniest joke. With more than 1.5 million votes the results of his research are in:

Two hunters are out in the woods when one of them collapses. He doesn't seem to be breathing & his eyes are glazed. The other guy whips out his phone & calls emergency services. He gasps, "My friend is dead! What can I do?" The operator says "Calm down. I can help. First, let's make sure he's dead." There's a silence, then a shot is heard. Back on the phone, the guy says "Okay, now what?"

Laughter

Research into laughter and the human brain at Stanford University in 2003 demonstrated that the same areas that light up when we experience monetary gain are also activated when we share a good laugh. The funnier we find the humour, the more blood flows to the area that makes us feel, even temporarily, like we have *Enough*. Laughter has also been shown to increase your focus, your mental energy, and your creativity, just like *Spirit*-inducing activities. Unlike most *Spirit* states, laughter is best when shared and can improve your sense of connectedness with the world around you.

> *Always laugh when you can. It's cheap medicine.*
>
> **LORD BYRON**

People who laugh regularly have better self-esteem and fewer negative thoughts. Choosing to laugh more—and it is a choice—may not immediately affect your external circumstances, but it will change how you perceive them. Positivity and laughing about life's failures and imperfections doesn't mean you're complacent and not acting to make a difference. You can still solve your problems while you laugh at them. Laughter has been shown to improve communication, empathy, and cooperation and de-escalate confrontations. Neuroscience shows that laughter does seem to share the same brain-wave patterns as the *Spirit* state. I like to think of laughing with another as shared good *Spirits*!

Laughter lets you regroup, relax, and reboot from a more positive place. Part of *Enough* is money, but the rest is pure perception. My suggestion is that you come at your *Enough* from both sides. Determine your *Enough* number. Adjust your spending and your attitude towards accumulating stuff. Make the money you need to while living within your means, but also cultivate *Spirit* activities. Strive for simplicity and balance. Connect to your community. Form friendships and share time with family. Make time for play and laughter. Find a way to practice philanthropy and give back.

Family and Friends

When I'm in the right company, and I'm authentic, I can allow myself to be completely naked, figuratively speaking. The communication and connection I share with another person, who's also being genuine, will just flow, and when that happens, I immediately know I'm connected with *Spirit*. When I feel free to laugh out loud, and I encourage the other person to do the same, humour and laughter lead to this amazing feeling that a particular moment just happened; laughter is at its best when it's a shared experience where everyone feels fantastic after!

In the company of real friends and family where I feel safe, I unwind and feel totally at ease and comfortable. I can just be myself, which is reassuring, and it's a very calming state of mind. All the feelings I associate with *Spirit* will manifest themselves when I'm at peace in another's company. I help family and friends without seeking compensation, and I sense they would do the same for me. That selflessness and generosity make me feel grateful, but they also make me savour what I have. Appreciating what you have during the process of reaching *Enough* will help you get there faster and will let you enjoy the journey along the way even more!

Family and friends have also taught me the importance of listening and being listened to. It's powerful to be able to speak and get things off your chest and also to reciprocate and to help others deal with whatever life is throwing at them. Listening is being present, and this being present, is also to be in *Spirit*. As with the moments when I go for a run or walk in nature, I've noticed that time flies when spending time in the company of those I love. When I'm a sounding board for a loved one, it's also a nice feeling just being there for them.

I've noticed that whenever I'm sick, I heal faster when those who love me take care of me. I have witnessed people in hospitals who have speedier recoveries when they have a strong support system. I have seen the connection between love and healing up close, and it's filled with an extraordinary energy.

That distinct type of energy is given off by those with whom I feel a connection. I can feel their energy even after they leave my presence, and that feeling will last for hours, days, weeks, months, even years after our time together has ended. I continue feeling as though we share an uncommon bond, even when we're apart, because of the power of a particular moment. I've come to attribute this relationship to the natural energy that comes from experiencing a state of *Spirit* together, either through shared laughter, or conversation, or because we are kindred souls, *sympatico* spirits that found each other serendipitously. Getting to *Enough* will require you to be lonely at times as you focus on your goals, but do what you can, whenever you can, to cultivate connections and to care for the contacts that you already have.

> *Friends bust balls; they don't break hearts.*
>
> **MICHAEL RULLO**

Pets

Pets also have an important role to play in feeling like you have *Enough*. Not only are they a source of unconditional love, the fact that they need your care and attention draws you out of the negativity that is often the result of too much self-focus and introspection. Having a pet has been shown to reduce stress and help with depression and anxiety. Science has also discovered that people with pets have fewer heart attacks and strokes, better immune systems, and lower blood pressure. Even individuals who do have heart attacks are more likely to survive if they have pets.

A 1996 study at the University of New York at Buffalo demonstrated that having a pet with you while performing a stressful activity is even more calming than having a close friend, spouse, or another family member in the room. Pets also seem to help reduce chronic pain (such as from irritable bowel, migraines, or arthritis) and improve surgical recovery times. They are currently being used to help treat post-traumatic stress in veterans who report that pets bring more joy into their lives.

Pets not only bring people comfort, and improve their overall moods, they also help them to socialize more. Being social and feeling connected is critical to feeling like you have *Enough*. Dog owners report meeting an average of eight to ten people regularly as they walk their dogs. The dogs take them out into the world and serve as a cultural bridge that causes them to view their neighbourhoods and the people who live there as friendlier.

Are pets part of the magical formula that will take you personally to *Enough*? If the name of the game is to stack the deck in your favour, then it's something else you should consider. Along with laughter, and connecting with friends and family, pets have been helping us meet the challenges of life and making us happier and healthier individuals for thousands of years. How far back does the human-animal bond go? In Cyprus, a wild cat was found buried alongside a person in a tomb that was 9,500 years old. Another archeological dig uncovered a 12,000-year-old skeleton in northern Israel. This individual had been buried with his or her hand resting on the skeleton of a puppy.

What's Love Got to Do with It?

I mentor a few younger gentlemen who are looking to become entrepreneurs themselves, and the same question keeps popping up:

Question: "I hear the secret to success is loving what you do; is that right?"

My answer: "Loving what you do is a part of it, but there are more times than not when you aren't going to love what you're doing. There are a lot of times in your life when you'll have to take jobs you just can't stand and maybe even hate with a passion. That's okay! We've all been there. The secret, however, is loving yourself enough to always do a good job. You don't have to love the work, but you do need to love yourself enough to give it your all!"

What happens next is usually silence and a long pause as the "Ah-ha" moment sinks in.

Love is the last topic I want to discuss, and I mention it here at the end of the book because it's the most important thing I need to convey to you. You'll never feel like you have *Enough* without love. I would never have achieved my goals, made money, and experienced *Spirit* without having love inside me and without giving that love to everything I do. Love creates a purpose and meaning for my life, and it's infinitely more important to me than money or material things. If I had millions in the bank, but my heart wasn't filled with love, I'd feel empty and bankrupt in more ways than one.

Who am I to speak of love? Who am I to give my version of love or tell you that you'll never get to *Enough* without it? Right now, as I write this, I'm single; does that mean I can't speak about love with any credibility? What does love have to do with anything, especially when it comes to goals, making money, and getting into *Spirit*? Let me explain; after all, we've come this far together.

I view myself as my Mom and Dad's son first and foremost, and I've shared with you a lot of the intimate details about how I was raised and the lessons they showed me in life. I can tell you my parents' story;

they came from nothing, started with less than nothing, and made something of their lives. My parents' generation didn't give up easily or discard things. Instead, they worked things out; they made the best of whatever life threw their way. They fixed problems and didn't run from them. They knew they had to "Make hay while the sun shines," as my Dad used to say. My perception of my generation and those growing up now is that the majority of people I encounter always seem to be looking for an external solution. They're looking for someone else to shoulder the blame when they should, and would be better off, doing something, anything, towards improving their circumstances and fixing their internal dialogues instead.

I witnessed how my heroes (my parents) lived their lives, and I observed how they made big things happen for themselves with so little. I did my best to replicate their life lessons with setting goals and making money, and I was fortunate beyond my wildest dreams. When that monetary success still didn't make me feel that I had *Enough*, I again turned to my parents' lives to see where I had gone wrong. I started to re-examine how they did things compared to what I was doing, and I began to find some pieces that had been missing. Love was one of those pieces.

My parents always did things from a place of love. I attribute my success to my parents' influence because I knowingly and sometimes unknowingly did things from a place of love in my heart, just like my parents did. The times when I've failed, or quit, I noticed my heart was not fully into it, and I didn't care enough about whatever I was attempting at the time. To be honest, I wasn't caring enough about me; that was my underlying problem.

The other day I was listening to a young friend of mine complain that his dad had told him to grow up and stop wasting his time with stupid things and foolish pursuits. His dad gave, as an example, his son's efforts at starting a business, his skiing and snowboarding, as well as his love of playing hockey. I told him, "It's fine to grow up, but it's not okay to give up on the things that put you in *Spirit* and make you happy. If you're not hurting anyone by doing what you love, the only person you'll end up damaging is yourself by not loving yourself enough to keep the things you enjoy."

I wanted him to understand that caring about himself was at the heart of a life well lived. It's important to continue to do activities or pursuits that you love, even if some people don't get, appreciate, or think about your passion the same way you do. If they look at you as being immature, that's fine. What's a must for you doesn't have to have the same meaning for someone else; it's a must for you because it's nourishment for your soul!

> *Neither a lofty degree of intelligence, nor imagination, nor both together, go to the making of genius. Love, love, love that is the soul of genius.*
>
> **AMADEUS MOZART**

When I do activities just for myself like going for a run or creating something, and I put myself into a state of *Spirit*, it's because I love myself enough to relax and put my mind at ease and stop stressing about things. Love works best when it's effortless. When I'm in *Spirit* and filled with wonder, during and afterwards, I'm manifesting that pure love for myself.

My Mom and Dad instilled in me the idea of feeling love for everything I do. "Then," they said, "It will never feel like work." When I address my goals, money, work, play, really everything I do, from a place of love, I start to feel like I have no limits! Without it, I sometimes feel defeated. Love inspires me not to give in or give up hope.

The secret to my success was setting financial and personal goals. Once I reached a goal, I always created a new one to tackle next. I could continue to make more and more money with no real purpose or meaning, but I recognized that this was a never-ending pursuit. I would still feel unfulfilled, on so many levels, afterwards. That just wasn't how I envisioned living my life. Alternatively, I could accept that there's such a thing as *Enough*, wherein I could have a real sense of satisfaction and an impression of absolute contentment.

The times in my life when I knew I had more than enough money, but still kept going for more, were the times I was filled with greed and not love. When I understood that there was a number that was *Enough* for me, all my money stresses stopped. I had my end point, my *Enough* number to work towards. If I made anything more, it was a bonus, not my goal.

If I gave up on a goal, I discovered that I wasn't in love with it enough to endure the journey that would allow me to accomplish it. The goals that I stuck with, even when I was feeling lost or running on empty, were those wherein I loved myself enough to keep pushing for a breakthrough. I look back now and acknowledge that the goals that I succeeded in accomplishing always came from an underlying feeling of love. When it came time to consider what my next goal was going to be, I found that if I started from a place of love first, I would have a better chance of accomplishing it.

The idea of *Enough* helped me to appreciate my life on a deeper level. I accomplished my goals and made lots of money, but I made time for the activities that put me into a state of *Spirit* as well. I looked for balance and made room for the energy and life force that's called *love!*

The ancient Greeks had at least six different words for what we lump under the one category we call love:

1. *Eros* referred to sexual passion.
2. *Philia* was their word for the love formed from long-term friendships.
3. *Ludus* was a playful love such as flirting.
4. *Agape* meant love for everyone, from which modern notions of charity arose.
5. *Pragma* referenced the love between a couple who had been married a long time and who had learned the language of compromise, compassion, and tolerance.
6. *Philautia* was labelled the love of self, from which all other types of love emerged.

The Greeks also understood that an obsessive love-of-self (narcissism) was unhealthy and led the sufferer to endlessly seek fortune and recognition, doomed to never have *Enough*.

Love is a deep sense of affection, tenderness, fondness, attachment, caring, and intimacy. It's the reason individuals create couples and couples create families. It's the reason for almost every song ever written, and it's at the heart of the majority of movies, plays, poems, and performances. Love is out there making the world go 'round, so why on earth wouldn't it be a necessary component in getting to *Enough*?

I'm not saying you need to start swiping right more often or fishing on the plenty-of-seafood sites because the Greeks instinctually had it right. There are a full five other kinds of love that can be cultivated if you're not currently someone else's seafood delight. To feel like you're *Enough*, start with *Philautia*, self-love, and *Agape*, which refers to the giving back of philanthropy and volunteering.

If you are a little low on self-love, how do you give it a boost? Start by giving yourself a break. Be nicer to yourself. Forgive yourself. Self-love is also acting on your goals so that you can appreciate your efforts to get to *Enough*. It's setting boundaries to protect yourself by saying *No* when you need to and practicing good self-care through nutrition and exercise.

Sharing the connection of love with another is also a powerful feeling. I view love as a mystery, but I know that when it happens, it's a truly magical experience that no words I use can adequately express. When I'm in love, and I'm feeling the love of another, and we combine our energy towards a common goal, love makes us both feel like we have no limits! The shared connection of real love is intoxicatingly divine!

When I mention making love with another, I'm not solely speaking about sex. I'm talking about making a meal with or for someone, or even holding someone's hand. I'm talking about writing something memorable for somebody or doing something creative to express love, such as making or choosing a special gift. The totality of love is selfless acts. You can even feel the love you and your loved one have for each other with a simple exchange of looks. Loving someone is a powerful feeling, but that feeling of being loved by another you care about is beyond measure. That love energy can push you to new heights, to take on new challenges, or to try things you've never done before.

There've been times when I didn't think it was possible for me to continue to do something, such as work on a goal or sort out a bad business deal. I had no energy and my spirits were low. With the love, encouragement, patience, and support from a loved one(s), I kept moving forwards. Love can push you past your limits, and it can stop you from giving up when times are tough. Love will help you get to *Enough*, so I encourage you to pursue it, in all its forms, with the same intensity that you pursue wealth or the other goals that will enrich your life. The Beatles were at their insightful best when they said, "All you need is love!" and "the love you take is equal to the love you make."

Maybe Love Is All You Need...

It was December 22, 2011, when my Dad passed away. I lost my father, hero, best friend, mentor, and the person I knew who loved me more than anyone, aside from my Mom, ever had. I was *devastated*!

I felt so lost after my Dad's passing. In the four years leading up to his death, I had given up major things like my company, even my home, so that I could help see him through the recovery after his accident and to take care of him after the cancer diagnosis. Before my father died, I had a long-distance romance with my girlfriend, and we had been tentatively planning to move in together. When my Dad was no longer around, life suddenly seemed so short. My girlfriend and I went ahead and moved in together. On a whim one night, I proposed.

She said, "Yes," and we went through the motions of preparing a wedding. However, our relationship couldn't withstand my grief or her feeling homesick and missing her friends and family. The relationship ended as quickly as the proposal. When it was over, I was heartbroken.

I bought two bicycles and started to do a lot of riding, but from the moment my Dad died, I honestly can't tell you much else of what I did as the months passed. I can't remember spending any time with anyone or doing anything other than running and riding. I do remember spending most of my time with my Mom or my sisters. For about a year and a half, I felt like I was in this dark fog, and I was never going to get out of it. Then things got even darker.

> *He who knows that enough is enough will always have enough.*
>
> **LAO TZU**

On July 7, 2012, I was in an awful bike accident. I broke four ribs and severely punctured my right lung. I was rushed to the emergency room at the hospital, where the doctors said that I was not to fall asleep or it could be fatal! I wish I could tell you I saw a calming white light filled with a beautiful energy and that peace came over me, but that wasn't the case.

I saw *red*!

I was angry that I hadn't listened more to my parents. I was mad at myself because my ambition almost ruined me. I was disappointed that my girlfriend and I broke up instead of working on our problems and supporting and loving each other. Lastly, I was mad at myself that I didn't have, and now might never have (just as my Dad had been trying to tell me!), *Enough*! I was having the ultimate pity party, splashed with a dose of the harsh reality that this night might be the night I die!

I'll spare you all the gory details, but I will say this, I lost my father, my company, and my girlfriend, and now I feared that I was about to lose my life. I wasn't having a run of good luck! As it happened, I didn't fall asleep, and the night passed in pain and anger, and mental, emotional, and physical fatigue. They released me the following day with instructions to return for a follow-up x-ray in five days.

When I went back for the x-ray, the technician came into the room looking puzzled. He asked, "Could you tell me again why you're here?" Somehow the follow-up x-rays showed no signs of any broken ribs, and my deep, dark purple bruising had gone away! I was asked to come back on the following Monday so that a senior technician could take another round of x-rays. On that Monday, I was still sore but mobile, and after taking another x-ray, the senior technician pulled me off to the side. Bewildered, he asked to see my identification again, and he quizzed me for some time about all the details surrounding the accident. He left to confer with his colleagues, and when he returned he was shaking his head in disbelief. There were still no signs of broken ribs on the x-rays. "Those take months to heal," he said, "The only thing I can tell you is you seemed to have experienced a miracle!"

That day was July 16, 2012. When I left that clinic, I made a decision. I was not going to put my life and dreams on hold anymore! I thought back to how my Dad had warned me that nothing was going to ever be *Enough*. It struck me that if I didn't define *Enough*, how would I ever know if I got there? I started to think about what I needed, what I desired, and how I envisioned living out the rest of my life. I calculated my *Enough* number. I realized that the cost of living a lifestyle I couldn't afford had been endless stress and sleepless nights filled with depression, worry, and unhappiness. I decided I needed to quit my previous way of thinking, and way of life, right then and there. I went from living in a 4,600 square foot home that was once appraised at $3.5 million to residing in a modest 2,500 square foot home that was worth about $600 thousand.

I started to question why I wanted certain things and whether or not I had been pressured into feeling that way by smart marketers and an economic system that manipulates and entices individuals into perpetual debt. I started to say *No* to impulsive purchases, and it got easier every time I did. I began to figure out just what exactly my means were and how I could live within them. It was a far cry from where I had been just a couple of years before, but I was happy for the first time since my Dad's passing. I sold off all the possessions that I didn't need, or that I didn't have any attachments to, and I simplified my life drastically.

I was still renting out some of the homes I owned, and I decided to sell off a couple of my properties to pay off my outstanding debts, mortgages, and lines of credit. Doing all these things radically decreased my gross worth, but it inadvertently increased my net worth. Suddenly, there I was, living within my means. I wasn't overextending myself, I was finally taking my parents' financial advice, and I had stopped letting my appetite for more money and more stuff overrule the size of my metaphorical stomach. I was starting to get an understanding of what my fill, my *Enough*, really was, and I didn't miss being a glutton! For the first time, I had the power to decide what I needed most. I had taken it back from the system and marketers, and I felt surprisingly good without the latest iPhone and the expensive cars that the smooth, well-dressed big shots were driving at the time.

I also started to practice *possible thinking*, as in, "If anything were possible, what would my goals be?" I researched goal setting, planning, and realization strategies and started to shut down my inner critic. What goals would take me to *Enough*? What was I missing in life and how could I go about getting it?

My first goal was to write a screenplay. I had told people that I was writing one, but I had never actually taken the time to even jot down some preliminary notes. To get started, I came up with a *MAP* (a plan and a process) to realize my goal. I began to follow the seven steps in my process:

1. Dream it!   2. Envision it!
3. Cement it!   4. Plan it!
5. Work it!   6. Adapt it!
7. Celebrate it!

I was selfish with my time and looked to mentors, apps, and the internet to help me, and I started to write like a madman. I also began to do my inspirational journaling daily. I started thinking more positively, made time to go for my runs, and I got out into nature more often so that I could experience the *Spirit* state that invigorates me. I wrote a screenplay; then I wrote another.

> *I have been impressed with the urgency of doing. Knowing is not enough; we must apply. Being willing is not enough; we must do.*
>
> **LEONARDO DA VINCI**

One day, someone suggested that I try to shop my screenplays to an agent. Getting to *Enough* requires taking some risks, so there I was speaking to an agent in Vancouver. The agent asked me how I was currently supporting myself. He assumed I was another broke, struggling artist until I began to tell him my story.

I told him that my Mom and Dad had arrived penniless to this country but with love in their hearts, searching for a better life. They used that love-energy to build a happy family and successful businesses. I told him about how they taught my sisters and me to work hard, view failure as feedback, and to always be caring. I told him about how connected they were to their community and how the love that they gave to people came back to them tenfold. I told him what my Dad had said about never having *Enough,* and how the more money I made, the more elusive *Enough* seemed to be. Finally, I told him about my father's accident and passing, my miraculous recovery from my bike accident, and how I had, at long last, figured out what my *Enough* was.

"Your story," he said, "is amazing! That's what people want to hear! How you got *Enough!* That's the story that's going to sell!" I was unconvinced. "Listen," he insisted, "Times are tough right now. You'd be doing some good. You could help people, maybe raise some money for a good cause that's close to your heart, and make a helpful difference." I thought about it. I let the reality of selling screenplays from Calgary, and not Hollywood, sink in. Then on the anniversary of my father's death, on December 22, 2013, I made a decision.

I knew in my heart that something was missing from my personal *Enough*, and it was philanthropy on a bigger scale, that giving back piece of the puzzle. "I'm going to write that book," I said, "I'm going to do my part in giving back to those who may be interested in listening to my story and maybe even learning something from my experience that could possibly help them to better their lives." I made a plan. I started my goal process (Remember? Dream it, envision it, cement it, plan it, work it, adapt it, and celebrate it.) and began to write, and now here we are, you and me.

It took me a long time to get here. It took the loss of my father. It took terminating a career and business that had ruled my life and was slowly sucking the energy and enthusiasm out of me. It took a personal relationship that ended abruptly, and it took almost losing my life in a bike accident for me to finally wake up!

Once I woke up, I immediately made the changes I had put off for so long! I felt like the universe was trying to tell me something all along, but I wasn't open to listening. Witnessing my Dad take his last breath was a haunting experience for me, but a real eye-opener as well. Maybe I needed to see that, to realize what mattered most to me in my life.

My Dad was an accomplished man in his own right and considered wealthy by many at the end of his life. However, what made me see him as a rich man was what happened when he passed away. In the last moments of his life, I witnessed those closest to him by his side, selflessly giving him all their love and support. I saw, felt, and experienced the love everyone had for him. I saw that he couldn't take his money with him, and he had left this world as he entered it. I knew that if I didn't change my lifestyle, it was going to kill me sooner rather than later. I reevaluated my beliefs, life, habits, and values, and I finally found my *Enough*. It was my Dad's final gift to me.

My Dad's spirit, and what he taught me, lives on through his example and through all those he touched with his big heart, kind actions, and generous nature. The very subject of money making one feel significant is sad to me now! I was one of those losers for whom money was everything, for about a second that is, until my parents set me straight. When I matured, money and status were not even a concern of mine. To those who matter most to me, what I am most proud of is that they know me to be an authentic and kind person.

When I set out to share what I had learned about *Enough*, I had no idea where it would lead me. I'm now a public speaker and an *Enough* consultant. My philanthropic goal is to personally help cancer-related charities and give back by sharing the message of how to get *Enough*.

My family doesn't treat me any differently because of what I've accomplished, and I, in turn, don't make them feel like they should! The only significance I associate with money today is something my Dad taught me, "How much money do I need to be free, so I don't have to kiss anybody's butt?" Money is the gateway to living life on my terms. When you attain your *Enough* number, and you can comfortably live within your means, that's real freedom!

Even though there are days I wish I could change some things that happened in the past, there's a reason the rear view mirror is so small & the windshield is so big, where you're headed is much more important than what you've left behind.

UNKNOWN

I still gladly take out my Mom's garbage, shovel her snow, and do many other things a good son does for his parent(s), and I know that my Mom and Dad's love is one of the things that matters most to me. They didn't care what I accomplished in life regarding wealth or business. They cared that I would always be a genuine and considerate person to others. I have them to thank for showing me that love is the most important thing in life, not money. We show our best selves when everything we do in our lives comes from a place of love. When I approach my life from a place of love, I feel as though I've reached my highest purpose as a human being and I'm my ultimate best self!

After spending so many years searching, chasing the never-ending quest for bigger, better, and best, what I found along the way was something more significant, and meaningful, and that gave me purpose. Love is the last piece of my *Enough* puzzle. Being truly loved and accepted by those I love is the greatest feeling I can reach for, and in my humble opinion, that's enough!

Not Had *Enough*? Well, Here's Some More:

- how philanthropy makes you happier:

  http://www.pnas.org/content/103/42/15623.full

  http://www.huffingtonpost.com/brady-josephson/want-to-be-happier-give-m_b_6175358.html

  http://www.lodestarfoundation.org/happiness-and-philanthropy

- why altruistic people have better sex lives:

  https://www.sciencedaily.com/releases/2016/08/160804141642.htm

- generosity reduces stress:

  https://www.mentalhelp.net/articles/socialization-and-altruistic-acts-as-stress-relief/

- why volunteers are healthier:

  https://www.helpguide.org/articles/healthy-living/volunteering-and-its-surprising-benefits.htm

- laughter and the brain:

  http://news.stanford.edu/news/2003/december10/laughter.html

  http://healthland.time.com/2013/05/09/the-laughing-brain/

  https://www.ccpa-accp.ca/the-benefits-of-laughter/

  https://www.scientificamerican.com/article/why-laughter-may-be-the-best-pain-medicine/

  http://abcnews.go.com/Health/laughing-makes-brain-work-study-finds/story?id=23393053

- pets and your health:

  http://www.health.com/health/gallery/0,,20810305,00.html#pets-relieve-depression-0

https://www.mnn.com/family/pets/stories/11-studies-that-prove-pets-are-good-your-health

http://www.buffalo.edu/news/releases/1996/03/3481.html

http://www.buffalo.edu/news/releases/1999/11/4489.html

https://www.health.harvard.edu/blog/therapy-dog-offers-stress-relief-at-work-201107223111

https://www.painpathways.org/pets-and-chronic-pain/

https://www.psychologytoday.com/blog/survivors/201107/why-dogs-heal-ptsd

http://www.smithsonianmag.com/science-nature/how-dogs-can-help-veterans-overcome-ptsd-137582968/

Chapter 13 • Takeaways:

1. Life can change in an instant. Don't wait for a tragedy to jolt you into getting your ducks in a row. Start your journey to *Enough* now.

2. Philanthropy that connects to your core values will help you feel like you have *Enough*.

3. Giving away money makes you even happier than when you received it in the first place, and the feeling lasts way longer!

4. People who volunteer are happier than those who don't.

5. Cultivate good karma by examining the motivations behind your actions and choosing actions that allow others to view you, and you to view yourself, in a more positive light.

6. *Always Be Caring* (ABC) and don't make your money by hurting others or it will come back to karmically bite you.

7. Laugh often. Laughter makes your brain feel like you have *Enough* by activating the same reward centres as when you get money.

8. Try to find the humour in your problems. People who laugh more often have better self-esteem and fewer negative thoughts.

9. Spend more time with friends and family.

10. Get a pet. Pets are a source of unconditional love that will boost your immune system, reduce your risk of heart attacks and stroke, and improve your mood.

11. Loving what you do is not as important as loving yourself enough to always do a good job!

12. You'll never feel like you have *Enough* without love. Develop your love for yourself and your love for others.

14

The Wizard of Awes:
Courage, Brains, and a Whole Lot of Heart

For I consider brains far superior to money in every way.
You may have noticed that if one has money without brains,
he cannot use it to his advantage; but if one has brains without money,
they will enable him to live comfortably to the end of his days.

L. FRANK BAUM

(The Scarecrow in *The Marvellous Land of Oz*)

IN the book *The Wonderful Wizard of Oz* by L. Frank Baum, the the Cowardly Lion asks, "Do you think Oz could give me courage?" The Tin Man announces, "I shall take the heart. For brains do not make one happy, and happiness is the best thing in the world," while the Scarecrow declares, "I shall ask for brains instead of a heart; for a fool would not know what to do with a heart if he had one." Dorothy's request seems simpler by comparison, but "Home," like *Enough*, is a concept whose layered complexities can only be defined by the person looking for it. We are all Cowardly Lions, Tin Men, Scarecrows, or Dorothys, looking for what we lack in order to feel like *Enough*.

It's been more than five years since my Dad's passing, and I've had more than enough time to do some soul searching on my own yellow-bricked journey and I've figured out some things for myself that I wanted to share with you, the reader. I've already shared with you how to set goals to keep moving forwards and to give your life purpose and meaning. I've talked about how to make more money, or keep more of what you have, because it takes money to pay for necessities, a lifestyle, and experiences. I've shared how important it is to make time in your day for the things you love to do most (activities that put you in *Spirit*). Finally, I discussed balance, simplifying, and living within your means, while looking for opportunities for philanthropy, creativity, community, laughter, and love. Ultimately, however, it all boils down to feelings! Having read this book, I hope you have a feeling that you're not in Kansas anymore, and that if you search for a bit of courage, use your brain, and put your heart into it, you'll find your *Enough*.

I set goals, make money to pay for things, and do things to put myself into *Spirit* for a feeling. I may forget what was said in a conversation, but I always remember what an interaction with someone felt like. To get to *Enough*, I had to understand that *Enough* is more than a number. It's all about reaching for and achieving things that bring this utopic feeling inside that lets you know you are *Enough*!

This book is not an ego-driven endeavour; it's the exact opposite! I love my anonymity, and I'm a very private person who had never even been on any social media sites until January 2017. When I set out to write this book, it was my way of giving back the wisdom, knowledge, and insight that brought me to my understanding of what *Enough* is. I wanted to share how I got there and to show how you can get there too, but I continue to learn about *Enough*, and how best to teach others to achieve it.

> *Enough doesn't necessarily mean rich.*
> *It means finding*
> *the right balance*
> *of all the things that*
> *are important in life,*
> *of which money is only one.*
>
> **MICHAEL RULLO**

As a result, I've created an *Enough* half-day seminar, a goal of mine is to take this message of *Enough* and share it with millions of people all over the world. My website www.michaelrullo. com is where you can follow my blog and discover additional current information I've gathered regarding *Enough*.

Another goal of mine is to use the platform of *Enough* to personally raise money for cancer-related charities. This cause is the one that speaks to me the most because it's the one that so deeply touched my life. As you know, my father passed away from cancer, so these are the charities I've committed myself to helping.

I've been wholly blessed in that I've always had a place to sleep, food, shelter, love, opportunities, and the support of those who championed me when I needed it most. When I was writing, living my life simply and without drama, I finally experienced firsthand the feeling that I had *Enough.* I wrote this book, with love in my heart, as my way to acknowledge those who taught me their life lessons and generously gave me their time, energy, support, patience, and knowledge. It took my Dad's passing, and my miraculous recovery, for me to realize how much I love my family, friends, and those closest to me. I encourage you to stop seeking more and to start figuring out what your *Enough* looks like, and feels like, for you.

> *Everything in life is unusual until you get accustomed to it.*
>
> **L. FRANK BRAUM**
>
> *The Scarecrow in The Marvelous Land of Oz*

If there is a Wizard at the end of your yellow-brick road passing out whatever it is you're missing, it would be awe-inspiring. I think it's more likely that even your own personal Wizard of Awes is going to suggest that you do more than tap your shoes together three times and make a wish in order to get to *Enough.* He'll probably suggest that you'll need goals to motivate you. He might tell you that a better understanding and respect for money will pay the bills, finance those goals, and give you enough time and inspiration to do things you love to do, things that put you in *Spirit.* He might tell you that giving is the best way to get or that there's no place like home.

He might give you some courage so that you can do things differently instead of doing what you've always done and hoping for a different result. It takes courage to go for your goals, courage to make money, and courage to simplify your life and live within your means in the face of megawatt marketing and its gold-plated promises. He might offer you brains so that you can give your life a good once over and figure out where you're losing money, how much you need, how to make more, and whether or not its really more money that you're after. It could be something else entirely that will take you to *Enough*, and you're sure to run into some winged monkeys that will try to ruin even your best laid plans.

If he offers you a heart, I would definitely consider taking it because an abundance of love—love of self, of others, and love *Enough* to see things through and not give up—are what most people find they are missing when they finally come face to face with the Wizard himself. I've come to understand conclusively that love is the feeling to aim for. Combine your goals with an understanding of money, begin doing more activities that put you in *Spirit*, and do it all from a place of love, then you'll have *Enough*.

> "You are both rich,
> my friends,"
> said Ozma gently,
> "& your riches are
> the only riches worth having
> —the riches of content!"
>
> **L. FRANK BAUM**
>
> *The Marvelous Land of Oz*

"But how about my courage?"asked the Lion anxiously. "You have plenty of courage, I am sure," answered the Wizard. "All you need is confidence in yourself. There is no living thing that is not afraid when it faces danger. The *true* courage is in facing danger when you are afraid, and that kind of courage you have in plenty."

With this book, my blog, speaking engagements, private *Enough* consultations, and with my half-day *Enough* seminars, I hope to pass along the message that *Enough* is attainable. I know it can be done because I did it. You can too. All you need is confidence in yourself and perhaps a bit of courage.

I don't take anything for granted anymore; I am committed to sharing the freeing message that *Enough* is a very liberating sensation with as many people as I can, but ultimately I hope those people will do something with that message. There's a saying that goes something along the lines of "When all is said and done, more is said than done." So with that, I genuinely hope that something I've said has made a little difference to you and your life. The rest is up to you. I sincerely wish you courage, brains, and lots of heart on your journey to *Enough*. May you find your *Enough* soon, or perhaps… instead…realize that you had it all along.

Peace & love,
Michael Rullo

Not Had *Enough*? Well, Here's Some More:

- *The Wonderful Wizard of Oz*: a free pdf ebook:

  https://www.gutenberg.org/files/55/55-h/55-h.htm

- to purchase additional digital and hard copies of *Got Enough?! A Rags to Revelations Story*:

  www.michaelrullo.com

- to stay up to date on the latest information about *Enough* and to be informed of upcoming seminars, speaking engagements, and personal consultations:

  www.michaelrullo.com

Selected Reading

Allen, J. (2007). *As a man thinketh*. New York, NY: Dover Publications

Bach, R. (1970). *Jonathan Livingston Seagull*. New York, NY: Scribner/Simon & Shuster, Inc.

Baum, L.F. (1996). *The wonderful wizard of oz*. New York, NY: Dover Evergreen Classics.

Benson, H., & Proctor, W. (2003). *The breakout principle: How to activate the natural trigger that maximizes creativity, athletic performance, productivity, and personal well-being*. New York, NY: Scribner/Simon & Shuster, Inc.

Cameron, J. (1992). *The artist's way: A spiritual path to higher creativity*. New York, NY: Jeremy P. Tarcher/Putnam.

Campbell, J. (1991). *The power of myth*. New York, NY: Anchor Books/Random House.

Canfield, J., & Switzer, J. (2005). *The success principles: How to get from where you are to where you want to be*. New York, NY: Harper Collins.

Carnegie, D. [1936]. (1981). *How to win friends and influence people*. New York, NY: Pocket Books/Simon & Shuster, Inc.

Chiltern, D. (1998). *The wealthy barber: The common sense guide to successful financial planning*. Roseville, CA: Prima Publishing/Crown Publishing/Random House, Inc.

Chopra, D. (1998). *Creating affluence: The a-to-z steps to a richer life*. San Rafael, CA: New World Library/Amber-Allen Publishing.

Chopra, D. (1994). *The seven spiritual laws of success: A practical guide to the fulfillment of your dreams*. San Rafael, CA: New World Library/Amber-Allen Publishing.

Clason, G.S. [1926]. (1989). *The richest man in Babylon*. New York, NY: Plume/Penguin Random House.

Coelho, P. [1989]. (2014). *The alchemist*. (25th Anniversary Edition). Toronto, ON: HarperCollins Canada.

Cousins, N. [1985]. (2005). *Anatomy of an illness: As perceived by the patient*. (20th Anniversary Edition). New York, NY: W.W. Norton & Company, Ltd.

Covey, Stephen. [1989]. (2013). *The 7 habits of highly effective people: Powerful lessons in personal change.* (25th anniversary edition). New York, NY: Rosetta Books LLC.

Csikszentmihalyi, M. [1990]. (2008). *Flow: The psychology of optimal experience.* Toronto, ON: HarperCollins Canada.

Dalai Lama. [1998]. (2009). *The art of happiness. A handbook for living.* (10th anniversary edition). New York, NY: Riverhead Books/Penguin Group.

De Roos, D. (2001). *Real estate riches: How to become rich using your banker's money.* (Rich Dad's Advisors). New York, NY: Warner Books Edition.

Dyer, W. (2010). *The shift: Taking your life from ambition to meaning.* Carlsbad, CA: Hay House.

Dyer, W. (2005). *The power of intention: Learning to co-create your world your way.* Carlsbad, CA: Hay House.

Dyer, W. (1998). *Wisdom of the ages: Modern master brings eternal truths into everyday life.* New York, NY: HarperCollins Publishers.

Gerber, M.E. (1995). *The e-myth revisited: Why most small businesses don't work and what to do about it.* New York, NY: HarperCollins Publishers.

Greene, R. (2012). *Mastery.* New York, NY: Viking/Penguin Group.

Greene, R., & Elffers, J. (1998). *The 48 laws of power.* New York, NY: Viking/Penguin Group.

Hemingway, E. [1952]. (1996). *The old man and the sea.* Toronto, ON: Simon & Schuster Canada.

Hill, N. [1937]. (2014). *Think and grow rich: For men and women who resent poverty.* Chicago, IL: Aristeus Books.

Kawasaki, G. (2011). *Enchantment: The art of changing hearts, minds, and actions.* New York, NY: Portfolio/Penguin.

Koch, R. (2014). *The 80/20 principle and 92 other powerful laws of nature: The science of success.* London, UK: Nicholas Brealey Publishing/Hodder & Stoughton.

Mandino, O. [1968]. (1985). *The greatest salesman in the world.* Hollywood, FL: Bantam/Frederick Fell Publishers, Inc.

McGraw, P. (2012). *Life code: The new rules for winning in the real world.* Los Angeles, CA: Bird Street Books.

Millman, D. (1995). *The laws of spirit: A tale of transformation: Simple, powerful truths for making life work.* Tiburon, CA: H.J. Kramer/New World Library.

Millman, D. [1980]. (2000). *Way of the peaceful warrior: A book that changes lives*. Tiburon, CA: H.J. Kramer/New World Library.

Pausch, R. (2008). *The last lecture: Lessons in living*. London, UK: Hodder & Stoughton.

Peale, N.V. [1952]. (2003). *The power of positive thinking*. New York, NY: Fireside/Prentice-Hall, Inc.

Pressfield, S. (2012). *Turning pro: Tap your inner power and create your life's work*. New York, NY: Black Irish Entertainment LLC.

Pressfield, S. (2002). *The war of art: Winning the inner creative battle*. New York, NY: Rugged Land LLC.

Redfield, J. (1994). *The celestine prophecy: An adventure*. London, UK: Bantam Books.

Robbins, T. [1991]. (2003). *Awaken the giant within: How to take immediate control of your mental, emotional, physical and financial destiny!* New York, NY: Free Press/Simon & Shuster, Inc.

Robbins, T. [1986]. (2003). *Unlimited power: The new science of personal achievement*. New York, NY: Free Press/Simon & Shuster, Inc.

Sharma, R. (2007). *The greatness guide 2: 101 ways to reach the next level*. New York, NY: HarperCollins Publishers.

Sharma, R. (2006). *The greatness guide: 101 lessons for making what's good at work and in life even better*. New York, NY; HarperCollins Publishers.

Wattles, W.D. [1976]. (2007). *The science of getting rich: Attracting financial success through creative thought*. Rochester, VT: Destiny Books/Inner Traditions International.

Disclaimer

I cannot teach anybody anything. I can only make them think.
SOCRATES

T HE book, *Got Enough?! A Rags to Revelation Story* shares with the reader life-lessons and the story of how Michael Rullo came to understand, and view the idea of *Enough,* and how he found it for himself. Michael describes what *Enough* looks and feels like for himself, and the views, examples, and opinions are his alone. The purpose and goal of the book, *Got Enough?!*, is to use Michael's personal *Enough* journey and philosophy, and hopefully it sparks the concept for the reader away from wanting more to instead finding what *Enough* is for themselves. It should not be considered a definitive guide on the subject of *Enough.*

Over many years, Michael has learned that a myriad of factors and influences were involved in helping him find his personal sense of *Enough.* While he hopes readers will be inspired to take action in their own lives, it remains the responsibility of each reader to connect the dots for themselves and to define, discover, and achieve their own sense of *Enough* in their own way. *Got Enough?! A Rags to Revelation Story* may be a starting point, but the goal to *Get Enough* requires readers to have many more in-depth conversations with themselves to determine what *Enough* looks and feels like for them. *Got Enough?!* might just provide readers with the impetus to take the next step, but ultimately only the reader can decide.

Realize that everything is connected to everything else.
LEONARDO DA VINCI

Acknowledgements

I'D like to thank Valerie Repnau of *Eurocom LLC*, Crescent McKeag of *Calgary Writing Services*, Jeremy Drought of *Last Impression Publishing Service*, and Bobbi Beatty of *Silver Scroll Services* for taking my writing and working with me to complete this book. It's because of their involvement that I am where I am today, and I'm forever grateful for these contributions.

About the Author

Michael Rullo is an author, real estate specialist, public speaker, and an *Enough-consultant* who paid off his first home by twenty-four, and made enough money and retired by the age of thirty-seven! He earned a stellar reputation as a new home designer and builder, and his exceptional success and financial savvy allowed him to enjoy life more and pursue his other passions without the stress of making more money! That's when he began to realize that even with all his prosperity and accomplishments, it just wasn't *Enough*.

Many of his affluent friends felt the same way, yet others, who seemed to have very little, radiated contentedness. Michael's remarkable journey to discover what makes someone feel like they have and are *Enough* became the basis for not only this book, but his lectures, seminars, consultations, charity work, blog, and website <www.michaelrullo.com>.

"I learned everything I could about money, goals, balance, flow, psychology, and the science of happiness so that I could share with other people how to get to *Enough*," says Michael. Today, he is passionate about giving back to make the world a better place and is using his experience to help others figure out what exactly is missing from their lives. He currently lives and leads by example a life of *Enough* and is available for consultations and public speaking engagements.

Contact and inquiries at <info@michaelrullo.com>